KENNETH WHITING

REMEMBERING A FORGOTTEN HERO OF NAVAL AVIATION AND SUBMARINES

FELIX HAYNES

PAGE PUBLISHING
Conneaut Lake, PA

First originally published by Page Publishing 2023

ISBN 979-8-88793-070-1 (pbk)
ISBN 979-8-88793-077-0 (digital)

Printed in the United States of America

DEDICATION

I would like to dedicate this book to Lt. Cdr. Felix T. Haynes, USNR, retired; deceased. Lt. Cdr. Haynes served as communications officer in the USS *Kenneth Whiting* AV-14 during the last year of World War II. Whether he was telling stories about being anchored for many days in such places as the Palau's Kossol Passage or the Ryukyus' Kerama Retto, supporting the *Kenneth Whiting*'s seaplane squadrons or about the kamikaze shot down by the *Kenneth Whiting*, my father provided the impetus for me to ask the question: Who was this guy Kenneth Whiting, and why isn't he better known?

As I began to research the life of Kenneth Whiting and his great but largely forgotten contributions to naval aviation and submarines, the questions morphed to these: Why has no biography about this man ever been published? Why did this Naval Academy graduate, whose accomplishments were well-known during his career, retire as a captain? And Why has he been largely forgotten?

So the questions grew, but their seeds came from my father. I like to think the book would have earned a "well done, son," and I know it has earned a dedication to him.

CHAPTER 1

WHERE ARE THE CARRIERS?

When America becomes embroiled in an international crisis, the first question leaders ask is, Where are the carriers? As the centerpiece of America's naval forces for operating forward, aircraft carriers operate aircraft that attack airborne, afloat, and ashore targets that threaten the freedom of the seas and lead in sustained power projection operations in support of US and coalition forces.[1]

Going back 80 years to December 7, 1941, as the pilots launched from six Japanese aircraft carriers over Pearl Harbor, Hawaii, just before 8:00 a.m., and looked down at 130 vessels of the US Pacific Fleet that arrayed beneath them—including 8 battleships, 8 cruisers, 30 destroyers, 4 submarines, and many assorted auxiliary vessels—the first thing that punctured the bubble of their excitement was the absence of aircraft carriers. Their absence may have saved the Hawaiian Islands from capture by the Japanese Navy and definitely gave the United States a chance at the dawn of World War II, so those Japanese pilots probably asked the same question: Where are their carriers?[2]

Pearl Harbor provided the ceremony for the passing of the torch from battleships to carriers; before Pearl Harbor, the battleship was the king of the seas, but after Pearl Harbor, battleships had been eclipsed by the aircraft carrier. Although some forward-seeing Navy leaders in the 1920s and 1930s anticipated aircraft carriers project-

1

ing striking power deep into enemy-held waters in the next war, too many black-shoe, Gun Club admirals expected this war to be decided by big battleship guns in a repetition of the world war's largest traditional naval engagement, the Battle of Jutland.[3]

Part of the reason carriers replaced battleships as the center of the fleet was the greater range at which carriers could strike the enemy, and although it has been used in other roles, the greatest use of aircraft carriers has always been as an offensive strike platform to project sea power. The greatest range ever achieved by the USS *Missouri*'s 16-inch guns was 23 miles; at the end of World War II, carrier-launched airplanes like the F6F Hellcat had a combat radius (maximum sortie range to target and back again carrying a full-combat load of weapons) of 945 miles. The combat radius of a current jet like the F/A-18 Super Hornet is 1,275 nautical miles. To this combat radius should be added the distance an aircraft carrier could move at a flank speed of over 30 knots during her sortied pilots' time aloft.[4]

When it operates in international waters, a carrier battle group has no need to seek the approval of host countries for landing or overflight rights. Nor does it need to go through the inefficient, time-consuming processes of building and maintaining bases in countries where our hosts may not fully support our presence.[5]

Contrary to the criticisms of those who say the need for carriers has diminished, they have played an expanded role since the fall of the Berlin Wall. Their hard-to-miss presence has indeed strengthened their traditional roles of deterrence, sea control, and showing the flag. Since the end of the Cold War, carriers have become more important in their role of kinetic-power projection, and ground troops have not been put into harm's way without the presence of a carrier air wing to secure the airspace and provide close air support.[6]

Two admirals, now deceased, have been universally credited with making the question "Where are the carriers?" important and keeping it relevant for so long. Both served their careers too early to be pilots (although they both earned the qualification of Naval Aviation observer in the aviation familiarization course of that name), but they have been credited with an early understanding of what Naval Aviation would become and putting aside the perspective of the battleship admirals and the "black shoe" surface Navy from which they came, leading "brown shoe" Naval Aviation's early growth and fueling its ability to reach the high altitudes to which it would ascend. Rear Admiral William A. Moffett, known as the Father of Naval Aviation, served as the first chief of the Bureau of Aeronautics (BuAer), oversaw the introduction of aircraft carriers, and fostered the effort to gain funding for the first aircraft carriers and aircraft. As a Medal of Honor winner, he was highly respected when he arrived at the BuAer post, and he soon surrounded himself with a coterie of young naval aviators like Henry Mustin, John Towers, and Kenneth Whiting whom he would empower to advance Naval Aviation's agenda. When Billy Mitchell led the Army's attack on Naval Aviation in the backwash of World War I, Moffett maintained a policy of official support for Naval Aviation and organized the Navy's defense of its new branch. His career ended with his premature death in the crash of one of the dirigibles for which he had fought so hard.[7]

The other nonpilot admiral who made an early philosophical transition from battleships and the surface Navy to the air was Admiral Joseph M. Reeves. Well-known in the Navy for being the first to receive the nickname "Bull," he was serving in Washington during World War II in a position to which he was assigned (a *billet*, in Navy terminology) and to which he was recalled from the retired list when his moniker was given to another admiral who would become even better known as William F. "Bull" Halsey.[8]

Perhaps because Moffett and Reeves achieved the high-profile rank of admiral, their names and the contributions to Naval Aviation they made during their careers are well-known.

But there is another naval officer whose career and contributions to both Naval Aviation and submarines have been largely lost to history.

Because of his sudden untimely death in mid-World War II from a cause the Navy did not want to admit publicly, because he was passed over for promotion to flag rank and mandatorily retired, or because he ended his career recalled to serve in lower-profile posts, many of his career achievements have been forgotten. The other man who made the question "Where are the carriers?" important kept it relevant for so long and who is the subject of this book is Kenneth Whiting. Although his biography has never been published, many who served with him or have written about him have awarded him the title Father of the Aircraft Carrier.

He was the first naval officer to begin to agitate continuously for carriers with formal proposals years before other Navy officers came aboard, and as the consensus that the Navy needed carriers was developing, he had the most comprehensive and accurate understanding of what they could become. Finally, after the Navy made its early decisions to build carriers, he played a major hand in taking five of the Navy's first six carriers through the long and sometimes politically risky process from obtaining congressional approval and funding for them, gaining international approval, laying their keels, constructing them, fitting them out, writing the book on their operation, and commanding two of them.

A Wright State University (the namesake of Orville Wright, who taught Kenneth Whiting to fly) library internet website says, "Whiting…was instrumental in the development of the aircraft carrier and is sometimes called the Father of the Aircraft Carrier."[9]

A summary of the career of Kenneth Whiting in his ZB file at the Naval History and Heritage Command may say it best:

> Captain Whiting was an early proponent of the aircraft carrier as a unit of the fleet. In the development of carrier designs, he displayed the same exceptional ability, energy, and enthusiasm which characterized his performance of duty throughout his naval career. Far more than any other, he is responsible for carriers, their main features of design, and for the types of airplanes operated from carriers. Again more than any other, the success and the honor and glory which Naval Aviation has attained may be accredited to this peerless leader and officer.[10]

One of the eulogists at Whiting's funeral said, "One cannot study Naval Aviation without considering Captain Whiting's achievement. In *The Queen of the Flattops*, a book about the *Lexington*, he is referred to as the Father of the Aircraft Carrier."[11]

Kenneth Whiting deserves to have his many accomplishments much more widely known, and the American people and the Navy he loved so much deserve to know them and him.

CHAPTER 2

THE FAMILY OF KENNETH WHITING

We are indebted for this history of the Whiting family to the two daughters of Kenneth Whiting, Edna and Moira, now deceased, who put together significant but never published journals of family photographs and memories of family stories to record the history of their family.

The Whiting family was from England, from which William Whiting, a gentleman of some means, emigrated. He arrived in Boston with his wife, Susannah, about 1630. He continued his travels to Hartford, Connecticut, where he became a founding father of that city, was treasurer of the Connecticut colony, and had a monopoly on all trade outside the colony. Several of William Whiting's descendants became clergymen in Hartford.

In the mid-1700s, the Whitings moved to Stratford, Connecticut, on the Atlantic coast, where one of them, Lieutenant John Whiting, served as an officer in the Continental Army. This qualified Lieutenant Whiting and all his direct Whiting male descendants for memberships in the prestigious Society of the Cincinnati.

Kenneth Whiting's grandfather, Francis Holland Nicholas Whiting, moved from Stratford to New York City in the 1840s and established a successful wallpaper manufacturing firm in Inwood, at the northern end of Manhattan Island. His son Eliot was born on February 10, 1850. Francis grew wealthy and invested his wealth. One of his investments was a rice plantation named Mount Holly, located in Goose Creek, outside of Charleston, South Carolina. Because Eliot hated the wallpaper factory, Francis sent him to South Carolina in 1877 to manage the plantation. This may not have been a good decision because Eliot was a charming, good-looking man of gentle temperament, but he was not resourceful.

A year later, Eliot made a trip back to New York City. There, he married Florence Daisy Day on December 31, 1878. The first Day had emigrated from England in 1634, settled in Hartford, Connecticut, where they also became founding fathers, and eventually moved to New York. Daisy, who had spent time in Paris in her youth while her parents were going through a divorce, was a force. She knew what she wanted and intended to get it, and these attributes were to play an important role in her eldest son's, Kenneth's, life.

Daisy was tall, with very red curly hair and blue-green eyes. With high cheekbones and slanty eyes, she was not pretty but very attractive. Kenneth's younger daughter, Moira, believed her grandmother Daisy and Moira's older sister Eddie favored the actress Katharine Hepburn, whose family was also from Hartford.

Eliot and Daisy returned to Mount Holly and started life with twin daughters, born in Charleston on April 12, 1880. Only one, named Katherine, survived babyhood.

Despite the happiness of Eliot and Daisy with their new family, the frequency of hurricanes hitting the South Carolina coast and plantation convinced Eliot's father, Francis, that the low country of South Carolina was foreign and unhealthy, and he sold Mount Holly. Bringing his again-pregnant wife, Daisy, Eliot unhappily returned to New York to work for his father at the wallpaper factory. Daisy was uncomfortable with the summer heat and went to Stockbridge, Massachusetts, in the Berkshires of western Massachusetts, where her second child, Kenneth Whiting, was born on July 22, 1881. The family fought over a name, and to settle the dispute, the name Kenneth was found in a dictionary.[1]

Two more children—Butler, "Butts" or "Buttsie," in 1882 and Virginia, or "Ginger," in 1885—followed Katherine and Kenneth into the family.

Eliot and Daisy settled in Inwood, but the family fortunes had dwindled. In 1887, Francis grew tired of labor unions attempting to organize his factory, and he sold it. This put Eliot, who had never trained for any gainful employment other than working for his father, out of work. Eliot eventually found work as manager of a Fifth Avenue hotel in New York City, where according to family lore, "He walked up and down Fifth Avenue with a gold-headed cane and was charming."

At this point, Kenneth's mother, Daisy, inserted herself into the world of work and family leadership. Having been warned by her father-in-law about the factory's sale before it took place and inspired by an article in *Ladies' Home Journal*, Daisy started an interior-decorating business to support the family and organized the children to do the housework. Armed with a book of wallpaper samples from her father-in-law's now-defunct business, her knowledge of a popular new way of constructing ceilings, and her considerable people skills, she made a proposal to a company that was building new apartment buildings in Queens. Convincing the apartment builders that they could charge more for their apartments if she decorated them, she began a business, which was to last thirty-five years.

For the first few years, the Whitings moved frequently seeking the lowest rent they could find. Daisy's last child, Francis Eliot Maynard Whiting (nicknamed Pete, Red, and F. E. M.), was born in Spuyten Duyvil, at the south end of the Bronx, in 1891, but Daisy maintained her business and returned to the Whiting apartment to feed the baby every four hours. The resulting strain caused a nervous breakdown, but she recovered and continued on as the family's main breadwinner.

In the summers, Daisy took her family to a rented house on Beach Avenue in Larchmont, New York, on the shore of Long Island Sound. In a few years, they moved there year-round. The Whiting family became members of St. John's Episcopal Church on Fountain Square in Larchmont, where Kenneth volunteered to pump the organ for the choir at services because he was tone-deaf and could not carry a tune.

After many years of working successfully in the field, Daisy ended her interior-decorating career as director of the John Wanamaker Department Store's Interior Decorating Department.

It was in still semirural Larchmont, with the water of Long Island Sound so close, that Kenneth Whiting developed the athletic and leadership abilities with which he was born. As the oldest of three brothers, he became the natural leader of a neighborhood gang of his family and neighbors. He was gifted with foot speed, a high level of gross and fine body coordination, and athletic skills, and he participated in sports year-round.

He avoided baths and haircuts, smoked Chesterfield cigarettes from age eleven, and drank alcohol. For fun, he developed a pastime of stealing pies. In the Inwood years, he learned to swim in the East River, whose currents range from over three knots in one direction to over four in the other. Then he taught his brothers and gang members to swim too. After the move to Larchmont, Kenneth entered all the swimming and washtub races at Horseshoe Harbor Yacht Club, near the Beach Avenue house, and won often.

Kenneth also became an excellent sailor and began a lifelong practice of borrowing small boats and yachts from others to enter in local sailing races. Once, while sailing a race with his dog as crew, the boat capsized while rounding a pylon. The dog was trapped under the boat, but Kenneth rescued him. He told the woman who owned the boat, and she gave the dog a large shot of brandy.

He taught his brothers Butts and Pete to box, so they could all represent the gang in bloody boxing matches held in a nearby barn.

The three brothers, close yet competitive, hauled wood for the family's heat and cooking and shoveled snow. Once, the two older brothers offered Pete a dime if he would haul the wood that day. He agreed to do so, and the older brothers ran off to sail. When Pete finished, he came to his brothers for his dime. They told him they would pay him next week. Pete said, "No nickel, no wood," and hauled all the wood back to where it started.

Kenneth walked nearly two miles from Larchmont each way every day to attend Mamaroneck High School. It was a long walk, but that was the only transportation he had. He also worked on a surveying crew.

Now fully grown, Kenneth stood 5 feet, 8 inches tall and weighed 150 pounds. He wore size 7 shoes.

As the time for college approached, with his high level of fine motor skills and manual dexterity, Kenneth became a good artist; he wanted to go to Paris and study art. Perhaps because of the time she had spent in Paris in her youth, Daisy refused to send him to what she described as a "cold loft in France." She wanted him to attend the United States Naval Academy at Annapolis, Maryland, instead.

Having suffered when her father-in-law, Francis, sold his business in response to the efforts of unions to organize the factory, Daisy joined the Republican Party and became active in politics to fight the Democrats in New York City's Tammany Hall machine. She had little trouble getting Kenneth an appointment to Annapolis.

Kenneth enrolled at Annapolis's Bobby Werntz Preparatory School and studied for the entrance examination for a year, but he failed the test the first time. After working on a road surveying crew for the summer, Kenneth went back to the Werntz School for another year. This time, he passed the entrance examination.

Kenneth entered Annapolis in 1900, a member of the Class of 1904. But he failed to make satisfactory academic progress the first year and was dismissed. Weak academic skills were to continue to plague Kenneth in the early years of his Navy career, and although there was no mention in any records of such modern diagnoses, one begins to suspect that he may have suffered from a learning disability or attention-deficit disorder. But Daisy once again used her political contacts and got him another appointment, after which, he passed the entrance examination and repeated the first year. Now a member of the Class of 1905, he was nineteen years, ten months old when he reentered.[2]

Academics continued to be a challenge for him, but he was very popular among his fellow midshipmen, and they helped him a lot with his studies. Perhaps related to the "tin ear" he had for music, he had particular problems with foreign languages. So his classmates got him some Spanish records to use for study.

Kenneth excelled in athletics, participating in football, boxing, swimming, and track. He played end in football, but to his great disappointment, in five years, the Navy football team never beat the Army, its archrival. In his last year, he was hurt in the first quarter of the Army game and had to watch the rest of the game from the bench. In boxing, he never weighed over 150 pounds, but with his speed and athleticism, he boxed as a heavyweight with great success. In his first-class year, he won the Athletic Sword, symbolic of the best athlete in his class.

He also excelled at leadership, and as a first classman, he was named commander of the Academy's Color Company.

In the social sphere, Kenneth had little interest in girls, which, in the Academy vernacular, made him a "Red Mike." His family speculated that he stayed away from girlfriends because his mother, Daisy, and his sister, Katherine, had such strong personalities.

However, Kenneth did enjoy another continuing area of midshipman life, engaging in fun behaviors like smoking and sneaking off Academy grounds. Some called these pranks, but the Academy called some of them rules infractions. Midshipmen committing such infractions were confined to the wooden-hulled, three-masted frigate USS *Santee*, a Naval Academy barracks ship built in 1855. Only once, in their second, or youngster, year, were Kenneth and his roommate, Theodore G. "Spuds" Ellyson confined to the *Santee*; it was not the only time the two would get in trouble together. While on the *Santee*, Kenneth decided to put his earlier experience with stealing pies to good use, and they planned to steal one from the captain's galley. The plan was for the smaller Kenneth to enter the galley through a porthole, steal one, and drop it through the porthole to Ellyson. Kenneth wiggled through the porthole but found himself in the captain's head, or bathroom, rather than the galley.

To the major social history contribution from the Journals of Family Memories put together by Kenneth's two daughters can be added the perspectives and stories of his fellow midshipmen. The 1905 Naval Academy yearbook, *The Lucky Bag*, included four nicknames for Kenneth given to him by his classmates—Ken, Vitings, Ting, and Hero. He had earned the nickname Hero in athletics, in which his list of activities included four years of football, boxing championship tribunal, track, hockey, and three years of swimming championships. His election his senior year to the presidency of the athletic association followed naturally. Other comments on his last nickname and its source in his athletic prowess were provided, "Handles a cat-boat to perfection…when shall such a hero live again?"

His weak study habits were noted by "Can study for hours at a time and never know what he has been reading."

Descriptions of his pleasing personality were "has the most charming smile you can imagine and uses it to great advantage in the Spanish department [perhaps also alluding to his weak study habits and how he used his pleasing personality to overcome them].

"Able, fearless, and modest as a maiden. Fond of night séances and represents New York in the Guvenurs [spelling is correct]. Twitch your finger at him, and he is as easily conquered as a shaven Samson [perhaps a reference to his relationships with women]."

Finally, the *Lucky Bag* made a prediction of his future success in the Navy, "Bring a bucket of medals for Vitings."[3]

Rear Admiral George Van Deurs, an Annapolis graduate himself, said this of him, "Though he never weighed over 150 pounds," he was one of the Naval Academy's most famous athletes.

He had starred on the hockey and track teams, won the swimming championship three years in a row, played varsity football… fought his way to a boxing championship against all comers, regardless of weight…and [was] a wizard with a sailboat.

With a friendly smile and modest manner, he was the most popular and influential midshipman in the school. At the Academy and afterward, he was a quiet, natural leader who, without even trying, usually had the wholehearted assistance of all near him. Regardless of rank, everyone who knew him always wanted to please him. Well-liked by his fellow midshipmen, he won election as president of the athletic association.[4]

However, against these strengths, despite innate ability on which he perhaps relied too much, he displayed a certain lack of academic urgency. "He never took out much time for studying. Textbooks seemed unimportant, and he graduated near the bottom of the Class of 1905."[5]

Kenneth Whiting graduated on January 30, 1905, according to the *1905 Annual Registry of the Naval Academy*, ranked 107th of the 114 graduates of his class.[6]

As a young man of twenty-four, his athletic body already contained the seeds of health problems, which would manifest themselves later in life. He had broken an arm, survived a two-month bout of pneumonia at age nine in 1890, and experienced the typical childhood diseases of scarlet fever, measles, mumps, and pertussis. He had paid for the prowess he had displayed in the Annapolis boxing ring and the earlier experience in the Larchmont barn where he learned to box by losing five molar teeth—three on one side, top and bottom; and two on the other, top and bottom. His Annapolis health record showed the broken bones and contusions, which he had earned from his all-sports, college athletic career.[7]

Such were some of the experiences with which Kenneth Whiting began his life and the raw ingredients with which he started his career as an officer in the United States Navy. In the early years of his career, more than one writer called him a daredevil, a man who lived to seek the next most dangerous activity, do it, and best it. The questions that must be asked about Whiting therefore are what changed him from a superb athlete, risk-taker, and a somewhat lazy student into a man who made early and experimental submarines work better and who envisioned, probably better than anyone else of his generation, the class of an entirely new warship, who led the campaign to get them, who built or led the first half dozen or so, and who developed much of the Navy's doctrine on how to employ them?[8]

For his contemporaries, those who knew Kenneth Whiting, he always seemed to live his life like a man on fire; he was always searching for new targets to incinerate. Whether the targets were submarines, airplanes, how the Navy was to fight World War I, or his greatest target of all, aircraft carriers, he lit his fires with a glint in his eye and a grin on his face, and the way he went about it made others want to follow him into the flames.

CHAPTER 3

MAKING A MAN AND
TRANSFORMING A NATION

Whiting's first fire came from an unlikely source—the son of a longtime professor of engineering and tactics at the United States Military Academy at West Point. It seemed natural that Rear Admiral Alfred Thayer Mahan would become a student and teacher of military history. The surprises were that Mahan specialized in *naval* history and that he based his theory on a major new use of a navy to support the economy of its nation.[1]

Since before its founding, the United States had had a robust economy, based on the economic system known as capitalism. (See Adam Smith's *Wealth of Nations*.) But the development of that economy, its international trade component, and some of the missions of its navy had been temporarily paused eighty years into the nation's development to settle questions about which the founding fathers had been unable to compromise, important questions having to do with the power of its national government vis-à-vis the states and how its national workforce would be organized. So during and after the Civil War, the American Navy had been focused internally on a revolution-suppression mission, blockading the ports of the Confederacy to prevent the South from getting the manufactured tools of war it needed to fight and navigating the rivers penetrating the South to support the American armies with the tools of war they needed to quell and control the South's drive for independence.[2]

Those questions had been settled on the battlefield in a bloody civil war, and with the Spanish-American War of 1898, America was ready to resume its march to international greatness, fueled by the power and wealth of capitalism and supported by its abundant natural resources, striving population, and geographic position protected by two oceans and a temperate climate.[3]

Mahan brought all these threads together in 1890 in an important and seminal work called *The Influence of Sea Power upon History*. He argued that a nation needed to maintain a robust international trade to acquire raw materials to fuel its economy and the international markets to sell its manufactured and agricultural products. To maintain that international trade, it needed a strong navy, which roamed the seven seas and projected sea power to keep the sea lanes open for merchant ships to move those raw materials and finished products between its mainland and the rest of the world. He based his theory on an historical analysis of strong countries like Great Britain, France, and Holland and the role their navies played in their strength.[4]

Mahan's work was read and digested by many nations that engaged in international trade, most of which already maintained some overseas possessions, which supported that trade. Many of the future and emerging leaders of those nations, like American cousins Theodore and Franklin Roosevelt, and Navy officers whose task it would be to lead navies in this international mission, read Mahan and used his theory to influence their countries' policies and actions. But one nation, the United States, had no such possessions yet, and the ideas in this book were to fuel an American drive for international power and possessions, including the Panama Canal, Cuba, Hawaii, Puerto Rico, and the Philippines. With that drive for international power and the support of those leaders, possessions and international trade came, and Alfred Thayer Mahan's ideas were a significant part of the impetus that made the twentieth century the American century.[5]

*****

Years of revolution by native *insurrectos* in Cuba and cruel responses by Spain and the government it put in place to rule Cuba flared into rebellion in the late 1890s. "Yellow journalism" reporting on these events, today known as fake news, by William Randolph Hearst, publisher of the *San Francisco Examiner* and *New York World*, and Joseph Pulitzer, publisher of the *New York Journal*, so inflamed the American public that it demanded the United States go to war with Spain to save the suffering Cuban people. President William McKinley tried to prevent the United States from repeating the bloodshed that he had seen as a soldier in the Civil War, but after the USS *Maine* was mysteriously blown up and sunk in Havana harbor, he succumbed to the pressure of public opinion and asked Congress for a declaration of war.[6]

The resulting war with Spain, well fought by both the American Army and Navy, ended with Spain surrendering Puerto Rico, the Philippines, Cuba, and other minor territories to a fledgling America as spoils of war. Suddenly, the United States had become a world power with an empire, and most Americans liked it.[7]

One American who particularly liked it was then-assistant secretary of the Navy Theodore Roosevelt. Influenced by Mahan, leading up to the Maine explosion, Roosevelt called for building up the Navy's strength and the ejection of Spain from Cuba. After the Maine explosion, Roosevelt, without seeking the approval of President McKinley or Navy Secretary John D. Long, transmitted orders to several naval commands directing them to prepare for war.[8]

After Commodore George Dewey's successful action against a Spanish fleet at Manila Bay, he gave partial credit for his victory to Roosevelt's unauthorized orders. Roosevelt resigned as assistant secretary of the Navy a short while later, and, along with Army Colonel Leonard Wood, formed the first US Volunteer Cavalry Regiment called the Rough Riders and made up of an amalgam of Roosevelt's fellow Ivy League students and cowboys he had met while out West. Then-Colonel Roosevelt led the Rough Riders up Cuba's Kettle Hill [mistakenly identified as San Juan Hill by some] to victory. The acclaim Roosevelt received from that feat propelled him to the governorship of New York, the vice presidency in 1901, and subsequently, the presidency after McKinley was assassinated.[9] Thus the nationalistic and aggressive Roosevelt ascended the steps to national leadership, a rostrum he did not relinquish until his death in January 1919, at the end of World War I.[10]

As president, after the twenty-year failure of the French to construct a Panama Canal, Roosevelt, among the first to become imbued with Mahan's dream of a trans-Isthmian canal, took the project over in 1903 through vigorous diplomatic and naval actions and completed it in 1914, with $23 million under budget and six months ahead of schedule. Facilitating the more rapid movement of American naval power around the world, the canal enhanced the ability of the American Navy to protect trade and commerce in the sea lanes.[11]

While president, Roosevelt ordered the Navy to paint its fleet white and have the Great White Fleet circumnavigate the world, calling at various ports to show the flag and demonstrating America's ability to project sea power around the globe.[12]

*****

In 1906, Roosevelt launched a project to prove the identity of the occupant of an unmarked pauper's grave in Paris, France. When the body of one of America's early naval heroes, John Paul Jones, was positively identified, Roosevelt had the body exhumed and brought back to the US Naval Academy. Jones's casket and body were installed in a crypt under the chapel of the Naval Academy, where it still rests. The message this act communicated to all Naval Academy midshipmen, as well as graduates of America's professional naval school, was direct. Jones was an aggressive combat leader who became a model for all American naval officers. When he engaged the British man-of-war HMS *Serapis* off the coast of France, he was outgunned. After an all-night duel, Jones's ship, the USS *Bon Homme Richard*, was burning and sinking. When the British captain yelled over the wreckage of both ships and asked Jones to surrender, his immediate response was "I have not yet begun to fight." Several hours later, the British captain surrendered to him. Jones transferred his flag, his wounded, and his crew to the *Serapis* and watched the *Bon Homme Richard* sink.[13]

In Roosevelt's eulogy that he gave at the Naval Academy's April 24, 1906, reinterment of Jones, he said as follows:

> Every officer of our Navy should know by heart the deeds of John Paul Jones. Every officer in our Navy should feel in each fiber of his being an eager desire to emulate the energy, the professional capacity, the indomitable determination and dauntless scorn of death which marked John Paul Jones above all his fellows... It is well for every American officer to remember that while a surrender may or may not be defensible, the man who refuses to surrender need never make a defense.[14]

Through academic naval leaders like Alfred Thayer Mahan, national leaders like Theodore Roosevelt, and naval combat leaders like John Paul Jones, at the beginning of the twentieth century, naval officers like Kenneth Whiting learned the preferred personality traits that their Navy and their country wanted them to exhibit. When the lives of many US Navy officers are examined, those traits frequently stand out at critical points in their careers.

CHAPTER 4

REFINING A MAN

Of such were the national and naval trends that influenced a young Kenneth Whiting as he grew up and began his career in the United States Navy. Like so many young men of his era, Alfred Thayer Mahan spoke to him. During Whiting's years as a Naval Academy midshipman and beyond, Teddy Roosevelt spoke to the nation and to Whiting from a megaphone with a growing volume. Indeed, it would have been difficult for Whiting or any of his Academy mates, with names like Nimitz, Halsey, Spruance, Mitscher, and McCain, to ignore Mahan's lectures and writings and Roosevelt's speeches and actions.

After Whiting graduated from the Naval Academy on January 30, 1905, as a passed midshipman, he reported on February 15 to the armored cruiser USS *West Virginia* ACR-5 to complete the then-mandatory two years of fleet experience prior to sitting for the written examination for appointment to the lowest naval officer rank of ensign. Soon after the midpoint of Whiting's service on West Virginia, he was transferred to the Asiatic Squadron, and aboard *West Virginia*, Whiting crossed the Pacific Ocean and the International Date Line, bound for her new duty station in Manila Bay, Philippines.[1]

A story from the Nisewaner and Walden Journals of Family Memories tells of the social life of a passed midshipman on an armored cruiser. Whiting and an Academy classmate were invited by some of their fellow passed midshipmen Academy graduates to a steerage party on the battleship USS *Alabama*. The two passed midshipmen rowed over and enjoyed themselves much but decided the battleship midshipmen were too conceited to be tolerated. They invited the battleship midshipmen back to the armored cruiser the next night. When the battleship midshipmen arrived, they were greeted by a rendition of "The Armored Cruiser Song" by Whiting and Academy classmate John Wilcox. Here are two of the verses:

> Away, away with sword and drum,
> Here we come, full of rum,
> Looking for someone to put on the bum,
> The Armored Cruiser Squadron.
>
> Here's to General T. M. Wood,
> Who took a drink whenever he could,
> But be it distinctly understood,
> The drinks were never on T. M. Wood[2]

But in the midst of fun among the young passed midshipmen, the work of the Navy continued. As the fleetwide ensign exams approached, Whiting's old academic laziness reasserted itself, and he did not study for them. As Admiral Van Deurs wrote, "He could not be bothered to study for final examinations. Anything routine bored him. He lived only to enjoy the exciting and unusual and to achieve the impossible." Despite his lack of preparation for the test, he did pass and was commissioned an ensign on January 31, 1907. "When his classmates were commissioned as ensigns [with better test scores ranked] ahead of him, he never worried about being the bottom man."[3]

With his mandatory two years of sea duty as a passed midshipman behind him and a wider gold stripe on the cuffs of his blues, in May 1907, Whiting was transferred to the supply ship of the Asiatic Fleet, the schooner-rigged steamship USS *Supply*. But he was barely able to unpack his bags before he was moved on to the USS *Concord*, a gunship that was also schooner-rigged and steam-driven, a veteran of the Battle of Manila Bay.

Whiting got to use his swimming abilities on the Asiatic station. In Manila, he dove off the deck of the *Concord* on a hot night and decided to swim under the ship and come up the other side. When he got to the keel, he found very little room between the keel and the mud at the bottom of Manila Bay. So he turned on his back and pulled himself through.

Another swimming experience resulted from one of the missions of the Asiatic Fleet to police the rivers of China, which was occupied by several of the great powers in the period leading up the 1912 Boxer Rebellion. While on the *Concord*, as a result of a police action, Whiting was ordered to dive into the Yangtze River and remove some of the Chinese casualties, about which he said, "I got the bodies out of the Yangtze, and they wouldn't take 'em."[4]

*****

In early 1908, Whiting was reassigned to the USS *Supply* and made a cruise from Yokohama to Guam. He found Guam to be boring, and he said, "The end of the earth." Perhaps as a way to chase away their boredom, on March 17, 1908, Whiting and his former Naval Academy roommate, Ensign Theodore G. "Spuds" Ellyson, as young men are wont to do, were having fun one night. But in their fun, they lost control, and they were charged with this offense:

> On midnight of March 17, 1908, they went aboard the Naval Ferry *Mindoro*…in an intoxicated condition and vomited over the chairs and benches of said ferry, and further, at 6:00 a.m., March 18, 1908, still showed the effects of having been under the influence of intoxicating liquor.[5]

Under charges, they were returned to the Philippines. A general court-martial was convened on board USS *Cleveland* (CL 21) at Cavite on August 5, 1908, by order of the commander in chief, US

Naval Force in Philippine waters, to try Whiting and Ellyson on two charges—conduct unbecoming an officer and a gentleman and conduct to the prejudice of good order and discipline. The court-martial found Whiting and Ellyson guilty of both charges and sentenced them each "to lose five numbers in…grade and to be publicly reprimanded by the commander in chief, US Naval Force in Philippine waters."[6]

Whiting said this put him back to the head of the Class of 1906![7]

The commander in chief approved the court proceedings and findings. Before restoring Whiting and Ellyson to duty, secretary of the Navy V. H. Metcalf referred to their former excellent reputations, their comparative youth, and the court's recommendation of clemency before approving their conviction and punishment. In the public reprimand portion of his approval, he said that "while it was deplorable that young officers of promise should bring disgrace upon themselves and the naval service, placing this stain on their good names should cause them to more strongly consider their duties to themselves, their families, and their naval brothers in the future and avoid any repetition of their actions."[8]

For perspective, another member of the Annapolis Class of 1905, Ensign Chester W. Nimitz [destined to end his active naval service as a fleet admiral] was charged with neglect of duty and also convicted in the Philippines by a general court-martial when a destroyer that he commanded, USS *Decatur*, ran aground on a mud bank on July 7, 1908. *Decatur* was pulled free the next day; Nimitz received a reprimand as his court-martial punishment.[9]

In the early-twentieth-century Navy, all three men overcame their early courts-martial and went on to have good careers. Would today's zero-defects Navy have the same level of tolerance for the mistakes of junior officers, or would the major future contributions of very promising young officers be lost to the service?

*****

A few months of service as a junior division officer on larger ships of war on the China station apparently convinced Whiting to volunteer for duty in a very new type of smaller warship, one fraught with danger and still working through the occasional confusion of determining operating doctrine—submarines. Because of the danger, a man had to volunteer to serve in one. Considered risky and primitive, it took courage to volunteer because no way had yet been developed to escape from a sunken submarine.

When the collier USS *Caesar* (AC-16) arrived in Manila with the submarines *Shark* and *Porpoise* cargoed on each side of her well deck, Whiting was in Manila. Painted with red paint, they looked like fat goldfish as high as two tall men. Each goldfish had a foot-high circular hatch mounted on their backs, like a dorsal fin. Their single-torpedo tubes protruded from their bows and looked like a parrot fish's mouth. After they were hoisted from the *Caesar*'s deck, submarine flotilla commander Lieutenant Guy W. S. Castle began recruiting an officer and six men each to man the early submarines.[10]

Intrigued by the challenge of these new, erratic, unreliable boats, Whiting and his good friend Ellyson volunteered for submarine duty. Whiting particularly liked the opportunity to display his confidence to handle any emergency that he might meet and to fix any of the new problems, which occurred on almost every dive.[11]

With very small crews, submarines were commanded by junior officers, which made them a fast route to one of the most desired billets in the US Navy, ship command. The challenge for such junior officers was that they had to learn all the operating systems of the entire boat.

Early Plunger-class submarines, which included USS *Shark* and USS *Porpoise*, were built with these specifications: displacement, 107 tons; length, 63 feet, 9 inches; beam, 11 feet, 8 inches; draft, 11 feet; speed, 8 knots surfaced or 7 knots submerged; test depth, 150 feet; complement, 7 men; armament, 1 eighteen-inch torpedo tube; torpedoes, 5.[12]

The first submarine billet to which Whiting was assigned was in USS *Shark* (SS-8), newly transferred to the Asiatic station along with her sister ship USS *Porpoise* (SS-7) for fitting out at the Cavite Submarine Base in Manila Bay. Whiting took command of *Shark* in October 1908.

Upon completion of *Shark's* fitting out, Whiting was transferred to USS *Porpoise*, and he took command of her on November 20, 1908. Ellyson replaced him in *Shark*.

By the time he took command of the *Porpoise*, Whiting had seen much of the Orient. He had swum in the Yangtze River, seen Shanghai, Tsingtao, Chefoo, and Tietsin. He had cruised through the South China Sea, calling at Hong Kong. He had tried smoking opium and sampled Chinese wine. In Shanghai, he had hired a rick-shaw to take him back to the *Concord*. But he became impatient at the slow pace of the coolie, so he changed places with him and ran him to the dock himself.[13]

Trading places with the coolie allowed him to demonstrate his hatred of the Chinese custom of "kowtowing" [acting in an obsessively subservient manner, such as kneeling or touching the ground with the forehead in worship or submission]. Putting the coolie on the rickshaw and pulling him must have made Whiting feel like he was leading his Larchmont children's gang or taking command of his submarine. He was charmed by having his own command, and he and Ellyson held Castle in high regard because he gave them such a free hand with their boats and because they could lead their small crews with eagerness and imagination.[14]

Because of the small size of Plunger-class boats, Whiting and his *Porpoise* crew of six men lived with other crews and their flotilla commander Castle on board the decommissioned gunboat USS *Elcano* (PG-3), moored near *Shark* and *Porpoise*, originally built by Spain, and seized in the Battle of Manila Bay on May 1, 1998.[15]

*****

Now that he had become a submariner, Whiting entered the debates about the continuing challenge of how to escape from a sunken submarine. On the evening of April 14, 1909, he was relaxing with Castle on board the *Elcano* when he declared, "In an emergency, a man could leave a submarine through her torpedo tube."

"Impracticable," answered Castle. "It was tried on a live dog at Newport. He was expelled by a shot of high-pressure air, like a torpedo, and he came up very dead, crushed to pulp by the air pressure."[16]

On the morning of April 15, 1909, Whiting walked down the pier dressed in dungarees, "an unremarkable-looking, remarkable young man. His ambition to try everything once had already involved him in numerous escapades," and today was to be no exception. When his chief gunner's mate reported the boat ready for its scheduled morning dive—everyone on board, battery and air banks full, and their charging lines disconnected—Whiting followed the chief to the *Porpoise*'s hatch, stepped a few rungs down the vertical ladder inside, and ordered the men on the pier to cast off the submarine's lines. His elbows on the rim of the hatch, he ordered the men in the little compartment below to start the gasoline engine. Then he conned the submarine toward the morning sun. After a few miles, he ordered the engine to be stopped and power transferred to the electric motor. A few moments later, he closed the hatch and stepped down the ladder to the boat's only compartment. At Whiting's order, the boat submerged to a depth of twenty feet. With the ballast adjusted so the submarine was slightly heavy, he ordered the motor stopped and let the boat settle to the soft bottom of Manila Bay in thirty feet of water.[17]

Not until then did Whiting announce to his crew of six sailors in the little compartment that he planned to go out the torpedo tube. He had never mentioned his intention to anyone nor asked Castle's permission to try it. He never wanted anyone else blamed or hurt if one of his ideas went sour. He always carried the responsibility and took the chances himself. He was obviously confident as he described to his men how he would do it. His confidence was contagious. Nobody ever thought of how they would explain their captain's death if his plan failed. His cool explanation to them was part of his carefully thought-out plan.[18]

Whiting stripped to his shorts as he gave each man his individual orders. Lying on his back, Whiting put his hands above his head and squirmed his shoulders into the eighteen-inch opening. He pushed himself with his heels until the end of the tube reached his knees. Then men pushed his feet until he could grab the crossbar that stiffened the outer tube door. When he said ready, his men closed the inner door and opened the outer door. Warm seawater rushed down his back and engulfed his body. He gulped his last breath of air before the water closed over his face. He opened the outer door, pulled himself out the tube, and swam to the surface.

His crew surfaced the boat and came out on deck with a heaving line. Whiting was floating on his back a few yards away. He rolled over, swam a few easy strokes, grasped the line, and scrambled aboard. It had taken seventy-seven seconds to get out of the tube and swim to the surface.

Of course, Whiting's method was not perfect because it was a way to save all the crew except the last man, who had to operate the torpedo tube door.[19]

That night, as stories of Whiting's exploit began to make the rounds of Manila's bars, reporters filed big stories based on the many erroneous descriptions of the feat. Some referred to "the whistling explosion of compressed air, which blew him into the embrace of the ocean." Some identified his submarine as the *Shark*, instead of the *Porpoise*. Incorrectly reporting that his flotilla commander was on the scene, some said he "gave Castle a snappy salute as he surfaced." However, Whiting's name in the stories was correct.

Whiting signed the *Porpoise*'s log for the week on April 17, 1909. It included the sentence, "Whiting went through the torpedo tube, boat lying in water in a normal condition, as an experiment." Flotilla Commander Castle filed a report with his superior officer, commander, Third Squadron, US Pacific Fleet, USS *Charleston*, dated April 21, 1909, which included, for the benefit of other submariners, that he had done it "without any crushing air pressure." In Castle's report, he also said, "Ensign Whiting has shown great zeal and ingenuity in devising practicable schemes for the improvement of the submarines in this station."[20]

Describing the experiment conducted from the USS *Porpoise* at the bottom of Manila Bay as "hazardous in the extreme," an extract from the *Army-Navy Journal,* dated Summer 1909, described Ensign Kenneth Whiting, USN, as clinging to the torpedo tube at its outer end, and when the second officer within carried out Whiting's command to open the torpedo tube port, pulled himself out, and used his fine swimming skills to swim to the surface and return on board. The journal said the trial showed that escape from a disabled submarine was possible in certain cases.[21]

Over the years, the rumors and stories rebounded through the Navy and were so embellished or incorrect that many believed it never happened. To this day, sometimes one hears the story about Whiting and the torpedo tube as "Whiting shot himself out of the torpedo tube." Whiting never tried to correct the reports.[22]

Trying to take care of his submarine crew and giving them the ability to be saved from a downed submarine was a harbinger of a career-long commitment of Whiting's; his subordinates always sensed his concern for them and responded with a great deal of loyalty to him. But perhaps because of his innate modesty, Kenneth was never proud of his torpedo-tube exploit and did not like to talk about it. Fame and publicity embarrassed Whiting. He did not feel his submarine experiment was so important, nor did he feel that it was his most important piece of work.[23]

Others, both in submarines and not, thought differently. In the US Navy submarine service and those of other countries' many experiments with equipment specifically developed to perfect the capability of the crew to escape from a sunken submarine followed Kenneth Whiting's daring maneuver, including the Momsen lung, the escape trunk, the Steinke hood, and the Davis submerged escape apparatus, but Whiting took the first successful step in making submarines safer to serve in. Risky though his step was, from descriptions of it, Whiting did not haphazardly put himself in the tube without thinking and propelled himself out of the tube with compressed air. He considered the risks and the history of the poor dog. He planned his action out as carefully as he could. He explained it to his crew calmly and rationally, so they would follow and support him, and carried his plan out in the same manner. Carefully analyzing the danger and developing a rational plan made the risk more manageable and contributed to his success. Such was a hallmark of the man and responded to the criticism of some who say he was an out-of-control risk-taker.

An August 21, 1909, *Tacoma Times* newspaper article, with an interior picture of a *Porpoise* or *Shark* type submarine and an identified picture of Kenneth Whiting in his Naval Academy uniform superimposed, explained well just how it felt then to sail in a submarine. With only one deck and the height at the center of the hull only six feet, six inches, the article explained, most cruises were for one day, and they ate, cooked, and slept on the boat. The men and officers got closer together because of the smallness of the space. They lived like one happy family, sharing all the perils and discomforts.[24]

While in command of *Porpoise*, Whiting taught himself to dive to depths of eighty feet using a breastplate and helmet. He also taught the crews of *Porpoise* and *Shark* the same skill. When the floating dry dock *Dewey*, which was important to the maintenance of the submarines in the flotilla, sank, he and the men he had taught to dive raised her. His men were all-important to him, and he would not ask anyone to do anything he could not or would not do himself.[25]

The physical examinations of Whiting during his time in command of *Porpoise* and *Shark* reflect well upon him as a young naval officer. He weighed the most he ever did as an adult, 156 pounds. After five to six hours of exercise, walking, or biking, his pulse was in the low to mid-90s. His vision in both eyes was 20/20.[26]

*****

On January 31, 1910, Whiting was promoted to lieutenant (junior grade), and on the same date, was given as an additional duty the command of USS *Shark*. From February until May 1910, Whiting replaced Castle as commander of the flotilla, consisting of the submarines *Shark*, *Porpoise*, and *Adder*.[27]

After nearly three years in command of *Porpoise*, over three years of Asiatic station command time in two different submarines and a short time as flotilla commander, Whiting requested a transfer to the US Atlantic Coast and was ordered there to assume command of USS *Tarpon* (SS-14), in October 1910.[28]

In the early years of the twentieth-century, travel of this length took Whiting more than fifty-seven days, nineteen days from Manila to Guam, nineteen days from Guam to Honolulu, nineteen days from Honolulu to San Francisco, and a long train trip from San Francisco to New York.[29]

But Asiatic service and commanding two submarines in three years had changed Whiting's perspective on submarine service. Other factors in Whiting's thinking could have included the fact that this early in his career, he had fulfilled major career expectations for ship command. He had learned Plunger-class submarines and could see no more challenges in that regard. The risk of submarine service may have seemed reduced and therefore less challenging because of his service in them. He could accept command of another submarine flotilla, his next logical career step in submarines, but no newer or better submarines would be built for a decade. What duty would he perform in submarines during that decade?

There was one other significant reason for Whiting's request for transfer to the East Coast. The "Red Mike" of Naval Academy days was approaching thirty years old, and a young lady named Edna May Andresen, four years Whiting's junior and with whom he had grown up in Larchmont, had said no to other suitors while she waited patiently for the one she wanted, Kenneth Whiting.[30]

The Andresens were originally from the cross-border area between the provinces of Schleswig-Holstein, Denmark, and Hamburg, Germany. They emigrated to Gloucester County, New Jersey, where an ancestor fought on the Tory side in the American Revolution and lost his plantation because of it. The Mays, the family of Edna's mother, Effie May, emigrated from Germany in the early 1820s, settled in Ohio, and moved to New York City about 1868.[31]

Ken and Edna were both natural athletes who enjoyed swimming and sailing. Their oldest daughter Eddie explained their attraction this way:

> I think from the beginning she loved him.
> He was a good-looking kid, brown eyes, really

brown, brown curly hair, and a kind of joking wildness about him. He was always very neat. No matter what he was wearing, even old sailing clothes, he was always neat. He was always trim, in good shape, and an athlete who played many sports, all to a degree of excellence without any apparent effort. He had lots of personal charm and was totally unaware of it. She was a blonde, with blue eyes, a round face, and sort of a tomboy. He told somebody during those early days that he was going to marry the girl with the fat, piano legs.[32]

Edna's father, Charles Andresen, was raised on West Forty-Third Street in Manhattan and built a successful hides and leather business there, but Edna was plagued with bronchitis, and Charles moved the family to what was then the country, 98 Park Avenue in Larchmont, which had been a boarding house without indoor bathing facilities whose residents bathed in Long Island Sound. As Charles's business prospered, he bought a yacht, had horses, and traveled in Europe and Russia. Edna attended a finishing school, where she excelled in piano and voice, but was never good in homemaker skills like sewing.[33]

Edna was also a very good athlete, a swimmer, sailor, golfer, tennis player, and horsewoman. In those days, women rode side saddle, with long skirts. At age eleven or twelve, she was thrown from a horse. Her skirt got looped over something, and she was dragged, which caused her discomfort for the rest of her life. An undiscovered injury to her pelvis from that fall caused her problems in later life with having children. But though she continued to burnish her athletic skills in horseback riding, swimming, and sailing, she never really mastered homemaker skills.[34]

Edna used her beautiful singing voice in the choir of St. John's Episcopal Church in Larchmont, her family's church, where she met her fellow parishioner Kenneth Whiting. Unable to contribute any musical skill to the choir, Whiting volunteered to pump the organ. One Sunday, he wanted to leave the church to participate in a sailing contest at the Horseshoe Harbor Yacht Club on the Sound, so he gave the organ a couple of extra-heavy pumps and left for the race. The organ gave out as the choir recessed at the end of the service.[35]

Ken trained Edna for swimming and washtub races, and she became a champion swimmer who liked to swim in cold water. She also continued, without much success, to practice her sewing and knitting, which she felt she would need to perfect if she were married to a low-paid junior naval officer. There were lots of postcards from China, Guam, wherever he was, but the shy "Red Mike" was still not even hinting about a commitment.[36]

When Ken returned to the East Coast, he spent his leave in Larchmont swimming, sailing, and courting Edna Andresen. He would walk from his family's house on Beach Avenue to Edna's house on Park Avenue, accompanied by a chow dog named Brockton Bennett, which he had brought back from the Far East, and sit with her on her front porch. Then he would whisper in the dog's ear, and the chow would walk back to Beach Avenue alone.[37]

*****

After his leave on September 1910, Whiting took command of the submarine *Tarpon*, operating in the Atlantic Torpedo Fleet. Then on January 11, 1911, he received orders to the Newport News Shipbuilding Company to fit out and commission a new, larger, experimental submarine, with many problems, the USS *Seal* (SS 19 1/2), later changed to the G-1 (or G-ONE, as many in the Navy spelled it because of the prevailing negative opinion of her).[38]

Seal was a product of an eager submarine-building competition between Simon Lake's Lake Torpedo Boat Company and Isaac Rice and L. Y. Spear's Electric Boat Company. Electric Boat had had the most success, mostly because of Lake's eccentric ideas about how submarines should be built and used and the unusual features he put in his boats, such as diver lockout chambers, wheels for rolling along the bottom, and watertight superstructures. These unusual features, which were usually inferior, and Lake's forceful personality, caused Electric Boat to win almost all the contracts for submarine construction. Lake sued the Navy, and to settle the dispute, the Navy offered the Lake Torpedo Boat Company a contract to build a boat, as long as it met the Navy's specifications. *Seal* was the result, and it had all of Lake's inferior features, plus trainable torpedo tubes in the superstructure that could shoot torpedoes to port and starboard.[39]

Seal was built to the following specifications: displacement, 400 tons; length, 161 feet; beam, 13 feet; draft, 12 feet; speed, 14 knots surface or 10 knots submerged; test depth, 200 feet; complement, 24 officers and men; armament, 6 eighteen-inch torpedo tubes.[40]

Doubting Lake's goofy features would operate properly, "the Navy hedged against the possible failure of the boat and assigned the *Seal* a hull number of 19 1/2." She was also renamed the G-1. In the Navy's entire history, *Seal* was the only ship to be assigned a hull number that included the number 1/2. As expected, she proved to be flawed but not as badly as the Navy feared. She was 2 and 1/2 years behind schedule in her development. The configuration of two of her four engines in tandem on each of her two shafts was unsuccessful. Her superstructure, which was supposed to be watertight, was not. She dived very slowly, and she did not meet the Navy's specifications for endurance. The wheels on her hull and the trainable torpedo tubes were especially disliked. Nevertheless, she was described as fairly reliable by Congress's Board of Inspection and Survey (INSURV), an oversight office staffed by Navy personnel.[41]

*****

Whiting was promoted to the rank of lieutenant on March 4, 1911.[42] It was during Whiting's *Seal* fitting-out assignment that his mother, Daisy, took command of his love life and sent his older sister Katherine and Edna Andresen to Newport News with this order to her daughter, "Don't come back until they're engaged!"[43]

The Nisewaner and Walden Journals of Family Memories continued:

> Daisy knew there was no one else for Edna,
> and knew, too, that she would take very good care

of him, which it seemed he would need. He was a Cloud Niner, smoked Chesterfields since age 11, liked to drink, and was already in experimental submarines, by no means a safe occupation.[44]

The trip was successful, and Ken and Edna announced their engagement in April 1911. "A year later, on April 24, 1912," according to the Nisewaner and Walden Journals of Family Memories, "they were married, *finally*, in Larchmont's St. John's Episcopal Church." Ken's best man was his younger brother Butler. Ushers were Lieutenant John Wilcox, Lieutenant Guy Castle, Lieutenant Lawrence McNair, and Ken's younger brother, Naval Academy Midshipman F. E. M. "Pete" Whiting. Edna's maid of honor was Mrs. William Higgen. A special car was attached to an express train to bring guests to and from New York City and Larchmont.[45]

Guy Castle was awarded the Congressional Medal of Honor for action at Vera Cruz, Mexico, in 1914. He died at sea on August 10, 1919, having achieved the rank of commander.[46]

John Wilcox went on to a long Navy career. As a rear admiral, he was in command of Task Force 39, consisting of the carrier USS *Wasp*, two heavy cruisers, eight destroyers, and his flagship, the battleship USS *Washington*, when he went overboard on March 27, 1942, under mysterious circumstances while on his way to the British Fleet base at Scapa Flow to provide support to the Soviet Union for convoys to Murmansk. His body was never recovered, and he was the only US Navy admiral ever lost at sea.[47]

The family practice of awarding nicknames for its members continued. Ken and Edna already called each other Chum, and this continued for their entire lives. Ken, who really liked his in-laws and had a good relationship with them, called Edna's parents "the Dickeys" or "the Dickie-birds."[48]

Second daughter Moira wrote in the Nisewaner and Walden Journals of Family Memories:

> I often wonder how it was for my mother
> in those early years, when she was thrown into

such a strange way of life, totally foreign to her, with full responsibility for this unusual man. Ken and Edna Whiting honeymooned in New York's Adirondack Mountains, wrapped up against the cold, poling rafts in cold mountain streams, far from the salt water that was home to them.[49]

The first summer of their marriage, Ken and Edna began a family tradition, which was to last throughout their married years. Ken would always take his entire annual leave allocation at the Andresen family home, 98 Park Avenue, in July or August, for the Horseshoe Harbor Yacht Club's annual Larchmont Race Week. He, Butts, and Edna would pilot big sailboats owned by others and enter other swimming and tub races. The Whitings were very competitive sailors and swimmers and won frequently.[50]

They participated in their first summer race week as a married couple in August 1912. Ken trained Edna, who was, of course, already a good swimmer. He placed her on a strict diet—no potatoes, only a small steak, and tomatoes for breakfast the day of the race, and nothing more until after the race.[51]

Edna had chosen a modest bathing suit with a big skirt that Ken did not consider hydrodynamically sound. There are two stories embedded in family lore about what happened next. The first is that Ken argued with Edna about the swimming suit, but she refused to change it. The second is that Ken tied a line to the skirt, and when she started the race, he pulled the skirt off as she dove in. Regardless of which story is true, she won the race, and the family has the gold medal to prove it.[52]

Edna was a fine sailor too and won the Yacht Club's 1912 Regatta in the middle of stiff sou'wester in a borrowed yacht.[53]

*****

With G-1's strange pieces of equipment, working with her was a challenge from the start. After Whiting fitted *Seal* out, his friend Ellyson was assigned to command her. But Ellyson was to apply for aviation duty, and when his application was accepted, Whiting would be ordered to replace him as commanding officer. Ken and Edna moved into the Montague Hotel in Brooklyn after their wedding while Whiting continued his efforts to solve G-1's challenges. Officers and men had offices in an old boxcar that was parked on a rail siding near the submarine. It was slow work, and G-1 was expected to be ready to go to New London before winter 1912. But she was still in Brooklyn Navy Yard in April 1913.[54]

In the summer of 1913, Clarkson Cowl—chairman of the board, vice president, and treasurer of James Hearn and Son department store; founder of the grain brokerage firm of Logan, Cowl, and Company; and president of the Central Mercantile Association— began loaning his two-masted schooner *Moira* to the Whitings every summer, as long as they continued to race her. This went on for many years, with the Whitings racing and cruising on Long Island Sound in Cowl's schooner.[55]

Whiting had run up significant debts from his bachelor days and Edna put the household on a strict budget to pay off the debts. They invited fellow officers and their wives to the Montague to play cribbage in the evening for small stakes. Their losing guests contributed to the "cocktail fund" and to the debt. The men were sure that Edna was watering down the gin, and she said each officer could only have one drink and a heeltap. The debt got smaller and no one really cared.[56]

By the end of 1913, the G-1 and the Whitings had moved to Newport, Rhode Island. The Whitings lived in a boarding house off Kay Street, and the major indoor entertainment was playing cribbage there with friends to continue to make dents in the Whiting family debt. As often as they could, they ice-skated on Easton's Pond, which was frozen the whole winter.[57]

Whiting continued to wrestle with G-1's many problems, like a fire caused by using hydrogen gas to recharge batteries, and progress was slow. It took Whiting until the spring of 1914 to make the radical ship perform properly, and along the way in October 1913, as the only officer on board, he took *Seal* to a new dive depth record of 256 feet in Long Island Sound. Whiting also set several other performance records and proved innovations still used to design today's submarines.[58]

Putting a fine point on Whiting's service in submarines and documenting one of his innovations was the US Patent Office's award of patent #1,097,700 to Whiting on May 26, 1914, for his invention of a piece of equipment to blow water from the exercise heads of torpedoes, which made them float to the surface after they had hit or passed their targets. This made them reusable, an early example of the Navy's sustainable use of resources. The Navy used this device for many years. This was not to be Whiting's only work in the field of patents.[59]

Another contribution made by Whiting as his six years of submarine service drew to a close was a plan he authored to standardize the training of submarine officers. He was given credit for this proposal by Admiral Yates Sterling at the Navy Submarine School at New London in July 1916.[60]

*****

Having succeeded in mastering the risk and challenge of submarines, Whiting looked skyward and saw a new challenge. Navy men were trying to master new pieces of primitive equipment called airplanes. In addition to courage, pilots would need the high level of all-body physical dexterity possessed by superior athletes like Whiting.

The idea to apply for pilot training had first risen with Whiting in command of Tarpon and Ellyson commanding G-1/*Seal* at a 1910 dinner hosted by then non-aviator William F. Halsey, with Ellyson and Whiting in attendance. As Halsey told it, he had his first contact with Naval Aviation at that Norfolk dinner with his two Naval Academy and submariner friends. Whiting asked Ellyson if he had thought anything about then-very new Naval Aviation. Ellyson replied that he had not, and Whiting said he was very interested. He said he had been watching early flyers like the Wright Brothers and Glenn Curtiss and had put in an official application to the Navy Department to learn to fly.[61]

Ellyson asked Whiting to send him a copy of his letter so he could apply also. To Whiting's irritation, Ellyson received Navy orders to learn to fly, which was to make him naval aviator number 1, and Whiting was ordered to take command of G-1/*Seal*. It was to be three or four years before Whiting was transferred to aviation and became naval aviator number 16.[62]

Telling the story in a slightly different way, according to the Nisewaner and Walden Journals of Family Memories, this was the first time either of them had thought about becoming a pilot. Soon after, both their applications had been submitted; both received replies from the Navy Department that their requests had been put on file.[63]

But the Navy Department decided to act first on Ellyson's application, and on October 22, 1912, Ellyson received telegraph orders relieving him of command of the G-1 and directing him to report to Glenn Curtiss in San Diego for aviation duty and pilot training. Curtiss was an airplane manufacturer and pilot who had asked for a naval officer to work with him at his plant. On the same day, Whiting got orders to relieve Ellyson as commander of submarine G-1, and he took command on October 28.[64]

Once in pilot training, Ellyson tried to return Whiting's favor by recommending him for pilot training, but Captain W. I. Chambers, in the office of the secretary of the Navy, wrote about Whiting in the margin of Ellyson's letter, "too slow, and his present duty too important." One assumes that Whiting's academic laziness had caught up with him and that, before deciding, Chambers had reviewed Whiting's Naval Academy grades and class rank as well as his performance on the fleet exam for ensign. Chambers was probably also referring to Whiting's present very challenging duty in command of the G-1.[65]

Ellyson, who became naval aviator number 1 as a result of his assignment to Curtiss, served in aviation until February 27, 1928, when as executive officer of the Navy's second aircraft carrier, USS *Lexington* (CV-2), he crashed and died on a night flight from Norfolk to Annapolis. This ended nearly thirty-year, close friendship of the two former Naval Academy roommates, who had together undergone midshipman punishment, court-martial, and early service in both submarines and Naval Aviation.[66]

CHAPTER 5

NEW RISK AND A NEW INSTRUMENT
TO PROJECT SEA POWER

Perhaps as a reward for the successes he had achieved with G-1, Whiting was finally accepted for pilot training on June 29, 1914, and ordered to report to the Wright Company in Dayton, Ohio, as the last Navy pilot to be taught to fly by Orville Wright. On the eve of this next great career challenge, as Whiting thought about the over seven years he had served in submarines, he might have had the same bitter taste in his mouth that many Navy submariners had about the difficulties of perfecting *Seal*/G-1, with so many experimental and never accepted features. When the Navy established a submarine school in New London, Connecticut, *Seal* was used as a school boat there. Those negative feelings on the part of the Navy eventually played out by assigning the unfortunate boat to undergo depth-charge tests in Narragansett Bay. When she was sunk in those tests, she was abandoned by the Navy on August 26, 1921, "unmourned and with a hearty good riddance."[1]

Had Whiting remained in the submarine service, it would have been six years before a larger, better, and less problematic class of submarines called S-boats would have come along. The specifications for the S-boat class were displacement, 1,180 tons; length, 219 feet; beam, 20 feet, 3/4 inches; draft, 16 feet; speed, 14.5 knots surface or 11 knots submerged; test depth, 200 feet; complement, 4 officers,

39 enlisted; armament, 1 four-inch deck gun, .30-caliber machine guns, 16 Mark 10 torpedoes, propulsion 2 diesel engines (surface), 2 electric motors (submerged).[2]

At this point, by being turned down for pilot training the first time, Whiting had probably learned a valuable career lesson about the negative impact of his poor grades and academic laziness on his career. He had applied himself mentally and physically in addressing *Seal*'s operational problems and had passed a final examination of sorts in solving those problems. Whiting probably could not have solved *Seal*/G-1's problems without conquering his academic laziness. Whiting's personal success, as well as the skills he had gained in ship command, would be important factors in his future Navy career in his new aviation specialty. He would carry with him a name and a reputation he had earned in submarines, well stated by Turnbull and Lord in their comprehensive history of Naval Aviation: "[The name] Whiting is standstill a tradition in the 'Pig Boats.'" In aviation, he had also found a new source of challenge and high risk, the importance to him of which he had already demonstrated. The high risk inherent in aviation had been proven by the deaths of two naval aviators during Whiting's seven-plus years of service in submarines. William D. Billingsley, naval aviator number 9, fell out of an airplane in turbulent weather over Chesapeake Bay in June 1913, and James M. Murray, naval aviator number 10, drowned following a crash in February 1914. But soon after Whiting's transfer to aviation, a series of accidents and fatalities occurred, with some of them by good friends of Whiting's, in the fledgling machines of early Naval Aviation.[3]

An indicator of how Congress and the Navy measured the risk inherent in piloting those early airplanes comes from Whiting's early pay records. A pay stub in the Whiting field files for the first four months of 1916 shows that, as a lieutenant with just over eight years of service, Whiting's base pay per month was $260. In addition, he received an extra stipend of 50 percent of his base pay, or $130 per month, to reflect his hazardous duty as a pilot.[4]

*****

Whiting's career turnaround presaged that of Army officer Dwight Eisenhower, born a decade after Whiting and with the same high athletic ability, the same likable personality, the same latent cognitive potential (during Prohibition, as late as the early 1920s, Eisenhower and his friend George Patton were using their cognitive abilities and creative ways to have fun by developing a new secret recipe for bathtub gin), and the same academic laziness that caused him to graduate in the middle of his West Point class and continued through the first decade of his career. Eisenhower had also received two written reprimands from US Army chief of Infantry, Major General Charles S. Farnsworth, one for filing for two housing allowances and one for publishing an article advocating the use of tanks in ways that violated 1920s Army doctrine about their use. Eisenhower achieved his turnaround through the mentoring and tutoring of Brigadier General Fox Conner during a tour in the Panama Canal Zone in the early 1920s. Whiting's contributions during and after his command tour in *Seal*/G-1 and Eisenhower's military career successes after his service under General Conner, from graduating first in his class at the Command and General Staff College to supreme commander of the Allied Expeditionary Force in Europe in World War II demonstrate well the strength of both men's career turnarounds. But it took Conner's efforts on behalf of Eisenhower's career to overcome Farnsworth's antipathy toward him and obtain the assignment to the Command and General Staff College.[5]

Overlooking the early weak performance and disciplinary incidents of both Eisenhower and Whiting, the Army and Navy probably noted the turnarounds of both officers and allowed their service to continue. Would today's zero-defects military allow their careers to proceed despite their misconduct?

*****

With Orville Wright as his instructor, after a physical, Whiting reported on June 29, 1914, to the Wright Flying School in Dayton, Ohio, for flight instruction.[6]

After the Wright brothers' historic flight at Kitty Hawk, North Carolina, on December 17, 1903, they tried to keep the details of their airplane confidential while seeking to patent it. At the same time, they became embroiled in a decade-plus series of patent lawsuits over wing-warping control systems with other early aviation pioneers like Glenn Curtiss and Alexander Graham Bell. During the lawsuits, the Navy hedged its bets and sent other officers like Ellyson and John Towers to Curtiss's flying school. The lawsuits also kept other companies from entering aircraft manufacturing, and they were finally settled on the eve of World War I by an agreement under which the federal government bought up patents and allowed all manufacturers to use them. Meanwhile, the Wrights continued their work to improve their airplanes and charged $250 tuition for student groups of no more than 4 or 5 (after reducing their initial fee of $500 for single students), opened up their Wright Flying School in 1910 at a field in Montgomery, Alabama (the site was later to become part of Maxwell Air Force Base). As the weather warmed in May, they relocated their school to Huffman Prairie, near Fairburn, eight miles northeast of their home in Dayton, Ohio; part of the instruction also occurred at Simms Station, another field just south of Dayton. Two years after the move to Huffman Prairie, Wilbur Wright, exhausted from the patent lawsuit fight, contracted typhoid fever and died on May 30, 1912. In addition to Whiting, other well-known graduates of the Wrights' School included naval aviator number 2, John Rodgers; Henry H. "Hap" Arnold, who commanded the Army Air Corps in World War II; and Thomas DeWitt Milling, the Army's first pilot to earn his wings.[7]

Wright wasted no time in beginning Whiting's pilot training. Huffman Prairie was an 84-acre rough cow pasture, so before a pilot could take off, the cows had to be shooed out of the way. For their license, they were required to take off, reach an altitude of 100 feet, do a figure 8 around the field, stay up for five minutes, and land safely. On August 6, 1914, Whiting was designated naval aviator number 16. "He was the last naval officer taught to fly at Orville Wright's school. To [Whiting], flying was just something else he did well easily, like swimming or sailing." The similar performance characteristics as airfoils of the sails on sailboats and of early aircraft wings probably facilitated Whiting's understanding of flying.[8]

The plane Whiting and his classmates trained in was the Wright Model B, a pusher biplane. Its specifications were as follows: crew and passenger—1 pilot, one passenger, seated in tandem on the lower wing; length—29 feet, 8 inches; wingspan—39 feet; height—8 feet, 9 inches; weight—800 pounds; power plant—1 Wright vertical 4-engine, 35 horsepower; maximum speed—45 miles per hour; cruising speed—40 miles per hour; range—110 miles.[9]

Whiting was happy to be in a new field. Submarines had become too well organized, too routine.[10]

The diary of Milton Wright, then a retired bishop of the United Church of the Brethren in Christ and the father of Orville and Wilbur Wright, makes it apparent that, from the beginning, the relationship of Orville and Kenneth and Edna Whiting was more than teacher and student.

> Sunday, July 19: Lieut. Whiting and wife called an hour, about 4:00.
> Sunday, July 26: Lieut. Whiting and wife dined with us, after one o'clock and remained till nearly bedtime.
> Thursday, August, 13: [Orville's sister] Katharine and Orville went down with Lieut. Whiting and came home at 4:30.[11]

Bishop Wright's diary also documented an early calamity of Whiting's pilot training:

> "Tuesday, August 18: Orville and Lieut. Whiting tried the airship on the River." They were flying over the Miami River three miles south of Dayton, Ohio, at 80 feet altitude. "The machine broke and Wright and Whiting plummeted into the river." Except for bumps and bruises, neither man was hurt, but they left the wreckage of the

plane in the middle of the Miami as they swam for shore. Whiting had replaced submarines with a new risk.[12]

*****

In September 1914, Whiting completed Orville Wright's course of flight instruction. He was ordered to the still small Pensacola Naval Aeronautic Station and designated as senior officer present (SOP) on November 23, 1914. He was instructed to establish a flying school, which was the beginning of NAS Pensacola and "to take over all government property from the present custodian," which was the US Marines. All government property consisted of a few sets of quarters, some office buildings, and lots of weeds. Being senior, Whiting relieved Lieutenant (junior grade) Godfrey DeCourcelles Chevalier (nicknames Chevy, Darp), USNA 1910 and naval aviator number 7.[13]

The US Navy's Pensacola Navy Yard, a ship-operating base, had been in Pensacola since 1826. Meanwhile, the Navy Department had made W. I. Chambers its first full-time officer in charge of Naval Aviation, and Congress had funded Naval Aviation development in its 1911–1912 Naval Appropriation Act. One of the Navy's first actions in its development of aviation was to establish its first naval air station at Pensacola. Seeking the much better climate for flying found in the Florida panhandle, on January 20, 1914, Lieutenant Commander Henry Mustin, naval aviator number 11, and Lieutenant John Towers, naval aviator number 3, debarked at NAS Pensacola from the USS *Mississippi* with all the nine officers, twenty-three enlisted men, and seven aircraft of the former Naval Aviation Camp at Greenbury Point near Annapolis, Maryland.[14]

Chevalier, one of the original nine officers from the Naval Aviation Camp, had served previously as SOP at Pensacola and had faced challenges. The station ship USS *North Carolina*, which held all the pay and records of the Pensacola Naval Aeronautic Station's officers and men, had suddenly sailed for Europe at the outbreak of World War I to help support neutral Americans caught in the growing fighting in World War I. Chevalier's men had not been paid in over five weeks, and Chevalier had to scramble to support them. The men had accrued debts to Pensacola merchants and needed money to subsist for their families and themselves. Chevalier convinced a local banker to allow his men to sign notes, promising to pay them when the Navy paid them. Next, he negotiated with a supply officer in Charleston, South Carolina, to pay for the men's meals in the station mess. Such were the challenges faced by the SOP at Pensacola Naval Aeronautic Station and the methods that he had to use, at the far end of the supply chain, to take care of his unit. Whiting would face many of the same challenges as the station's new SOP.[15]

In his first two weeks as SOP, Whiting received a letter dated September 22, 1914, from Captain Mark Bristol, office of the secretary of the Navy and his superior officer. Bristol discussed the pay and supply problem caused by North Carolina's absence, which Whiting had inherited from Chevalier, and directed Whiting to write him weekly, describing the problems he was facing. Bristol's letter included a directive to fly as much as he could with Chevalier, Whiting's new instructor, and obtain his Navy air pilot certificate as soon as possible. Though Chevalier was lower in rank and had less leadership experience than Whiting, he was a more experienced pilot; there was much Chevalier could teach Whiting about airplanes to round out the training Whiting had received from Orville Wright. Besides, there was much experimental aviation work to be done, and Bristol wanted Whiting as well prepared as possible to carry it out. Along the way, Whiting and Chevalier became very good and close friends.[16]

Retired Rear Admiral George Van Deurs provided one view of the leadership of Whiting and Chevalier of the fledgling Pensacola installation. Unlike Whiting, Chevalier had not yet developed a service-wide reputation, but the two men were alike in important ways. They built a common vision of the possible future of Naval Aviation not shared by many of their fellow naval aviators. They concentrated on the essentials of putting men and machines in the air and scorned the details. They focused on making Navy planes and the small number of pilots assigned there better.[17]

Working within the low resources of early Naval Aviation, when the money was spent and the work done, drinking was pleasanter than addressing problems, which were not possible to solve. Early Pensacola was a loose organization, and men worked because leaders like Whiting and Chevalier were well-liked.[18]

Another perspective on the issues raised by Van Deurs about Whiting's leadership of the Navy's first naval air station is provided by the Kenneth Whiting files at NAS Whiting Field. The files contain a continuing series of letters back and forth between Bristol and Whiting during Whiting's assignment as SOP discussing the many administrative issues that plagued the station and documenting the actions Whiting took to address and solve them. In these efforts, it helped that Whiting had the administrative experience commanding submarines and a submarine flotilla, which Chevalier did not have, but as senior officer present, he lacked the full authority of a commanding officer to implement solutions.[19]

With the Navy Department's Congressional authority and funding for the development of Naval Aviation now formalized, it moved to tighten up its aviation chain of command and the authority of those in the chain. Bristol replaced Chambers, but with the new title of director of aeronautics. No longer would there be a mere senior officer present at NAS Pensacola; there would be a commanding officer with all the authority inherent in that title. Since Mustin outranked Whiting, Bristol appointed Mustin to the commanding officer billet in January 1915 and relieved Whiting as SOP Whiting remained as executive officer, and as executive officer, he started a catapult school for the pilots. As one of his first actions as commanding officer, Mustin, who had previously had to operate an unofficial air station with inadequate help and money, wrote to Bristol and said both Whiting and Chevalier "were just swamped and had done wonders under the circumstances."[20]

On April 10, 1915, under Chevalier's instruction, Whiting qualified for his Navy pilot certificate and became naval air pilot number 11, which after a complete renumbering of its pilots by the Navy Department morphed into naval aviator number 16. At about the same time, Whiting and another pilot, Walter Brookins, were involved in a crash. Chevalier said, "Be careful, Mr. Whiting, for the love of Mike. Let some of us worthless bums do the tumbling stuff… tell Mrs. Whiting that I have a corner on all the tumbles and smashes from now on."[21]

On May 10, 1915, Ken and Edna's first child, named Edna (nicknames Eddie, Ant) was born in the Whiting quarters. Since NAS Pensacola was the Navy's first naval air station, Edna was "the first child to be born on a naval air station, and at that time, the only one." Because of Edna's undiagnosed pelvic damage from being thrown from a horse as a child, her daughter Eddie was born with a withered right arm. When Eddie was a very young child, Edna tried to get her to carry out a program of regular exercises and treatments to strengthen the limb and hand. Eddie resisted vigorously, and after eight years, Edna gave up trying to make her do them. However, all was not lost, and despite Eddie's arm and hand, Ken and Edna raised Eddie to be a strong, independent, and effective member of the family. She could sail a boat with one hand, and later on, when she sometimes recruited boys to go sailing with her, she was always the captain. Later on, Eddie taught herself to print beautifully with her left hand; as an adult, she used her skill to prepare one of the two Nisewaner and Walden Journals of Family Memories, so import-ant in telling the personal side of this Kenneth Whiting biography. Her arm was rarely photographed in any family pictures. With a hair band to keep her curly hair in place and her photographs always reflecting the savvy look in her eyes, it would be a mistake for anyone to see her as handicapped.[22]

With Whiting serving as best man, one of Pensacola's pilots, Wynne Spencer, married Wallis Warfield. Later, Warfield divorced Spencer and married the Duke of Windsor, heir apparent to the British throne.[23]

Another accomplishment of Whiting's during his tour at Pensacola was his acquisition of a civilian pilot's license from the Aero Club of America. In a letter to Whiting dated June 24, 1915, Secretary Howard Huntington, Aero Club of America, informed Whiting that he had been granted an expert certificate (pilot's license) from the Club on June 23, 1915. The Aero Club of America began issuing optional private pilot's licenses in 1911. Congress passed the Air Commerce Act in 1927, and the Federal government took mandatory authority from then on for the issuance of pilot's licenses.[24]

Among other actions as commanding officer, NAS Pensacola, Mustin used his new authority to rein in excessive drinking by the pilots by requiring them to sign this statement before getting in the cockpit: "I am ready for flight," meaning, "I certify on my honor that during the preceding twenty-four hours, I have not taken a drink of any alcoholic liquor, and my physical condition is normal in all respects." This forced the pilots to confine their drinking to Saturday night dinner dances at a Pensacola hotel named the San Carlos. The signed statements "and the Saturday night dinner dances at the San Carlos were Pensacola institutions long after Mustin's time."[25]

In September 1915, a hurricane blew away the hangars and damaged airplanes. The crash boat also burned. On July 5, 1916, another hurricane causing over $20 million in current dollars in damage hit the station, leaving the flying school in a shamble and without any working planes. Times were hard for the aviators, but work at Pensacola continued. Planes were tested. Swept-back wings, triple pontoons, altimeters, and bombs were some of the things that were a part of the daily routine.[26]

*****

Whiting's relief as NAS Pensacola's SOP in January 1915 had allowed him to concentrate on perfecting his flying skills. One other major sequence of activities would test him perhaps even more than *Seal* had and reveal other significant professional strengths; the sequence also uncovered what would become major comprehensive professional disagreements between the non-aviator Bristol and aviator Mustin, who was backed by all the Pensacola pilots. Although the Navy had only experienced the deaths of two of its pilots in airplane crashes until the beginning of 1915, over the next few months, three more of its pilots were to crash and die. As the appointed chairman of the crash investigation boards, Whiting was to play a significant role in these investigations and in the conflict between the Pensacola pilots and the non-aviator senior officers at the Department of Navy over their causes.[27]

The pilots who died in those crashes were Melvin L. Stolz, James V. Rockwell, and Richard C. Saufley, and all the aircraft involved were Curtiss-manufactured "pusher" aircraft. A pusher aircraft's center of gravity was near the center of the aircraft, where the engine was mounted between the wings and behind the pilot, and his seat was located far forward (to better see the ground or water underneath the craft). The non-aviator senior officers in Washington purchased these aircraft and were ideologically and financially committed to them. Pilot error caused by a shortage of aircraft and not flying frequently enough was cited by the senior officers as the causes of all three crashes. The junior officer pilots believed that pusher aircraft were less stable than "tractor" aircraft, which had engines mounted far forward and the pilot seated behind the engine. This instability of pusher airplanes caused the airplane to be more likely to stall and go into a spin, a condition from which no pilot had yet discovered a way to recover. After each crash, a three-man board was appointed to investigate the crash and determine its cause. In each case, Whiting was appointed the chairman; all three boards, reflecting the prevailing opinion of the Pensacola pilots, concluded that the instability of the center-mounted pusher engine was the proximate cause of the crashes and deaths. Aviator Mustin supported each board's findings and forwarded them to Washington, where they were disapproved by the Navy's non-aviator senior officers. Whiting's signature on each board's report put him squarely in the sights of his Department of the Navy superiors, and it is not difficult to imagine the pressure the young officer was under. It was another early test of his mettle, but with Mustin's support, Whiting stood his ground.[28]

In one of only two articles dealing with the characteristics of good line and staff officers published in US Naval Institute's *Proceedings* between 1867 and 1960, Vice Admiral George C. Dyer discussed the personality traits that make up a good officer of the line [who command] and staff [who support commanders] of the United States Navy.

The one essential characteristic of the senior naval officer of the line is "marked leadership... The marked leadership characteristic includes three qualities...(1) a fighting spirit, (2) physical courage, and (3) a complete and sympathetic understanding of, and a wholesome respect for those who serve under and support the leader.[29]

In most cases, the only arena for the true test of fighting spirit—a hot war—is not available. In peacetime, an officer displays a fighting spirit when he "risks his official neck over a piece of paper, an idea, a sound principle, or his service." Over his career, Whiting risked his neck many times over all these things.[30]

Fighting spirit can be measured by the vigor and resolution with which an officer battles the enemy or his opponents under favorable or unfavorable conditions. It can also be measured by an officer's ability to live and grow stronger from day to day while under frequent and heavy attacks of the enemy or his opponents. Physical courage is fighting spirit, plus continuing to think and act offensively when an officer is under great hazard.[31]

The third quality "encompasses an interest in and a real knowledge of humanity and the humans who support the leader in his endeavors, and it produces loyal shipmates to admirals and seamen, airmen, and firemen." In his earlier service in locations like torpedo tubes in a submerged submarine, in his chairing of crash investigation boards, and in his future testimony before the Morrow Board and the Mitchell court-martial, Whiting displayed all three of these qualities: a fighting spirit, physical courage, and understanding and respect for those who served under him. Particularly, in the case of the three crash investigation boards, he risked his "official neck over a sound principle" and the pieces of paper containing his signature on which that principle was documented. In the future, he would display the same traits fighting for another idea which, when the Navy adopted it, was to have an enormous impact on the future ability of the Navy to perform its mission worldwide. From day to day, he must have been under frequent and heavy attacks from his opponents, the senior officers of the Navy, yet he kept thinking and acting offensively despite the great element of hazard to his career. Finally, he was making his fight over the future of pusher aircraft for his fellow pilots and their lives, and Van Deurs documented well the loyalty Whiting earned from them.[32]

On March 10, 1916, Bristol, in an obvious career move to acquire time in command at sea and to avoid a continuing conflict with Chambers, his predecessor, arrived in Pensacola and assumed command of the Air Service and of the USS *North Carolina*. Bristol immediately became embroiled in another conflict with Mustin. These two strong personalities differed on many things, and their relationship was marked by continuing disagreement. Mustin had backed a proposal of Whiting's that a big seagoing train ferry owned by Henry M. Flagler's Florida East Coast Railway and named for Flagler be acquired and converted into an experimental airplane carrier because "her double-deck construction, providing both protection for planes and a landing platform, made her ideal for experimental purposes." Bristol, who believed that ships should have catapults only, had stopped it.[33]

Another example of the continuing conflict between the Navy's senior admirals and the young pilots came when one of those pilots, Harry Bartlett, crashed his plane. Whiting borrowed Admiral Albert Gleaves's barge to rescue him. After the rescue, Gleaves put Bartlett on restriction for destroying government property. Chevalier [and many of the other pilots] deplored the attitude of the Navy's non-aviator admirals toward planes and its junior officer aviators.

Over the next twenty-plus years until those junior officer aviators were promoted to senior rank and could make more knowledgeable decisions to positively impact Naval Aviation, non-aviator battleship admirals were to evaluate the performance of aviators in ways that caused great harm to their careers. Until then, the Navy sometimes sacrificed the potential contributions of Naval Aviation and its aviators. Near the end of that twenty-year period, Whiting was to become one of the naval aviators whose careers were harmed.[34]

In the midst of the continuing conflict between Bristol and Mustin, one might miss the genesis of the greatest thread of American

Naval Aviation, the development of aircraft carriers, and the man who began to sew it, Kenneth Whiting. In early 1916, Whiting began publicly agitating [within the Navy] for a new ship he called a plane carrier, which was destined to revolutionize the Navy and naval warfare. Whiting is sometimes referred to as the US Navy's Father of the Aircraft Carrier, and it was at this time that he began to earn the title.[35]

But the ebb and flow of the continuing conflict between Bristol and Mustin would continue well into 1916, with Whiting continuing to agitate for plane carriers and studying and discussing other ways his goal could be achieved.

Bristol wasted no time in using his authority as commander of the Air Service, and on the day he took over, he had all the student aviators; station officers Chevalier; Harold W. Scofield, naval aviator number 28; William M. Corry, naval aviator number 23; Albert C. "Putty" Read, naval aviator number 24; Harold T. Bartlett, naval aviator number 21; and Patrick N. L. Bellinger, naval aviator number 8; and twenty-four enlisted men report aboard the *North Carolina*. That morning, they all began standing deck watches aboard the moored ship, and the ship took on coal for a voyage. Four seaplanes were also taken on board. When coaling was complete, the ship sailed for Guantanamo Bay, Cuba, taken in the Spanish-American War.[36]

Bristol's plan was to demonstrate and develop the roles that Naval Aviation could play with the fleet at sea, including spotting naval artillery rounds using radios with which Bristol had equipped the ship. But the ship had no way to fly off planes. No one knew how to pick up or land a plane at sea. Everyone aboard knew they were unprepared to be a fleet aviation ship, and Bristol knew that his time was running out.[37]

Over the next two weeks, attempts were made to develop the new roles Bristol envisioned, but there were mostly unsuccessful. Bellinger wrote up a complete and optimistic report on the operation, but the best facts could not refute the opinion of the senior line officers who believed that aircraft had no use at sea. The best he could do was to document the lack of success in these trials and recommend more trial-and-error testing in the future. Disapproving Bellinger's further testing recommendation, Bristol, in forwarding the report to the Navy Department, recommended that Pensacola should only train pilots, and the *North Carolina* should develop tactics.[38]

There was one achievement that was to have significant long-term consequences; however, that came to final fruition about the time the *North Carolina* returned to Pensacola. With the leading of the two pilots left behind on the Guantanamo cruise, Whiting and Holden C. Richardson, naval aviator number 13, a catapult had been successfully developed and mounted on a coal barge. Flown by Bellinger the first time, an AB-2 seaplane was launched from the barge. Mounting catapults on plane carriers in the future would enable these new ships to launch airplanes, one of the key evolutions of a carrier.[39]

*****

Returning to the investigations of the three accidents and deaths, Mustin, Whiting, and the Pensacola pilots won their battle because after the third death and investigation board report, Rear Admiral William S. Benson, the Navy's first chief of naval operations (or CNO, the Navy's title for its senior officer), asked Mustin to review all three accidents and deaths. In a lengthy report, which marked Mustin in Navy annals as the pilot's champion and which saved many lives, Mustin summarized the causes of the three crashes as faulty workmanship, poor plane design, and a stubborn refusal to look at the problem from a pilot's point of view. He said he had already addressed the workmanship issues by creating an inspection department that reported directly to him and which maintained a continuous review of all maintenance work performed on aircraft at the station. This was to become standard air station procedure for the entire Navy. Then he addressed all the issues on which he and Bristol had differed over two years. He documented twenty-one different steps he had taken to improve the plane situation. He listed incidents in which Bristol had either delayed action or taken none. He maintained that a non-aviator could not understand all the issues of aviation, that Bristol had only taken two short flights as a passenger since becoming commander of the Air Service, and that Bristol had no real understanding of either aerodynamics or flight instruction. Mustin argued that, as a pilot, all his opinions should be accepted as expert testimony by the Navy Department; if the Department was unwilling to do so, he requested an investigation of his competence by the department. This paper was to become a milestone in the over twenty-five-year path to the Naval Aviation community's commanding its own ships and air stations.[40]

But one victory in a battle did not constitute final victory in the war between the naval aviators and the rest of the Navy. As the battle raged, Bristol gave Mustin a poor fitness report; as a result, Mustin was passed over for promotion to commander, detached from Pensacola on January 31, 1917, and his naval aviator designation revoked. These were not the last prices paid by aviators who battled the surface-dominated power structure of the Navy for the independence of Naval Aviation.[41]

While Mustin's report was being reviewed by the Navy Department, by previous action, Bristol's span of authority over Naval Aviation was reduced by removing shore-based aviation from his command. As a result of Mustin's report, CNO Benson grounded all pusher engine aircraft except for testing pontoons, directed that no more be purchased, and ordered that in the future only tractor-type aircraft be purchased for Pensacola. This may have been the first victory of the Naval Aviation community in its battle for control.[42]

But another victory came on the first one's heels. At the same time, as Benson was reversing Bristol's decisions about tractor aircraft, Benson promoted Mustin and restored him to aviation command.[43]

Perhaps the final event emanating from the three-crash sequence occurred in February 1917, when Marine aviator F. T. Evans was flying a Curtiss N-9 above the beach at Pensacola and decided to try a loop. In the midst of the loop, the aircraft stalled and went into a spin. Prior to Evans's effort, such a spin had always caused a fatal crash. Counterintuitively, instead of pulling the stick backward, he pushed it forward and then applied rudder to stop the spin. On his way back to NAS Pensacola, he realized what he had done and successfully replicated it several more times above the airfield so Navy witnesses could see his feat. The deadly nose dive that had plagued aviation since its beginning had been cured, and "from that day, spin recovery became a part of every student's first instruction… Sixteen years later, the authorities finally awarded Evans the Distinguished Flying Cross for discovering the spin recovery technique."[44]

*****

By now, Naval Aviation had split into several tracks, lighter-than-air dirigibles and blimps, seaplanes launched from and landing on land or water, seaplanes catapulted from battleships and cruisers, and at least one man had begun thinking about a fourth track. Whiting's service at Pensacola had included working in every existing track but lighter-than-air, and the fourth track for which he had begun agitating in early 1916 was ships with long covered decks and hangars underneath, which could carry airplanes anywhere in the world and offensively project naval power. He called these plane carriers. He made his first formal proposal to create plane carriers soon after he had begun talking about this important new idea, when he had recommended that the Navy purchase from the Florida East Coast Railway a big railroad ferryboat, the *Henry M. Flagler*, and convert her into a plane carrier. With her double-deck construction providing both protection for planes and a launching platform, she seemed ideal to begin experimenting with this totally new type of craft.[45]

The *Henry M. Flagler*, constructed at William Camp and Sons Philadelphia shipyard, had the following specifications: displacement—878 tons (2,699 tons fully loaded); propulsion—2 triple expansion engines, 2,700 hp; length—337 feet; beam—59 feet. She was launched on September 22, 1914, and at the time, she was reputed to be the largest car ferry in the world. In service, she ran from Port Everglades, Florida, to Havana, Cuba.[46]

Though Whiting's proposal was not accepted at the time, it is noteworthy that during World War II, the Navy did purchase the *Henry M. Flagler* and two other ferries—the *Joseph R. Parrott* and the *Estrada Palma*—from Flagler's Florida East Coast Railway and converted them for aircraft transport, net laying and mine warfare operations. Nets were strung out near the entrances of friendly ports to deny entrance to unwanted ships, and with the three vessels' large cargo-carrying capacity, the converted ships' service included Africa, Sicily, Tarawa, Kwajalein, Eniwetok, Saipan, Peleliu, Iwo Jima, Leyte, and Okinawa. After the war, the Navy sold all three ships to the West India Fruit and Steamship Company.[47]

In one more footnote to Whiting's tour at Pensacola, in his last year there, he returned to his earlier interest in patents. Perhaps because of their 1916 investigations of the accidents and deaths of their fellow aviators, Mustin and Whiting worked together on the design of seaplanes. This culminated in their joint filing of a patent application on October 17, 1916, for a new design for hydroaeroplanes.[48]

*****

On November 16, 1916, Whiting received orders transferring him to the USS *Washington* (ACR-11), as aviation officer and aide to the commander, Destroyer Force. In this billet, he would report to Rear Admiral Albert Gleaves, commander, Destroyer Force, Atlantic Fleet, and have a unit of seaplanes under his command. On January 4, 1917, after a Christmas leave and time to move his family, Whiting boarded the ship at Portsmouth, New Hampshire, only now the ship's name had been changed to the USS *Seattle* because the Navy decided to change the names of all cruisers to cities and leave only battleships named for states.[49]

Seattle's specifications were as follows: length—504 feet, 5 inches; beam—72 feet, 10 1/2 inches; draft—25 feet; displacement—15,733 tons; speed—22 knots; complement—41 officers, 850 enlisted; propulsion—28,500 horsepower, 2 sets 4-cylinder engines, 2 propellers; main armament—4 ten-inch guns, 16 six-inch, and 22 three-inch, 4 torpedo tubes.[50]

With Edna pregnant with their second child, Ken sent Edna and baby Eddie off to Larchmont and packed up their baggage alone— the only time he packed their household goods alone. He packed Edna's best hat with the flat iron inside and a nest of furniture tables arrived with a ten-penny nail through their tops. Thereafter, he was not entrusted with the role of packing and preserving family items.[51]

Whiting had already built a catapult on a coal tender in Pensacola, and they used the knowledge they had gained in that experiment with the Seattle's catapult before she sailed for the Caribbean early in 1917. But none of the cruiser's planes had a reliable engine, and during her short cruise, most flights had trouble taking off. Those that flew averaged flights of twelve minutes, and many ended with forced landings or crashes. Given Whiting's already-begun agitation for plane carriers and his then active proposal to purchase the *Henry M. Flagler* and convert her, Whiting and his other pilots—William M. Corry, George D. Murray, and Lawrence B. Sperry—joined the *Seattle*…and wished that she were a carrier.[52]

With Whiting's leadership, making the trip rugged and active, the *Seattle* pilots pioneered useful shipboard aviation. He believed in trying new things to learn how, and he had unlimited confidence in his pilots. He was able to persuade the conservative Admiral Gleaves, who had earlier put aviator Bartlett on restriction for destroying government property when he crashed an airplane, and the *Seattle*'s captain to let him try a variety of experiments. A March 16, 1917, memorandum from Whiting to Admiral Gleaves, subject "Options for Recovering Seaplanes on Ships," contains a complete, detailed analysis of those options, not only for recovering planes on ships but also in the water and by which ships. Gleaves' responses to the memo and to Whiting's techniques of persuasion are illustrated by comments in his memoirs, "Whiting was a bold and fearless aviator and did excellent pioneer work in the development of Naval Aviation."[53]

The pilots flew at Port-au-Prince and from Hicacal Beach at Guantanamo [although the United States was not yet in the war, they practiced] patrolling for German submarines. R. A. Lavender, the staff radio officer, flew with them repeatedly in the course of improving their temperamental wireless sets, and for the first time, an American ship, while she was firing, received radio spots from a plane.[54]

Whiting and his pilots also began pondering how to install and use the arresting gear, then called retarding gear, which they had already made to work on a coal barge, so airplanes could perform the second important plane carrier evolution and land on ships.[55]

While Edna was living with the Dickeys and expecting their second child, before going off to war, husband and father Whiting wrote Edna a letter from the *Seattle* and provided evidence of his growing maturity by giving thought to the growing family he was leaving behind. As reported in a *Pensacola News Journal* article by NAS Pensacola historian Hill Goodspeed, he told his wife, Edna, the following:

> Should anything happen to me, I would like our kids brought up much the same way you and I have been...not confined to any one religion nor taught to live in a way that would prejudice them toward one religion, taught to live a clean life, to live in the open, to sail and swim, to rough it, and be independent and honest. They will know right from wrong without being told, for I have always known that; to think for themselves and never to "kowtow" to anyone except you.

With Edna pregnant with their second child, Whiting continued his letter and said the following if they had a son:

> And if he wants to, he can follow in my footsteps in the sea and the air for when it comes time, the air will be more important, though there is an unlimited field of work under the water.[56]

CHAPTER 6

WHITING LEADS THE FIRST
AMERICANS "OVER THERE"

World War I began with the assassination of Archduke Ferdinand, the heir to the Austro-Hungarian Empire throne by a Serbian patriot. As most of the major world and European powers lined up and declared war on each other in response to secret treaties between the parties, the United Stated held back. Public opinion was for neutrality, and President Woodrow Wilson promised in his 1916 reelection campaign "to keep us out of the war."[1]

In February 1915, Germany announced a campaign of unrestricted submarine warfare, including American-flagged vessels and others carrying American citizens and cargoes that Germany suspected were carrying munitions across the Atlantic for Britain and France. After the May 7, 1915, sinking of the Cunard ocean liner RMS *Lusitania* and bitter complaints from the United States, Germany backed down for a time. However, on January 31, 1917, Germany resumed its unrestricted submarine warfare campaign. One month later, German Foreign Minister Arthur Zimmerman sent a secret diplomatic note to the Mexican government inviting Mexico to declare war on the United States. When Germany and its allies won, Zimmerman promised Mexico's share of the spoils would be most of the territory it had lost to the US in the 1848 Mexican War, including the states of California, Arizona, and New Mexico. Britain intercepted the communication and [as part of its ongoing campaign to convince the US to enter the war on the side of Britain and France] leaked it to the American press. On March 1, 1917, the Zimmerman Note was published. American public opinion, already moving after Germany restarted unrestricted submarine warfare, swung rapidly from neutral to anti-German. Following the swing in public opinion, Wilson quickly changed his mind and asked Congress for a declaration of war. On April 6, 1917, Congress declared war on Germany.[2]

The change in public opinion and the actions of Wilson and the Congress took place in little more than a month, and the Wilson administration and the US military were caught flat-footed and unprepared for war.

When war was declared by Congress, the Navy possessed only 54 technologically obsolete aircraft, fewer than 300 pilots, and naval personnel held aviation ratings, and many of those were assigned to other billets. Further, within the Navy Department, aircraft procurement, maintenance, and armaments responsibilities were divided among several semiautonomous bureaus. Advances by the other combatants since the war began in 1914 placed Naval Aviation even further behind.[3]

Eighteen months later, the Navy had established 27 naval air stations, and aviation strength totaled more than 1,150 officers, 18,300 bluejackets, 400 aircraft, 50 kite balloons, and three dirigibles; more than 120 naval aviators lost their lives in foreign service. The Navy Department accomplished this large mobilization by initiating massive recruitment, training, and building programs in the United States, contracting with domestic and foreign manufacturers for thousands of aircraft, engines, and equipment, and shipping huge numbers of men and equipment to Europe in the time span of 19 months.[4]

The process of transforming Naval Aviation from its very weak state to its great growth during World War I began when CNO Benson decided to form the Navy's First Aeronautic Detachment, known as the FAD, with 100 men, put it under the dynamic leadership of Lt. Kenneth Whiting, and sent it to Europe for training. Benson issued orders to execute his decision on May 9, 1917.[5]

Whiting took command of the First Aeronautic Detachment in May 1917, with instructions from Admiral Benson to gather sufficient sailors and supplies as soon as possible. These were inexperienced men with the primary mission of providing a visible, early token of the United States' military commitment. The seven officers selected by Whiting included pilots Lieutenant Grattan C. Dichman, Lieutenant (junior grade) Godfrey DeCourcelles Chevalier, and Lieutenant (junior grade) Virgil Griffin, Paymaster and Lieutenant Omar Conger, Supply Corps, Assistant Paymaster Frederick Michel, and Assistant Surgeon Arthur Sinton. He also selected 122 enlisted men, and Benson instructed Whiting to embark his unit on two coal supply ships, the USS *Jupiter* (AC-3) and the USS *Neptune* (AC-8), and take them to France. Whiting was to be responsible for the administrative control and discipline of the unit; orders to the group would come from him, although it would operate under "the commander of the French force to which it was assigned."[6]

A twenty-year-old enlisted man named A. M. Pride, who was to make major contributions after the war as an aviator and commissioned officer in the fields of engineering, hydraulic gear, and arresting gear, was also listed on the FAD's *muster roll*, the US Navy's term for a roster of personnel.[7]

In the only mention of a chain of command for Whiting by the Navy Department, he was to keep the US naval attaché in Paris, Lieutenant Commander William N. Sayles, aware of his location and of where he was working. Whiting was to interpret this order as also identifying Sayles as the man to whom he should address the many reports he would produce during his tour as FAD commander. Despite Sayles relaying to Washington much of what Whiting communicated to him, this would further exacerbate confusion caused by parallel chains of command in Europe and other independent officers senior to Whiting vying for command of Naval Aviation there. Those involved in this situation, which affected Whiting's activities directly, included Admiral William Sims in London, soon to be designated by secretary of the Navy Josephus Daniels as commander of American Naval Forces operating in European waters, and uninformed by the Navy Department of Whiting's presence in Europe; Captain Richard Jackson, sent to Paris at the request of the French to serve as Sims's liaison only (but who was to attempt to assume much more authority); and Sayles. Whiting's mission required him to negotiate with the French; the confusion caused by these conflicting chains of command in Europe also required him to negotiate with his fellow naval officers, all senior to him.[8]

Marc Wortman whose Ivy League background made him ideal to document the history and growth of the Navy's World War I Yale volunteer naval reserve aviation unit attempted in the book he wrote for that purpose, *The Millionaires' Unit*, to analyze the organizational confusion experienced by the Navy at the beginning of the war. However, he may have been limited in this analysis because of lack of awareness of the American military's tradition of giving general, mission-type orders to field commanders and allowing them to interpret them based on their professional education and more immediate awareness of the environment in which they operated. This doctrine was heavily driven by technology available at the time of World War I, which did not allow for secure, timely communications between a unit deployed overseas and its headquarters in the United States.

The command and control method known as "mission command" was developed by the German military in the 1890s to take advantage of potential opportunities evolving from the confusion of battle through decentralized decision-making. On-scene subordinate commanders were better able to sense an emerging opportunity than a higher commander, who was limited not only by not having a complete and accurate on-scene sense of the battlefield but also by the communications technology of the time, and capitalize on situations in which split-second decisions were pivotal. It allowed subordinate commanders to take ownership of their actions and allowed greater flexibility for responding rapidly to changing combat situations, dealing with unforeseen problems, and exploiting fleeting opportunities. It encouraged initiative and creativity by subordinates and greatly enhanced motivation and morale.[9]

"Mission command is considered the principal method of command and control in the US military."[10]

It is considered the most effective method of command and control ever devised to take advantage of the risk, chaos, and unpredictability inherent in war and of opportunities within the fog of war to gain a decisive advantage. Control of risk can best be achieved by pre-deployment communication by a higher commander of his intent and then giving the subordinate commander sufficient freedom of action to exercise his initiative and creative skills in executing the assigned mission. Better commanders and subordinates learn to trust each other by the clear communication of the commander's intent, by the support of the subordinate commander by the higher commander in whatever mission-pursuant actions the subordinate take in good faith, and by clear, complete, and critical reports from the subordinate commander on the results achieved. A good example of control of risk by a clearly communicated commander's intent came in the planning leading up the Battle of Midway, June 4–7, 1942, in which the commander in chief of the Pacific Fleet, Admiral Chester Nimitz, very clearly communicated to Rear Admirals Spruance and Fletcher his desire that they account for the pre-battle Japanese superiority of resources by the principle of calculated risk.[11]

Although the mission-command methodology had only been developed some twenty years previous to the FAD's deployment to France, it certainly appears to describe the actions of CNO Benson. Almost certainly the important commander's intent had been given by Benson to Whiting in their verbal discussions about the mission, and within the descriptions of his aggressive operating style reported by many, Whiting appears to have been operating within the methodology in his pursuit of the FAD's mission.

Whiting had been described by various observers as a "fire-eating, compulsive daredevil who participated in every dangerous naval enterprise he could reach," "impulsive, fire-eating," "aggressive and energetic," a "hard-drinking mischief-maker," and "a natural leader of men, not very tall, perhaps five feet, nine inches, of athletic build, compact, and strong." He walked with a natural spring in his step, moving purposefully, and with a "keen eye, ruled by a strong hand in a velvet glove," and many believed he flew for the "pure, wholesome hell of it."[12]

When Whiting started his European mission in early May, Rear Admiral Leigh Palmer, chief of the Bureau of Navigation [the Navy's name for the Bureau of Naval Personnel, to which it was renamed in 1942], had given him written guidance vaguely connecting his written aeronautical training development mission anywhere he needed to go in France with the oral instructions he had been given. Before leaving Washington, Whiting also received a letter of introduction to Commander de Blanpre, French naval attaché in Washington. This letter described the need to train detachment members as pilots with the specific request that they also be qualified as seaplane pilots, and Whiting was also given verbal orders to negotiate with the French government to complete the training of pilots, mechanics, and other men in the unit. The letter went on to say that duties after training might include, for example, patrolling, sea scouting, and expeditions. Whiting also received authorization to conclude an agreement with French authorities, which determined the exact status of the detachment and avoided confusion. His attempts to extract more specific information from his supervisors proved unsuccessful; if he wanted to get to France quickly, he should leave as soon as possible before someone revoked or changed his orders.[13]

Critical of Benson's choice of Whiting, Wortman wrote the following:

> [He] may not have been the most judicious choice for the first American military officer to deal directly with the French. An impulsive daredevil…[who] found ways to take part in every risky naval enterprise he could…he reviewed the situation in France, [and] without waiting word from Washington, he committed the United States to the creation or takeover of a chain of naval air stations along the French seaboard, including one, at Dunkerque, the Allies themselves considered largely indefensible.[14]

From another perspective, Benson's choice may have been exactly the right one. After the quick about-face by President Wilson and Congress to enter the war, the military was under some pressure to get to France. The group did not take any aircraft and was sent over primarily to show a war-weary France that United States forces were actually "coming over there and thus be an antidote to the epidemic of unrest, nearly amounting to mutiny, affecting the French forces" [Actually, some French units did mutiny in the trenches, and severe punishments had to be imposed to restore order]. Benson also wanted to create a symbol to demonstrate that the Navy was *on board* with the decision. He kept the Navy's risk for that symbol low by organizing a small unit to put an immediate toehold on French soil. Given Benson's 3,000-mile view of the situation on the ground in France, the instructions he gave Whiting were vague and flexible. From the reputation Whiting had gained in the Navy over his 12 years of peacetime service, with a congressional declaration of war now in effect, Benson probably expected Whiting to interpret his mission and instructions even more aggressively and broadly, and as a strong and popular leader, to be able to achieve the maximum impact from his 131 officers and men and open the door to future cooperation with our French ally on a much larger scale.[15]

Either by accident or because Whiting's style was well-known in the small prewar Navy, the results of Whiting's appointment as FAD commander were to be much more important and far-reaching because of his enthusiastic personality and constant initiative. His vague written orders told him only to proceed to France and to keep the United States naval attaché there informed of his movements. When he had asked for a more specific interpretation of his orders, the only response he received was that, if he wanted to go the war zone, he had better get started before some change of policy in the midst of the fluid situation of just-declared war should cancel his orders. With this as his only guidance, he embarked his FAD as soon as he could; when he reached Paris, he began to act totally on his own discretion and judgment.[16]

Whiting embarked the officers, enlisted men, and supplies of the First Aeronautic Detachment on May 23–24 in the two colliers,

Neptune and *Jupiter*. But his campaign for a new type of warship was probably never far from Whiting's thoughts. Given his continuing outspokenness about the need for plane carriers and his previously submitted proposal to purchase the Florida East Coast Railway's large ferry *Henry M. Flagler* and convert her into a plane carrier, it is easy to imagine Whiting walking about the collier *Neptune* during his two-week transatlantic crossing sizing her up as another option for conversion to a plane carrier. After the war, when he was assigned to the Navy's Bureau of Aeronautics and had begun a formal campaign for plane carriers, it is just as easy to imagine that he was still remembering those walks around the *Neptune*.[17]

After a German U-boat fired two torpedoes at them sixty miles off the Gironde River mouth and missed, *Jupiter* arrived at Pauillac, France, on June 5, 1917, and *Neptune* at Saint-Nazaire, France, on June 8, 1917. Benson achieved his symbol with *Jupiter* and its contingent, the first Americans in France. Whiting and his *Neptune* contingent reached there five days before General John J. "Black Jack" Pershing's American Expeditionary Force headquarters contingent.[18]

On June 20, shortly after Whiting arrived in France, his recommendation [the first of several similar Whiting recommendations to come] to purchase the Florida East Coast Railway's ferryboat and convert it into an airplane carrier was disapproved by the Navy Department, but twenty-five years later, in World War II, the *Henry M. Flagler* and two other ferryboats were purchased by the Navy and converted into transports, net layers, and mine warfare ships.[19]

After Whiting arrived in France, sadly the Whitings' second child, named Virginia, was stillborn on June 26, 1917. The cause was determined to be the undiscovered injury to Edna's pelvis, which had occurred in her fall from the horse as a child.[20]

With the loss of Virginia and with Whiting in France, Edna became very active in volunteer work, like the American Special Aid Society and the American Red Cross Automotive Corps. For this, she took a class on the care and repair of motor vehicles, which enabled her to maintain the family vehicles the rest of her life. Baby Eddie was cared for by Edna's mother, Effie May Andresen.[21]

Whiting received word on June 28, 1917, of his promotion to lieutenant commander, which was backdated with a date of rank of May 23, 1917. The happiness of his promotion must have been dampened by word of the loss of his and Edna's second child received two days before.[22]

In the first six weeks of the FAD's arrival in France, Whiting dedicated himself to an exhausting period of research and travel in France in the pursuit of his assigned mission. His activities included inspections of many potential sites for bases and extensive negotiations with his French hosts. Places visited, many multiple times, included Paris, Dunkerque, Saint-Pol, Tours, La Rochelle, La Pallice, Fromentine, Sables-d'Olonne, Marennes, Saint-Trojan, Royan, Lacanau, Verdun, Lake Hourtin, Bordeaux, Arcachon, Pauillac, Saint-Nazaire, La Baule, and Le Croisic.[23]

Agreements reached with the French, which became recommendations he authored in a twenty-plus page, July 20 report (the first of several) transmitted through Naval Attaché Sayles to the Department of the Navy in Washington, included the following:

1. The United States Navy should construct and assume responsibility for four stations, seaplane bases at Le Croisic, Saint-Trojan, and Dunkerque and an American training school at Lacanau. For the sites he considered, Whiting included detailed summaries of the strategic, logistical, and topographic advantages and disadvantages for his decisions to select or reject them.

2. Given the need in France for ten support personnel for every pilot aviator, the Navy should rebalance the flow of Naval Aviation personnel to France and begin the training of pilots at the French Army school at Tours and observers and mechanics to the French naval school at Saint-Raphael.

3. The Navy should establish and construct a supply and maintenance base on the protected Gironde River in Pauillac.

4. Given the shortage of available freighters and the space efficiencies inherent in shipping American seaplanes in parts

rather than assembled, the US Navy should manufacture seaplane parts, ship them that way, and construct a plant in France to assemble the parts into completed seaplanes.

5. Having seen how advanced the British Navy's aerial photography support function was, the US Navy should catch up.

6. Finally, given the French determination of the need for fifty seaplane bases beyond those already recommended to protect France and its ports from the German U-boat threat, the Navy should accede to an additional French request to take responsibility for twelve bases of the fifty.[24]

The FAD was to exist until October 24, 1917. Everything that happened in France during the previous five months, the life of the FAD, can be attributed to Kenneth Whiting's inspections and negotiations with the French government, according to his fellow Navy men and other authors who have written about him. He had been described as peripatetic, hugely energetic, and demonstrating a high level of energy and initiative. His senior officers in Washington probably looked on in wonder as they beheld the spate of actions Whiting took as he pursued the mission they had given him with their vague orders. [It is safe to say that as FAD commander Whiting functioned far above his pay grade and displayed extremely high initiative in negotiating and implementing the plan for the Navy's prosecution of the war in France.][25]

Wortman further described Whiting's efforts from the standpoint of the Yale naval reserve pilots who shortly began arriving in France. Upon arriving in France, he immediately began negotiations with the French and agreed to send pilots to the French base at Tours to complete training and mechanics to Saint-Raphael. In return, since he had only been given enough money to pay and subsist his unit and not enough to pay the French for the training, he agreed that the Navy would take responsibility for a Navy training station at Moutchic on the shore of Lac Lacanau and three coastal bases, Le Croisic, at the mouth of the Loire River, Saint-Trojan at the mouth of the Gironde River, and Dunkerque, at a very vulnerable point for attacks on the coast of the North Sea and at the northwestern end of the trench lines that had divided France for three years of the war. Le Croisic, Saint-Trojan, and Lacanau are on the Bay of Biscay. Over the next few months, as the Navy began to send men to France to fight the war (including the Yale Unit of Naval Reservists), Whiting operated from his Paris headquarters and assigned pilots and mechanics out to the bases to complete training. He also trained French pilots.[26]

Rossano provided a more detailed explanation of Whiting's activities from the time the First Aeronautic Detachment arrived in France. Whiting and the *Neptune* contingent disembarked at Saint-Nazaire on June 8, were greeted by Sayles, and took the train to Brest, ten men to a compartment. Expenses were paid from a $30,000 supply of gold bullion, which Conger had brought with him. When Whiting found out that some of the enlisted men had brought along a supply of alcohol to make the trip more pleasant, he conducted a surprise search. Fortunately, the men had finished a bottle of Benedictine but lost their cognac when Whiting confiscated it. In Brest, officers rode to their hotel in a car flying an American flag while enlisted personnel were greeted on the street by local men and pretty French women before occupying temporary quarters on the site of the future Brest Naval Air Station, where they enjoyed a meal with wine. Insufficient by US Navy standards, the French served them two meals per day, at 10:00 a.m. and 4:30 p.m. The men claimed the food was lousy, often serving only black coffee strong enough to poison any ordinary man and sour war bread. Sailors received liberty the first day and evening, along with their pay in the form of $20 gold pieces from Conger's stash. With champagne at $0.80 a bottle, the gold went far.[27]

Whiting immediately undertook a round of official calls to various local military figures, and from those meetings, he decided to move everyone to the French aviation station at Camaret, about fifteen miles away on the other side of Brest harbor. There, they conducted a modest ceremony, raising the stars and stripes over the building and yard where they were staying.[28] Whiting left for Paris with Conger on June 12 to begin the negotiations with the French government, which were part of his assigned mission. After another round of official calls in Paris, following his mission orders to proceed independent of command oversight, Whiting initiated negotiations with Admiral de Bon, head of the French naval staff; Commander Cazenave, chief of the French Naval Air Service; and Capitaine de Fregate De Laborde, in charge of seaplanes. It soon became apparent that the French were also suffering from the fog of war [or perhaps the FAD had crossed the Atlantic faster than French communications about them]; this French delegation was not aware of the commitments made by another group of French officials who had visited Washington earlier in the spring, about welcoming untrained student pilots and mechanics and instructing them quickly in France. In addition, the French held that the American did not have sufficient support personnel for the number of student-pilots it brought. To match the French program of instruction with the mix of personnel would require additional negotiations, and none of these additional factors could have been known by the Navy Department when Whiting's mission was put together. Finally, the French wanted to decentralize the FAD and place the men under French command, while Whiting, in keeping with his instructions to avoid confusion by negotiating an agreement concerning the status of his unit, decided [as did Pershing for most of his AEF units] he wanted to keep his personnel together for training. To settle these matters, the French proposed that all the unit's pilots be sent to Tours for initial training, to be followed by seaplane school at Lac Hourtin (a likely site of a future American facility). They further proposed that mechanics be sent for training to Saint-Raphael on the Mediterranean coast and then rejoin the unit's pilots at Hourtin. Whiting agreed, and as the unit made these moves, he also addressed the men's food complaints by assigning a commissary steward, two messmen, and a mess attendant. FAD personnel were to be fed according to American standards.[29]

In return for all this training, the French proposed that the FAD become the nucleus for operating three coastal patrol stations and a flight school in France, to be augmented by additional Navy personnel expected to follow Whiting's unit. Although this French proposal fell beyond the specific parameters of Whiting's vague instructions, as the man on the ground, he concluded that, since he lacked the funds to pay the French for training his men [his gold bullion was only to pay and subsist the men of the FAD], this quid pro quo was necessary to obtain French agreement for his primary mission, training his men; by agreeing to the French proposal, he did open himself to criticism by some of going beyond the authority of a lieutenant. The final agreement listed the three station locations as Le Croisic, Saint-Trojan, and Dunkerque. From the mouth of the Loire River, Le Croisic would screen the approaches to Saint-Nazaire and provide a base to attack U-boats in the vicinity of Belle Isle and Ile d'Yeu. Saint-Trojan would protect the Gironde River route to Bordeaux. It was expected that Le Croisic and Saint-Trojan would also become American disembarkation bases for troop and supply convoys. Site of an established primary seaplane school, Lac Hourtin would fulfill two purposes. It would become an American training center and fulfill Whiting's special instruction to qualify his pilots to fly seaplanes.[30]

Rossano questioned Dunkerque as the final French location to which Whiting agreed. He recognized that the North Sea coastal site possessed the strengths that no American convoys navigated the region and that the location provided a good opportunity to take the fight to the Germans by attacking their submarines sortieing from the Belgian coast bases of Bruges, Ostend, and Zeebrugge. But the site was the continuous target of major bombing and shelling that would make it difficult to keep its facilities at operational standards.[31]

Whiting's unit was to have primary responsibility for providing workers to construct the bases, with the French supplementing the crews. Responsibility for construction supplies would be split between the two countries. Each base was estimated to cost $1 million, and the negotiators agreed that construction of the bases should be completed by September. None of these specifics were to be free of glitches, including budgets and timetables. With the four-base agreement in place, several additional stations were added to the list. Whiting's agreement laid the foundation for much of the Navy's wartime aviation program in France, but its budget and timetable challenges were not to be solved until the Navy created its very effective construction battalions in World War II.[32]

In Turnbull and Lord's *Naval Aviation History*, Whiting immediately began negotiations by going into conference with the French Naval Chief of Staff Admiral De Bon and the Chief of the French Naval Air Force Captain Cazenau. Although technically quite without authority to make commitments, Whiting agreed that the American pilots would be trained at the French Army School, Tours, while American mechanics went to the machine school at Saint-Raphael. Further, he agreed to a plan for manning certain French stations at Le Croisic, Saint-Trojan, and Moutchic.[33]

Although these agreements were cabled to Sayles and hence to the Navy Department, through some unexplained administrative oversight, Admiral Sims was completely unaware of Whiting's existence, his mission, or the specifics of Whiting's agreements [because Whiting had no instructions to report to Sims]. It was the British Admiralty who first became aware of this oversight, informed Sims, and inquired about the extensive planning for France while relatively little had been done about England. After admitting to the British that he was unaware of Whiting's mission, he immediately sent for Whiting. "When Sims had studied what Whiting had done, he approved of the whole plan and commended Whiting for his initiative. Any question of action without authority was dropped into the files."[34]

Whiting forged ahead; the negotiations were followed by an inspection tour of the proposed sites, and Whiting and De Laborde led a joint group that departed Paris on June 18. Whiting got his first view of the war-torn rubble of Dunkerque, and having selected the specific ground for the American base at Dunkerque, Whiting and his party returned to Paris on June 21. After two more days of discussions, they left on a longer inspection tour of the selected station sites along the southwestern coast, including Tours, Le Croisic, and Lac Hourtin. Judging the Lac Hourtin site to be too crowded, Whiting selected another site for the proposed American flying school a few miles south at Lacanau. At the end of the tour, Whiting prepared his July 20 detailed report of all the sites and their advantages and disadvantages and submitted it to Sayles. The negotiations proceeded with the French offering a complete analysis of the defense of their entire coastline; from this, they concluded that they would need fifty more coastal stations, and they requested the United States to take responsibility for twelve of them.[35]

Whiting sat down to write his July 20 report of all the results of his negotiations and inspections to his Navy superiors. Conger had already submitted a lengthy report on June 18, after eight days on the ground, to Rear Admiral Samuel McGowan, chief of the Bureau of Supplies and Accounts, which included a very brief summary of the proposed aeronautic program.[36]

In the midst of these six weeks of intense negotiations and extensive travel to inspect potential sites for coastal stations, Whiting received word of the stillborn death of his second daughter and of his promotion to lieutenant commander. One wonders at the impact on the negotiations of these important messages.[37]

Sayles followed Conger's report shortly, forwarding Whiting's July 20 report to him of his itinerary of travel and inspections [meeting one of Whiting's specific instructions] and of his support of the three-base, one-school agreement. Whiting's major July 20 report ended with the recommendation to enlarge the program to fifteen bases, including the twelve seaplane bases and a few dirigible and kite balloon stations, and asked for his unit to be immediately reinforced with eight hundred more construction and support personnel to construct and operate the four new bases. After a trip back to Dunkerque to see the progress of construction of the new station and his initial reporting responsibilities fulfilled by his July 20 report, Whiting continued to move on four fronts, overall planning and organization, pilot training at Tours, mechanics or observers' instruction at Saint-Raphael, and creation of an American flying school at Lacanau. The unit also received a name more permanent than the First Aeronautic Detachment [although the initial FAD name continued to be used] and became the United States Naval Aviation Forces Foreign Service (USNAFFS).[38]

As Admiral Sims supported the decisions Whiting had reported on July 20, he began to consider how to deal with relieving Whiting as FAD commander with a more senior officer. Meanwhile, Whiting sent another major planning memo to Washington on August 26, in which he restated some of the points in his July 20 report and added more visionary, offensive-minded proposals to attack German U-boats. It was titled "Information and Suggestions for the Use of Seaplanes," [which he had already concluded would be the most efficient weapon against submarines] and described the characteristics of the German U-boat offensive and new strategies for how the Allies could use seaplanes to counter it. In another forward-thinking proposal, which was eventually implemented in the escort carriers of World War II, he recommended the conversion or construction of Great Lakes-type rail carriers to carry seaplanes to operate against submarines in the deep water of the western Atlantic. He advocated establishing twenty-four naval air stations, twelve on each shore, to control the English Channel [in just a few months, Whiting would take command of the largest English Channel base at Killingholme]. He reemphasized that German bases on the North Sea could be bombed using his continuing proposals for large seaplane carriers. Perhaps realizing the large overall size of the Navy's European presence, which he had proposed in all his reports and the need to efficiently transport aircraft and equipment overseas in parts for eventual assembly in Europe, he added that the department should assemble a corps of men to operate an overseas assembly and repair facility.[39]

In this most detailed missive, Whiting proposed that each station should have two hundred officers and men and that pilots, observers, gunners, and signalmen be sent to France for training as rapidly as possible. He also proposed consideration of a much larger plan in which the United States would take over twelve seaplane stations and three dirigible bases. To explain the French plan, Whiting arranged for Marine Corps Captain B. L. Smith to return to Washington to personally present the plan. On August 8, the secretary of the Navy approved the first four bases, one at Tours for training and three more for coastal patrol, and a month later, the Navy Department approved the plan for all fifteen bases.[40]

This report proposing a large-scale bombing campaign against German naval facilities like Kiel, Heligoland, Cuxhaven, and Wilhelmshaven triggered the possibility of Whiting being assigned to command NAS Killingholme. Whiting was particularly well-suited to write this report, analyzing German U-boat operations and proposing strategies using seaplanes to counter them because he was qualified in both submarines and aviation.[41]

The primary German submarine bases were at the bases of Ostend, Zeebrugge, and Bruges, he said, and in their operations, they placed great importance on taking advantage of the congestion of shipping close to shore, in and out of French and British ports. Thus, the Allied anti-submarine efforts should focus on either bottling U-boats up in their home ports or driving them away from French and British ports and out to sea. Because the North Sea near Ostend and Zeebrugge is shallow and thickly interspersed with shifting sandbars, the German U-boats were forced to run on the surface until they reached deeper water closer to the center of the North Sea.[42]

Carrying out the French plan to build more seaplane bases along the French coast and following the British goal of building more bases on the southern coasts of England and Ireland would give the Allies the ability to drive the U-boats away from the Allied ports and to attack them close to their German and Belgian ports. He therefore proposed the following strategies:

1. In the Mediterranean, establishing four seaplane bases at Nice, Corfu, a point near the Straits of Gibraltar, and a point on the African coast south of Sardinia.

2. Acquire large ships presently used by maritime businesses to transport cars and trains in the Great Lakes and between Havana and Key West and construct decks as long and wide as the ships from which to launch seaplanes.

3. Make use of four Navy ships equipped with seaplane catapults—*Seattle* [on which he had recently served], *North Carolina*, *Huntington*, and *Pittsburgh*—to conduct offensive operations against German U-boats.

4. Conduct offensive operations against German U-boats in their bases by either obtaining a base in Holland or Denmark from which to operate large bombing planes against the German U-boat bases or acquiring and con-

verting 15 or 20 ships at least 500 feet long and capable of carrying at least 30 seaplanes each to overcome the 250-mile width of the North Sea (which Allied airplanes based at currently existing bases could not do). [Of course, strategies 2 and 5 would involve creating airplane carriers, Whiting's next proposal for this new type of ship.][43]

While Sims and the Navy Department considered Whiting's report and proposal of August 26, his approved July 20 plan for constructing and operating seaplane bases in France was being implemented. The first base to be completed was at Moutchic, commissioned on July 7, 1917. Le Croisic followed very shortly, Saint-Trojan, and Dunkerque soon had skeleton American squadrons flying from those stations. Construction of the remaining bases could not keep up with the optimistic schedule laid out in Whiting's plan, but they were eventually completed.[44]

However, on August 16, the first students completed the first flight course at the flight training base at Tours and transferred to Lac Hourtin for seaplane training.[45]

Summer 1917 turned into fall, and after Whiting had submitted his August 26 comprehensive analyses of the war in Europe and how Naval Aviation should fight it, Admiral Sims decided to deal with the issue of Whiting's rank by reorganizing the fast-growing Navy effort in France and placing Captain Hutchinson I. Cone in command. A junior lieutenant commander like Whiting was just too junior to command the large Navy presence, which Whiting's plan and growth had created on the Continent, and Sims wanted his own man in command. Hutch Cone took command of the Navy in France on September 27, 1917; at the same time, the Navy Department approved Whiting's proposal for the Navy to take responsibility for fifteen bases in France. With the Navy firmly wedded to the plan he had negotiated and written, US Naval Aviation Forces Foreign Service chief Cone relieved Whiting; Whiting shut down the First Aeronautic Detachment on October 24, 1917.[46]

Any summative evaluation of Kenneth Whiting's performance during the five months in which he commanded the FAD must be

75

judged by his extraordinary zeal, lack of experience, the Navy's flat-footed start of its war effort, the government's overwhelming pressure on the Navy to achieve full mobilization overseas as quickly as possible, and the unplanned end of the war via an unexpected armistice. Viewed from the welcomed perspective of the post-armistice calm, some of Whiting's actions were likely misguided. His decision to establish and defend a patrol station at Dunkerque, for example, can be seriously questioned while we search for alternative strategies of how to deal with this important piece of key terrain at the nexus of the lines of the combatants and the British Channel shore. After the armistice, the size of the American establishment in France probably exceeded the needs of the Navy; if the armistice had not occurred, the size of that establishment might have been proportional to the need to seek a German surrender. But as we view Whiting's activities and accomplishments through the lens of these important factors, we must stand with Rossano in this summary of Whiting's Great War FAD work.

> During his few months of largely unsupervised activity, Kenneth Whiting provided extraordinary drive, initiative, and leadership. Almost single-handedly he created a framework for future aviation efforts in France. Whiting arranged training for a critical nucleus of pilots and mechanics, selected sites for a dozen patrol stations, outlined needs and priorities for the aeronautic campaign to come, and negotiated a series of agreements with the French. With these actions he set the agenda, and Washington reacted to his initiative, not the other way around.[47]

Dunkerque begs more analysis. Located as it was on the North Sea and at the extreme northwestern end of the trench lines in France, it was undoubtedly key terrain and would have had to be defended from sea and land. Comparisons can be drawn to World War II's Guadalcanal, but perhaps Culp's Hill and Little Round

Top of Gettysburg, at the extreme flanks of the Union line, provide even better comparisons to Dunkerque. Guadalcanal and Little Round Top were bitterly and savagely contested by the adversaries in those wars, and the South's failure to follow up its early success in driving the enemy on the first afternoon of Gettysburg by exerting a maximum effort to take Culp's Hill at sunset of that first day is usually listed by military historians as one of the reasons the South lost that pivotal battle. Whiting should not have placed offensive aviation assets at the extremely hot Dunkerque location, but as key terrain, it was vital that the Allies strongly defend it. Whiting should have worked close air support by Navy or Army air into the defense of Dunkerque while finding another location near the coast, less exposed to German bombing, behind the Allied lines, and southwest of Dunkerque on the North Sea in order to prosecute the very important aviation missions of North Sea anti-submarine warfare and attacking German forces in and behind their trenches.

Upon arriving in Britain in September 1917, Cone initiated a thorough overhaul of Naval Aviation efforts by following Whiting's plan to prosecute the war in France and responding to the British appeals for help with organizing and expanding efforts to fight the War from British shores. He conferred with Sims, Whiting, Conger, and others; reviewed existing correspondence; met repeatedly with the Admiralty; and undertook a tour of potential station sites in Ireland and England. Cone then crossed over to France and relieved Whiting on October 24, assuming command of the US Naval Aviation Forces Foreign Service. [Much of Cone's analysis and planning of necessity was focused on Britain and Ireland. Whiting's plan for France had been done and been approved by the Navy Department, but no similar analysis and planning for Britain had been done. In France, Cone inherited Whiting's command and his plan.][48]

Original FAD officers went on to fill a variety of posts: Grattan Dichman, USNA 1907, naval aviator number 30, commanded the aviation school at Moutchic, later commanded NAS Brest, returned to destroyer service, and was a full commander serving on the staff of the commander, aircraft squadrons, battle fleet when he was killed in a crash of his aircraft on October 16, 1924. Godfrey Chevalier became commanding officer at NAS Dunkerque. Flights from there were begun September 1, 1918, but were only to last ten days when the challenges of protecting Dunkerque from German attack caused the Navy to decide to abandon the base. Chevalier transferred to his final World War I billet at the Northern Bombing Group assembly and repair base at Eastleigh. Virgil Griffin, USNA 1909, naval aviator number 41, served on the Paris staff, spent several weeks at RNAS Yarmouth, assumed command of NAS Saint-Trojan, retired as captain, USN, and passed away March 27, 1957. After the war, Chevalier and Griffin were to continue to be part of Whiting's team in the development of the aircraft carrier. Omar Conger oversaw the supply effort until late in the war; was a part of the team that selected naval air station sites in England, Scotland, and Ireland; went with a team to Italy to negotiate a plan for Naval Aviation bombardment of Asiatic ports; and ended the war working with the French Naval Ministry. Surgeon Arthur Sinton carried out numerous inspections at Tours, Moutchic, and Pauillac, and ended the war as chief operating surgeon at the US Naval Base Hospital at Brest.[49]

After serving as an enlisted machinist mate in FAD, Alfred M. Pride volunteered for flight training at NAS Pensacola; he earned his wings and commission there. He was integrated into the regular Navy and sent by the Navy to the Massachusetts Institute of Technology to complete a degree in aeronautical engineering. He was considered one of the best pilots of his generation. He then served as part of Whiting's team in several more billets, including developing Langley's arresting gear and fitting out Saratoga. He was one of the pilots who flew in the air show at NAS Norfolk in 1930. On September 23, 1931, he became the first to land a helicopter, XOP-1 autogiro, on an aircraft carrier, the *Langley*; then-Captain Kenneth Whiting was flying with him as his passenger. He distinguished himself commanding World War II carriers groups and retired in 1959 as a vice admiral. He was promoted to full admiral from the retired list, based on his distinguished wartime service.[50]

CHAPTER 7

WHITING TAKES COMMAND AT NAS KILLINGHOLME

T he squeaking wheel got the grease, and because the French reached out to America first in World War I and America sent a very aggressive Naval Aviation leader to work with them, France initially received much more attention than Britain. Whiting negotiated and brought to life the shape and depth of the American war effort in France.[1]

Had the Navy conferred with the British high command before Whiting acted, supporting aerial operations against U-boat air bases in England and Ireland would probably have been addressed ahead of any bases in France. But the bases in France were important in forcing the enemy U-boats out into the open sea, where targets were more widely separated and their danger to Allied shipping was relatively less. If establishing the bases in France before those of Britain could not be justified from a strategic standpoint, by the end of the war, their existence could clearly be justified.[2]

When Hutch Cone arrived in London, the British proposed beefing up the anti-submarine effort around the British Isles by adding more coastal aviation bases [where the creation of American stations had received much lower priority] to the American destroyers already operating in Ireland, where U-boats preyed on the convoys passing daily; two North Sea base in particular, RNAS Felixstowe and Killingholme, could be designated as the bases to implement the plan. Cone accepted the plan.[3]

CNO Benson ruled out the use of seaplane carriers, which Whiting had proposed in his August 26 report, but the chance to attack the German fleet directly in its lair using a similar strategy proved tempting to the American administration. In October, the British Admiralty proposed a plan to build a fleet of 80 fifty-foot lighters, to be towed by destroyers, which would carry large flying boats to within 50 miles of the German fleet bases at Cuxhaven, Kiel, Heligoland, and Wilhelmshaven. The aircraft would be offloaded at sea, attack their targets, and fly home [or fly back past the lighters and be recovered at sea]. The original British F2A flying boats, powered by Rolls-Royce engines, could reach a top speed of 84 knots [96 miles per hour], with a fully-loaded weight of 10,250 pounds, and remain aloft for 4 hours and 36 minutes at full speed and 6 hours and 36 minutes at cruising speed. The Admiralty plan also involved the United States' strengthening its F2A flying boats by incorporating new, more powerful Liberty motors.[4]

The British proposal used an analysis similar to the one Whiting had used in his August 26 report and incorporated strategies and technology equivalent to those Whiting had proposed in that report. New lighters, based in Felixstowe and Killingholme, towed by destroyers and carrying seaplanes within striking distance of the German bases at Kiel, Wilhelmshaven, Cuxhaven, and Heligoland (enabling the Allies to attack these German bases as easily as they could already reach Ostend and Bruges) should overcome the short cruising radius of the seaplane bombers.[5]

Ultimately, the Navy Department chose to strengthen the British F2A modification proposal even more and to build a new flying boat, a larger version of the existing Curtiss H-12, to be called an H-16 "Large America" and equipped with the more powerful Liberty motors. Measuring 46 feet in length, the H-16 had a 96-foot wingspan. Its two 400-horsepower Liberty motors provided power and generated a top speed of 95 miles per hour. The plane could remain aloft for 4 hours at maximum speed or up to 9 hours [about 2 1/2 hours more than the original British H-12 version] at cruising speed.

The H-16 had a loaded weight of 10,900 pounds, including a crew of 4, radio equipment, 4 or 5 machine guns, and two 230-pound depth bombs.[6]

The British proposal represented a decisive shift away from defensive activity [that had been implemented by Whiting in France] along the Brittany and Bay of Biscay coasts to a more offensive strategy based in England and Flanders.[7]

The British were also considering such a plan for their coastal station on the North Sea at Felixstowe. At 58 feet in length, the lighters would be sufficient to carry flying boats weighing up to five tons. They would be constructed of steel and would incorporate an airtight trimming tank in the stem that would be flooded by high-capacity pumps and emptied with compressed air. Flying boats would be launched or retrieved from the water by lowering the stem and by using a trolley or cradle and winch. The lighter hull shape and a special bridle would allow destroyers to tow them at speeds of up to 30 knots. After the first sea trials in June–September 1917 completely met the designers' expectations, the British Admiralty asked the US Navy to operate the British Royal Naval Air Station at Killingholme on the east coast of England and to support 30 lighters and 40 planes there (all American built).[8]

Benson visited London in November, approved the general plan, and directed the Navy Department in Washington to begin construction of the necessary flying boats at once. Despite Whiting's general enthusiasm for proposals like this, combining the risks inherent in pioneering new strategic concepts and technology with large decks to carry planes over water, he generated a new maturity by compiling an extensive list of questions and reasons he believed the plan to be unrealistic. Perhaps matching the fast pace at which Whiting worked and the need for speed in a war, the department selected him to head the American portion. Whiting immediately visited the Admiralty and the RNAS station at Felixstowe, from where the English portion of the plan would be managed. He was soon ordered back to the United States to push the project and received assurances from Benson that it would receive top priority.[9]

When the typical problems with construction of new, untested equipment and conversions of older equipment arose while he was in the United States, Whiting worked closely with Curtiss to resolve them; because of the urgency of war, all the problems were not resolved at the factory, and the Navy Department decided to ship completed Curtiss products to Europe with any necessary modifications to be done overseas. Work on the lighters also moved ahead, with Whiting as the man in charge of rounding all the new pieces of equipment into shape for combat.[10]

Gathering up the large number of pilots and enlisted men required for the Killingholme initiative was also a challenge, but Whiting already had experience in creating and coordinating a decentralized training system and moving men through it to their ultimate combat unit. Some of the manpower was already in Europe and only needed to be sent to British bases for further training and to gain war experience, but much of it was still in the United States and had to go through schools as diverse as the Royal Air Force school at Fort Worth, Texas, the Packard factory in Detroit (Liberty Motors), Savage Arms Works (machine guns), the Philadelphia Navy Yard (Delco radios), New York (lighters), and Hampton Roads, Virginia (large flying boats).[11]

After coordinating all the intricately moving pieces of this temporary logistical system from the Office of Naval Operations in Washington, Whiting finally achieved a critical mass of equipment and manpower. Embarking 23 crated H-16s, 8 lighters, 8 officers and 150 men, he duplicated the Atlantic transit he had made just over a year ago on *Neptune* and departed for Europe on May 18, 1918, aboard USS *Jason*. Three destroyers escorted the ship and its valuable cargo on the voyage. During the last 40-mile leg of the trip into the Humber River, the first All-American H-12 flying boat flew top cover. *Jason* reached the Immingham Docks on May 30.[12]

Whiting and the Navy took over operations at NAS Killingholme on July 1 and assumed formal control on July 20, 1918. By then the base had grown large, mustering 67 officers and 902 enlisted men, extending across 135 acres of low-lying ground beside the River Humber. Eight hangars had been built; the concrete apron covered

10 acres of shoreline, and two 800-foot slipways of stout planks and piles driven into the riverbed to carry aircraft from the concrete apron across the wide Humber mudflats and into the water. A city of brick-and-frame huts stood at the southern edge of the station, replacing a veritable tent city, and illustrative of the base's growth; by September, it had 46 planes and 1,900 personnel.[13]

During the time Whiting was in command at Killingholme, he had a dream one night that his sister Katherine had been killed in a car accident. The worldwide flu epidemic of 1918 had already begun, and instead of a car accident, Katherine died of influenza. She left five children, and her and Ken's mother, Daisy, became their guardian and raised them.[14]

After Katherine's death, Captain N. E. Irwin wrote a letter to assistant secretary of the Navy Franklin Roosevelt requesting that Whiting be ordered home as soon as possible because of the shock of Katherine's death to their mother, Daisy, and because Whiting's only remaining work was in supervising the return of the Killingholme base to the British. Irwin specifically stated that Whiting had had nothing to do with the request [yet another example of Whiting's character trait of modesty preventing him from advocating for himself], which had come from another officer familiar with the Whiting family's situation.[15]

*****

Even with some limited success, by July, the British decided to terminate the lighter-bombing initiative, and in early August, Sims notified Cone of their decision. The British cited weather conditions and the difficulty in forecasting them, resulting in three or four failures for every successful action. Flying boats were vulnerable to the Germans' improved antiaircraft defenses, and by then, better land-based bombers had been developed. However, despite suffering from the same problems experienced by the British, under Whiting, sporadic experiments at Killingholme to transport seaplanes to German bases by lighter continued.[16]

NAS Killingholme never carried out the great lighter project, for which it was created, but it still compiled a substantial record of conducting anti-submarine and scouting patrols over the North Sea. At the armistice, the Killingholme muster roll included 91 officers and 1,324 bluejackets, the largest naval air station in Europe. Sixty of the 91 officers were pilots, the most of any American facility. From July 20, 1918, when the US took formal control until November 21, when the German fleet surrendered, they conducted 233 patrols, flew 968 hours, and 57,647 patrol miles. Their aircraft convoyed 6,243 ships and made 35 forced landings at sea. Of their 10 attacks on enemy submarines, four achieved positive results. Two officers and 7 enlisted men died in accidents.[17]

A product of the Yale naval reserve pilots' unit, Robert S. Lovett applied the knowledge he gained in analyzing railroad operation for his father's company, the Union Pacific Railroad, and evaluated the effectiveness of the operations at Felixstowe and Killingholme. Over the life of Felixstowe, he found that a seaplane needed to cover, on average, 22,000 square miles of the North Sea before ever sighting an enemy submarine, several weeks of largely fruitless crisscrossing of an empty sea nearly half as large as all of England. Next, he looked at U-boat operations of the German enemy, and he found that at any one time, about 85 percent of the German U-boat fleet of 350 submarines would be berthed in ports like Kiel, Zeebrugge, Ostend, and Bruges for maintenance and repair and being provisioned for their next patrols. Instead of chasing the Huns separately in the wide North Sea, he concluded that a better strategy was to attack them when they were clustered together in their home ports [Whiting had drawn the same conclusion in his August 26, 1917, report].[18]

To this point in his analysis, Lovett supported Whiting's plan to bomb those same ports using lighters and seaplanes. However, the difficulties realized and never overcome in Whiting's plan was getting the seaplane-carrying lighters across the North Sea and close enough to those ports to make a difference. In the first ever plan to bomb the enemy using the concept of land-based strategic bombardment [several years after the war, the Army Air Service and ultimately the US Air Force won the strategic bombardment mission and make it a primary one of their own], Lovett proposed the Navy bomb them using long-range, land-based bombers based at stations around Dunkerque. Sims and Cone approved the plan and the creation of the Northern Bombing Group to implement it, but problems with the effectiveness of the Italian aircraft purchased to carry it out also greatly limited this plan's success.[19]

Then in a harbinger of mission-related conflicts over the next thirty years, first between the Army and the Navy and next between the Army and its Air Corps, head of the Army Air Service Major General Benjamin Foulois challenged Lovett's plan, on the grounds that land-based strategic bombardment should be the Army's mission; the Navy should strike from water in water-based seaplanes, and the Army should attack land-based forces using land-based machines. Pershing disagreed with Foulois and went along with the Navy's plan, but the fight escalated to Washington. There, the War Department was able to force the Department of the Navy to scale back the scope of the Northern Bombing Group.[20]

*****

With the armistice signed on November 11, 1918, World War I was over, and on December 26, the British Navy's Vice Admiral E. Charlton, who commanded the east coast of England, wrote a letter to the Admiralty commending the services rendered by the American Naval Air Station at Killingholme. In addition to documenting the over two hundred flights and fifty thousand flying hours flown from the base, he mentioned two flights of special interest. On August 5, a night flight of over four hundred miles was made during a raid of enemy aircraft, and on October 30, an H-16 with Liberty engines achieved the plane's maximum cruising time of nine hours. All the work of the American units at the base had contributed largely to the prevention of successful attacks on convoys by enemy submarines.[21]

NAS Killingholme was disestablished on January 6, 1919. After the breakup of the largest naval air station in Europe, for Whiting's service in World War I beginning in May 1917 with his leadership of the First Aeronautic Detachment, his negotiation of the plan for the defense of Allied ships plying the waters around France from German submarine attacks, and then with his command of NAS Killingholme, he was awarded the Navy's second highest award, the Navy Cross, and France's highest award, the Croix de Guerre (Chevalier). Signed "For the President, Josephus Daniels, Secretary of the Navy," the citation for his Navy Cross read as follows:

> For exceptionally meritorious service in a duty of great responsibility as Commanding Officer of the first US Aeronautical detachment to reach France, and later in command of the important US Naval Air Station at Killingholme, England.[22]

With his decorated World War I service, Whiting definitely outgrew his early reputation of using his great athletic skills to take on personally risky and dangerous activities in submarines and airplanes. He applied the cognitive skills he had learned in overcoming his academic laziness in his performance breakthrough in *Seal* to wartime duty involving a higher level of complexity in the leadership of men, the management of logistical and organizational challenges, and the international diplomatic skills required to negotiate partnerships with wartime allies.

For his daring flying and for his successful command of the first naval air station on foreign soil, Dunkerque, Whiting's good friend Chevalier was awarded the Distinguished Service Medal and the French Croix de Guerre (Chevalier).[23]

After World War I, Chevalier made the first successful torpedo drops from an American plane and flew from battleship turrets. Then, on USS *Langley*, with Whiting as executive officer, he worked to develop the arresting gear and landing techniques of the Navy's first carrier and made the first landing on that ship in an Aeromarine 39B aircraft. Chevalier and Whiting served together frequently until Chevalier was killed in an airplane crash on November 24, 1922, when he took off from Norfolk Naval Air Station, circled over a friend's house, crashed, and died.[24]

CHAPTER 8

CONTINUING THE BATTLE FOR A PLANE CARRIER

During World War I, Chevalier and Whiting watched with admiration as the British Navy tried to operate planes from ships and had had long conversations about how to build and operate plane carriers. As the war neared its end, Whiting and Chevalier began to focus on the three aircraft carriers the British had either constructed or converted, HMS *Hermes, Eagle,* and *Argus,* and they visited several of the ships to observe operations. Germany also converted the merchantman *Stuttgart* into a carrier. Whiting returned from the war far ahead of his time in the conservative Navy of the 1920s, and he continued to advocate for his all-consuming obsession with the need for aircraft carriers for fighters and other land planes, not just seaplanes. With Whiting's strong advocacy, these ideas began to receive more support from the United States Navy, and for the Navy, the decade of the 1920s became the decade of the aircraft carrier.

In 1909, French inventor Clement Ader had accurately predicted in his book *L'Aviation Militaire* the flattop aircraft carrier with an island superstructure and a hangar bay, very different from other ships of the day, to operate airplanes at sea. The deck would look like a landing field, as flat and wide as possible, and aircraft would be stored below and anchored to the deck so as not to be affected by the ship's pitching and rolling. The ship would have deck elevators that were long and wide enough to hold airplanes with the wings folded, with traps to keep rain and seawater from penetrating below. The US naval attaché in Paris, Commander F. C. Champin, reported the book to the Department of the Navy in Washington.[1]

Experimental flights to test the concept followed, and American civilian Eugene Ely was the first pilot to launch an airplane from a stationery ship on November 14, 1910. He took off in his Curtiss Pusher aircraft from a temporary, eighty-three-foot-long structure fixed over the deck of the armored cruiser USS *Birmingham* at Hampton Roads, Virginia, and landed nearby at Willoughby Split after about five minutes in the air. On January 18, 1911, Ely became the first pilot to land on a stationery ship. He took off from the Tanforan Racetrack and landed on a similar temporary structure on the aft end of the USS *Pennsylvania* anchored at the San Francisco waterfront. His aircraft was then turned around, and he took off again. The improvised braking system of sandbags and ropes used to stop his airplane led directly to the wires and hook arresting system later used. Tragically, he crashed and died in Macon, Georgia, on October 19, 1911, and Congress awarded him the Distinguished Flying Cross posthumously in 1933.[2]

Although other navies were soon to surpass them, the British Navy's Royal Naval Air Service then began a series of activities and accomplishments that temporarily placed it at the world's forefront of Naval Aviation and aircraft carriers. The British Royal Navy's Charles Rumney Samson became the first pilot to take off from a moving ship, the HMS *Hibernia*, steaming at fifteen knots, on May 9, 1912, at a Royal Fleet Review at Weymouth, England. Britain's HMS *Ark Royal* was converted while under construction to be a hybrid airplane or seaplane carrier with a launch platform. Launched on September 5, 1914, she served in the Dardanelles Campaign and through World War I.[3]

The British Navy also modified another battlecruiser, HMS *Furious*, in 1917 to be a hybrid battlecruiser and aircraft carrier. *Furious* had originally been equipped with two huge eighteen-inch naval guns. In her 1917 modification, a partial flight deck was erected over the bow of *Furious*, where one of the eighteen-inch naval guns had been; left on the stern of the ship was the other huge gun. When the stern gun was first fired after the modification, its massive shock caused structural damage to the forward partial flight deck. Plans were immediately made to remove the stern gun.[4]

Flying a Sopwith Pup on August 2, 1917, Royal Navy Squadron Leader E. H. Dunning became the first man to land a plane on a moving ship. But *Furious* lacked arresting gear like that used when American Eugene Ely had performed the same feat six years earlier, so as Dunning adroitly held the airplane just off the deck in prevailing wind that equaled the Pup's speed, ten other pilots from Dunning's squadron had to drag the craft to the deck by grabbing straps attached to the Pup's airframe. Dunning was killed five days later when his airplane went overboard during a similar landing attempt, and he drowned before a boat could be launched to rescue him.[5]

After Dunning's death, the British added, first, a separate landing deck to *Furious*, and then, a continuous deck running the length of the ship. An American naval officer saw them experimenting with sandbags on lines similar to those Ely had used. After off-center landings caused planes to swerve, the cross-deck lines were discarded, and *Furious* went to sea in March 1918 with her landing deck covered with taut fore-and-aft wires high enough so that a plane's landing gear axle skidded along them with the wheels clear of the deck. Anchor-like hooks protruding from the axle snagged the wires and kept the plane from bouncing.[6]

On July 19, 1918, the British also conducted the first air strike launched from a carrier, when seven Sopwith Camels, next generation airplanes from the Sopwith Pup, launched from *Furious* to attack the German Zeppelin base at Tondern with two 50-pound bombs each. One had to abort with engine trouble, but first flight leader Captain William D. Jackson and his two wingmates destroyed two zeppelins, L.54 and L.60, and the second flight set a balloon afire at its moorings. For the return flight, two of the pilots reached *Furious* but ditched into the sea alongside the ship. One force-landed off Denmark and drowned, and the three remaining landed in neutral Denmark. Britain was forced to go through diplomatic channels to retrieve the pilots who had landed in Denmark.[7]

*****

Whiting's early return from Europe in late 1918, after his sister Katherine's death and the letter from Captain Irwin to the Navy Department requesting his early return to deal with the ensuing family crisis, came just in time for Christmas. There was much tree trimming, singing, and midnight snacking on Welsh Rarebit and beer in Larchmont.[8]

While he was taking his homecoming leave, Whiting received orders to the Navy Department's Bureau of Navigation in Washington, where he relieved John Towers on the aviation desk. He reported in February 1919, and the Whitings took an apartment at the Dresden on Connecticut Avenue. During this tour in Washington, the Whitings moved to the Brighton Hotel on California Street Northwest. Wynne Spencer and Wallis Warfield also lived there, and in a harbinger of the divorce to come, it was not unusual to get a midnight telephone call from Warfield to help resolve an argument. Whiting would struggle into his clothes and go mediate the dispute, which often took most of the night.[9]

This was an ideal location for him to continue the battle for plane carriers that he had first begun in January 1916 and continued until the end of World War I with at least three unsuccessful proposals to acquire certain ships and convert them to carriers. Even though he did not like Washington duty, he used the platform for his campaign.[10]

During his 1919–1921 tour in the Bureau of Navigation, Whiting and other converts fought against the Navy's senior officers—most of whom were "black shoe" battleship admirals, and many in Congress, who still thought more and bigger battleships were the right way to go—to promote carriers and catapults and the use of land planes at sea. They tried to explain to unbelievers the possibilities for devastating air raids on land, sea, and other fleets.[11]

In the years between World War I and World War II, Whiting would continue his battle for aircraft carriers from a much more advantageous position in the Navy, gain success in similar future proposals, and be instrumental in the construction of the Navy's first six aircraft carriers.

After crediting Eugene Ely for pointing the way to aircraft carriers when he became the first pilot to land on one in December 1910, Van Deurs summarized the pivotal and leading role Kenneth Whiting played in bringing them to fruition in the 1920s and 1930s. Many people, both in and out of the Navy, deserve credit for these radical ships. With big hangars opening in their centers, most naval architects said they would not be practical. Conservative surface officers believed they would handicap the fleet in battle. Led by Whiting, a small group of persistent men should receive credit for overcoming opposition to carriers and solving their problems. From the spring of 1916 to 1919, Whiting agitated for carriers; the first significant victory was achieved when the *Langley* conversion was authorized. Then he led in the development of her plans, supervised her construction, organized her, and supervised the pilots who used her as a laboratory to figure out how to efficiently operate planes at sea. Later, he planned and supervised the construction of the *Saratoga* and *Lexington*. Finally, he served as the *Saratoga*'s executive officer and commanded her. "Whiting deserves credit as the parent and guardian of our Navy's aircraft carriers."[12]

One of those conservative sea officers in 1919 was Chief of Naval Operations William S. Benson. After World War I, when Benson could not "conceive of any use the fleet will ever have for aviation," he tried to abolish the Navy's Office of Aviation. But assistant secretary of the Navy Franklin Roosevelt reversed the decision because he believed Naval Aviation might someday be the principal factor at sea with missions to bomb enemy warships, scout enemy fleets, map minefields, and escort convoys. Over the next 20 years, from its near obliteration, the Navy built up Naval Aviation to the decisive edge it became under Commander-in-Chief Franklin Roosevelt in World War II, and it remains today as the centerpiece of the combat striking arms of the US Navy.[13]

Into this headwind caused by the conservative battleship admirals, in 1919, the proposal of Whiting and the Office of Aviation to convert the coal ship USS *Jupiter* into the Navy's first aircraft carrier came. With his negative opinion about Naval Aviation, knowing of Roosevelt's support of Naval Aviation, and perhaps looking for a compromise on how to deal with the proposal, Benson referred it to the Navy's General Board. Although their recommendations carried great weight within the Navy Department, the General Board was a strictly advisory group of senior admirals, most near the end of their careers, who brought considerable expertise to bear but also had time to devote to problem-solving without the press of day-to-day decision-making. The General Board did not control its own agenda; it could only consider matters like strategy and ship characteristics, which had been referred to it.[14]

Whiting had experience testifying before the General Board. The first use of artillery spotting from an airplane had been recorded in early 1917 on USS *Seattle* in the Caribbean, in the seaplane unit under Whiting's command. Later in 1919, after the battleship USS *Texas* experimented successfully with the use of aircraft to spot her gunfire and found that the aircraft spotters provided her greater accuracy, Whiting testified before the General Board, attesting that aircraft spotting could increase the accuracy of ship gunnery by up to 200 percent. The success of these experiments led the General Board to advise the Navy to embark floatplanes aboard all its battleships and cruisers.[15]

On an issue closer to his heart, Whiting testified before the General Board with other leading naval aviators, including Mustin and Towers, about the need for aircraft carriers and the interference within the Navy that stifled aviation development before the world war. Whiting offered two options to non-aviator Captain T. T. Craven, director of Naval Aviation, for how to acquire the first carrier, which he wanted to use to experiment with the many details of how a carrier should operate. The first option involved the conversion of two ships the Navy already had in its arsenal, high-speed passenger liners. During World War I, the Navy had taken the two over, which were fast enough to meet their purpose of traveling between

San Diego and Seattle faster than a train could [and thus fast enough to operate with the fleet], to use as transports.[16]

The second option he offered was to convert into the first carrier the coal collier USS *Jupiter* (AC-3), one of the two ships in which the First Aeronautic Detachment had traveled to France in 1917. In the first recorded suggestion to use a large fleet collier as an airplane ship, Whiting argued that *Jupiter*'s advantages outweighed her disadvantages. Whiting expected resistance because *Jupiter*, *Neptune*, and their sister ships were the first fleet coaling vessels ever built, but he knew it would take years to build a new plane carrier designed for the purpose (even if Congress would appropriate the money), and an experimental ship, quickly converted, would open the door to building better carriers. Although she was probably too slow to keep up with the rest of the fleet, she had the necessary length for takeoffs, had a hold large enough for a hangar bay large enough to stow many planes with high headroom and open sides exposed to the elements, and the space requirement to berth her smaller operating crew meant there would be space for the aviation support crew, workshops, and storerooms. Built beginning October 18, 1911, at Mare Island Navy Yard in Vallejo, California, *Jupiter* was one of several ships built to supply coal to the fighting ships of the US Navy before oil-fired boilers became the norm. She was 542 feet in length and weighed 19,360 tons. She drew 27 feet, 8 inches of water. She had twin-propeller shafts, and fully-loaded could achieve a top speed of 14.5 knots. Her two experimental General Electric turbo-electric generator sets could generate 7,200 shaft horsepower, and she was the first Navy ship to be built with this then-advanced type of propulsion. She had a crew complement of 163 officers and men and was armed with 4 four-inch guns. She had large coal-carrying holds, which were considered ideal for conversion to living quarters for the larger crew she would require as an aircraft carrier and for aviation workshops and storerooms. The hangar of the converted carrier, below her flight deck, would be totally exposed to the elements on both sides.[17]

Although Mustin, Whiting and Towers were unified in their testimony before the General Board in supporting the conversion of the Jupiter to an experimental aircraft carrier, they did not necessarily share Whiting's long-term vision for what carriers should be or how carriers could transform naval strategy. Some of the General Board members' thinking leaned closer to that of Mustin and Towers about ships to merely transport seaplanes, instead of Whiting's vision of ships on which planes could land and take off. For example, Towers had "flirted with the idea of a flight-deck aircraft carrier," but "many of his ideas were not well formed." He had not seen the recent British carriers (Whiting had), and he was perhaps unaware of the damage that firing HMS *Furious'* large naval gun had done to the ship's partial flight deck. Towers had the greatest experience with the rigid airship and the big flying boat, and thus, he assigned them the immediate priority of his preferred solution. Because of the difficulty of recovering them, he was most troubled by the problem of operating smaller planes from ships; flying airplanes from ships in wartime seemed suicidal to him. Towers saw aircraft carriers as only a makeshift solution, a floating platform not necessary beyond 1925. They could be used now to carry and launch aircraft for spotting and scouting. Once these scout planes could be developed, the functions of battleships, battle cruisers, and aircraft carriers would merge; by 1925, all ships would carry aircraft and be designed to do so.[18]

After his retirement from the Navy in the early 1960s, Vice Admiral F. W. Pennoyer Jr., a member of the inner circle who had worked under Whiting to design and build *Langley*, prepared a paper titled "Notes on USS *Langley* (CV-1)." Pennoyer said that the story of the *Langley* began right after World War I with a few young maverick naval aviators returning from overseas. They were excited about the tremendous potential of the aircraft carrier developed by Britain during the war. "The leader of the mavericks was Commander Kenneth Whiting supported by Lieutenant Commander Godfrey de C. Chevalier, Captain Henry Mustin, and Commander Theodore Ellyson." Though Whiting was quiet and deceptively inconspicuous, his reputation from Annapolis, submarines, and aviation preceded him with the General Board, and his personality caused both seniors and juniors to want to agree with him.[19]

At that time, Pennoyer explained, all matters concerning naval policy, including the type and principal features of all new construction, were decided by the General Board. The group was made up of about nine especially selected senior flag officers. A junior officer appearing before them would suffer the same qualms as the accused before a general court-martial. One member of the Board had a huge mustache with the points groomed upward forming a fearsome arc. He was nicknamed Handlebars. The General Board hearings proposing the conversion of the collier USS *Jupiter* into an experimental aircraft carrier were long and stormy. Responding to the General Board's request for specifications and details, Whiting worked closely with Captain C. M. "Pop" Simmers, chief of the Bureau of Construction and Repair. After convincing Simmers that an experimental ship about 500 feet long, with a flat top, large holds, and a small crew was the best choice, Whiting moved on to the need to divert the ship's exhaust smoke and to include a plane elevator, shops, and stowage for planes. To help with the dimensions of spaces, Whiting gave Simmers scale silhouettes of some existing planes. "Handlebars roared his disapproval, shouting, 'We are robbing the Fleet of a perfectly good coal collier for Lord knows what.'"[20]

Pointing out the inadequacies of divergent ideas and supporting convergent ones, Whiting sat through several more weeks of General Board hearings in which Simmers and other pilots testified. Simmers's final recommended plan mirrored Whiting's, and near the end of the hearings, former submariner Whiting successfully added storage for live and dummy torpedoes to support torpedo planes that were then only on the drawing boards, catapults countersunk into the deck to launch planes, and an air compressor to support catapults and charge torpedoes. Whiting and Simmers were also able to negate discussion about different engines for the ship conversion [which would have added time to the conversion] and even different kinds of ships. The final vote of the General Board was closely split and barely passed, but on April 15, 1919, Craven and the General Board selected the *Jupiter* option and gave its support to the plan; the next step was to take it to Congress for authorization and funding.[21]

Another perspective comes from Ryan David Wadle's Texas A&M University master's thesis. Numerous hearings, he wrote, were held before the General Board during and after World War I on the potential of Naval Aviation and of a proposed new type of ship called an aircraft carrier. Most leading naval aviators, including Mustin, Whiting, and Towers, testified before the Board, "whose members appears to have been skeptical of those who believed that aviation held promise not just in a support role but also as another means of attack against an opposing force," but this "did not prevent the board from recommending the conversion of the collier *Jupiter* in April 1919."[22]

As part of the Navy's campaign to gain authorization and funding from Congress for the Jupiter's conversion, Whiting was one of several naval officers who testified before the House and Senate Committees on Naval Affairs. He wrote a memorandum to the House of Representatives Committee on Naval Affairs:

> When the War ended those who had chosen the Navy as a life work, and especially those who had taken up Naval Aviation, revived the question of "carriers" and "fleet aviation." They found the sledding not quite so hard as formerly, but the going was still a bit rough.[23]
>
> The naval officers who had not actually seen Naval Aviation working retained their ultra conservatism; some of those who had seen it working were still conservative, but not ultra; they were in the class "from Missouri" and wished to be "shown." Others, among the ranking officers who had seen, had conquered their conservatism and were convinced.[24]
>
> This latter group, headed by the General Board of the Navy, and including Adm. Henry T. Mao, Adm. N. C. Twining, Capt. Ernest J. King, and Capt. W. S. Pye, both on the staff of the commander in chief during the war, Capt. H. I. Cone and Capt. Thomas T. Craven. Both Cone and Craven incontinently demanded that "carriers" be added to our fleets.[25]

The net result of those demands was the [General Board] recommendation that the collier *Jupiter* be converted into a "carrier" in order that the claims of the naval aviators might be given a demonstration.[26]

On July 11, 1919, Congress authorized the conversion of *Jupiter* "into an airplane carrier," which would be named USS *Langley* (CV-1).[27]

Fully converted, *Langley's* displacement would drop from *Jupiter's* 19,960 to 11,500, which would increase her top speed by 1.5 knots to 15.5. Her length would remain 542 feet, and her beam, 65 feet. With less displacement, her draft would drop from 27 feet, 8 inches to 18 feet, 11 inches. Adding the pilots and aviation support crew, her complement would increase from 163 to 468. Her 4 four-inch guns would be replaced with 4 five-inch.[28]

The *Langley* was named after Samuel Pierpont Langley, an American astrophysicist and aeronautical engineer who served as secretary of the Smithsonian Institute, invented the bolometer to measure the amount of radiation emitted by the sun, and built the first significantly sized, heavier-than-air machine to achieve sustained flight. After his pilotless aerodrome number 5 flew over 3,000 feet over the Potomac River on May 6, 1896, he received a $50,000 federal grant to further develop it. But he ran out of the grant money and was never able to make it fully controllable.[29]

In March 1920, *Jupiter* entered the Norfolk Navy Yard to begin her conversion. The general requirements for the conversion, provided by Commander Henry Mustin in the Office of Naval Operations, were based on the flexibility of the *Langley* being able to support seaplanes and landplanes and being able to reverse the arresting gear so airplanes could be landed over the stern or bow; the reversible arresting gear requirement was later abandoned. Beyond the general requirements, plans for the conversion were nowhere near complete, with many major questions remaining about the design of the ship, its deck, and the aircraft that would fly from its deck. In answering the questions, Kenneth Whiting would lead in fulfilling her designation as an experimental ship and provide the blueprints for America's future carriers.[30]

One of the most important unanswered questions about deck design was how *Langley* was going to arrest or "trap" airplanes landing on her deck. As soon as it received all the important General Board and congressional spending approvals for the *Langley's* conversion, the Navy paid the British $40,000 in 1920 for the right to use the arresting gear the British had first developed and installed on HMS *Furious* in 1918.[31]

Two years later, when the arresting gear equipment had been installed on a large turntable with a 100-foot diameter on Chambers Field at NAS Hampton Roads, Whiting and Chevalier began to experiment with it. But they eventually turned the work over to Lieutenant (junior grade) Alfred M. Pride. Meanwhile, as the number of trial landings on the replica deck began to multiply, Whiting and Chevalier tried to accelerate their work by returning to their former wartime allies, the British. The British were not helpful. All information concerning their carriers was now highly classified, and the British denied that information to their former World War I allies. The team tried to trade information on the British airplane arresting gear for drawings of the American Navy's hydraulic catapults, but the material provided by the British consisted of worthless photostatic copies of a few rough sketches, devoid of details.[32]

Rear Admiral Jackson R. Tate, who served with Whiting on *Langley*, said in an article written for the US Naval Institute's *Proceedings* the following:

> Ken Whiting did most of her design, got building authorization and money and wet-nursed her entire conversion. Whiting developed Naval Aviation as we know it today…and was a man far ahead of his time in the very conservative Navy of the 1920s.[33]

On *Langley*, Whiting, who stayed in Washington as prospective executive officer while the conversion was ongoing, led a team of aviators he handpicked, composed of Lieutenant Commander Godfrey D. Chevalier (prospective air officer), Lieutenant Commander Virgil Griffin (prospective assistant air officer), Lieutenant A. Melville Pride, and Lieutenant Fred W. Pennoyer. Before the war, Whiting and Chevalier had flown together a great deal at Pensacola and developed a strong friendship. Pride was a reserve officer with a degree from Massachusetts Institute of Technology with a brilliant engineering mind and was one of the best pilots of his time. Pennoyer was a dedicated construction engineer, the only Construction Corps pilot in the Navy, to whom fell all the details of designing all the gear of both *Langley* and her planes. Because of his construction engineering background, Pennoyer initially focused on the development and testing of the aircraft arresting and catapult installations. After the conversion was completed, the scope of his work covered every feature of the ship affecting the operation and maintenance of the aircraft. Pennoyer and Pride teamed up in the designing and building of the arresting gear and hydraulic gears, and Whiting consulted frequently with civilian design engineer Carl L. Norden, who also invented the Norden bombsight.[34]

When Pennoyer reported to the Norfolk Navy Yard in early 1922, a few weeks before *Langley's* scheduled commissioning, her deck was unfinished, with thin steel plating that felt like a tin roof when walked on, and the yard was unable to provide finished drawings to complete it. Detailed specifications for completing the deck were in the hands of the turntable test unit at Hampton Roads. Pride was in charge of the unit, acting under the direction of Whiting, Chevalier, and Griffin. At Hampton Roads, the unit had constructed a scaled-down replica of a flight deck for developing and testing all elements of airplane arresting gear. Mounted on a turntable, the deck could be rotated into the wind by hand. Using trial and error, the team made *hundreds and hundreds of landings* to prove each element before editing the design specifications and passing them on to the Navy Yard.[35]

To develop proficiency in deck landings onto the platform, the flight schedule of all the pilots was rotated. A landing score for each pilot on every landing was calculated and plotted, and the competition was spirited because the one with the best overall score was expected to make the first landing on the completed *Langley* deck. Pride maintained a strong lead in the competition, and Chevalier, while he carried out his prospective air officer duties, had the least opportunity for practice and the lowest score.[36]

When the *Langley's* deck was completed according to the specifications developed using the Hampton Roads turntable replica of the flight deck, the unit went aboard *Langley*, which was still under construction, and all testing activities shifted to the real flight deck. Despite Pride's strong lead in the competition, when the day came to select the pilot to make the first landing on *Langley*, Whiting chose Chevalier, the most senior pilot and the most popular one. According to Pennoyer, Chevalier "was one of the finest and most likeable officers I have ever served with." Unfortunately, Chevalier's Aeromarine number 606 skidded slightly on landing and ended up on its nose and wing tip. When the deck was cleared, Pride made the next landing. It was perfect.[37]

Although Pennoyer said in his notes that the dynamics of arresting and handling aircraft in those early *Langley* years differed from those used in subsequent carrier aviation in later years, the unit had to work through them to lay the groundwork for the eventual perfected methodology. In the design and construction of the *Langley's* arresting gear, great efforts were made to match the landing gear and tail skid originally installed in the Navy's early aircraft. The initial arresting gear consisted of half-inch steel cables under high tension and installed both ways, fore and aft and athwart, on the deck, and the cables were mounted to enable the entire system to be lowered to the deck or raised not less than six inches above the deck to "trap" the landing airplane. The number of cables to be raised or lowered was variable, depending on the weight of the aircraft to be landed, its anticipated landing speed, and the relative wind across the deck. The cables also were equipped with hand brakes, to clamp the cables after each landing; operation of those brakes required split-second timing. At either end of each cable, there were five-foot steel levers, and these levers were a serious menace. A man standing in the nets abreast of one when a crosswire was engaged was certain to get a broken jaw or worse. According to Pennoyer, these levers caused the only serious injuries from flight operations, and they were soon replaced by safer tensioning devices. Also, each cable had a string of control devices called fiddle bridges, and the number of fiddle bridges was well over a hundred. Initially, the fiddle bridges had to be set manually between landings, and the time to reset them for each landing was about five minutes. Later, they were connected to a power supply to enable operators to change them simultaneously, and the reset time was considerably shortened.[38]

The landing tolerances of the fore-and-aft wire complex were tight, and a landing that was even slightly canted or skidding would cause a nose-over, a cartwheel, or other crash, which led to broken wheels, blown tires, bent or nicked propellers, or damaged wings. Such damage would require the pilot to divert and land at the nearest beach. Pennoyer's records documented one minor accident for every ten landings and a major crash for every one hundred landings. Forty years later, when Pennoyer was writing his "Notes," the accident rate in landing on Navy carriers, day and night, had been reduced by large advances in the technology of carrier arresting gear to one minor accident for several thousand landings.[39]

Early on and after many trials, the *Langley's* arresting gear developed by Pride consisted of British fore-and-aft wires, moveable up and down, superimposed on cross-deck cables invented by Ely connected by lifting weights. When a plane landed, it caught a cross-deck wire, came to a quick halt, and was held down by the fore-and-aft wires.[40]

A few years later, the Navy concluded that the fore-and-aft wires not only slowed up operations but were also the major cause of the accident rate. "Although they had already been installed on the decks of the Navy's second and third carriers, *Lexington* and *Saratoga*, they were all eliminated in 1929." Since then, the Navy's carrier arresting gear has been the system first used by Eugene Ely, adapted to larger planes by strengthened, cross-deck heavy steel cables, and attached to higher-capacity energy absorbers instead of his jury-rigged sandbags.[41]

As the team worked on perfecting the design of the *Langley's* arresting gear, they also worked the other end of the landing challenge—reengineering the Navy's aircraft to enable them to land on the *Langley's* deck. At that time, no aircraft in existence or under construction had been designed to land on a carrier. New equipment had to be designed in the field and installed on their aircraft by the *Langley's* crew. The drag of the added equipment plus their weight, Pennoyer said, would give nightmares to any aeronautical engineer. This equipment was heavy and well made, but its drag took at least fifteen knots off the airplanes' speed with a related reduction in range. The first piece of equipment was a tail hook to engage the cross wires, and there was no point on any of the aircraft, which was strong enough to attach a hook without major alterations. The challenge was to attach the hook at a point where its pull would line up through the airplane's center of gravity, and after several attempts, the after section of the fuselage of each airplane had to be rebuilt to provide a centerline hook jointed universally. Other alterations in the aircraft were an extension in the propeller to reduce damage from the fore and aft wires and the installation of the heavy, non-aerodynamic axle hooks for engaging the cross wires; the team claimed a major success when they were able to reduce drag by rotating the axle hooks to a horizontal position in flight. The lower wings of some aircraft also required modifications to cut down damage to the tips.[42]

The Navy yard was not particularly involved in rebuilding the ship. They were not sure what the aviators wanted, except a deck, catapults, and arresting gear, so Whiting and Chevalier had to be involved in almost daily conferences with Navy yard officials. Among the many glitches that Whiting led in overcoming in the conversion to the *Langley* were the disposal of boiler smoke and gases with a flush flight deck, the airplane elevator between the flight and hangar decks, maintaining visibility from the navigational bridge under the flush-flight deck, a large and complete photo lab, the pigeon house for communications, adding a ten-foot-deep layer of cement in the old coal holds to lower the ship to the desired draft, where to place stations for the control of the flight deck and arresting gear, and designing the arresting gear.[43]

True to Langley's designation as an experimental ship, two systems for disposing of boiler smoke and gases were installed. A system with jets of salt water to cool and smother the gases discharged to starboard was installed below the flight deck while a couple of hinged smokestacks, which could be lowered below the flight deck level during flight operations for discharge to port, were used. Because the fumes would asphyxiate anyone near the jets by swirling over the flight and lower decks, the salt water jet system was abandoned. Along with conning the ship with the wind a few degrees off the starboard bow during flight operations, the hinged smokestack system proved to be much more effective and was adopted for use on the *Langley*. The practice of conning the ship with the wind a few degrees off the starboard bow during flight operations has survived and is still in use today.[44]

Langley's single airplane elevator between the flight and hangar decks was the largest attempted by the Otis Elevator Company until that time. Operated by cables on large drums electrically powered, it took about two minutes to be raised or lowered. More than the device's speed, in a rolling sea, the counterweights would frequently jam and leave the elevator stalled between decks and held by its emergency brakes. Langley developed a technique for freeing the counterweights in a seaway without accident, but it was quite tricky. Modern hydraulic carrier elevators when Pennoyer wrote his "Notes" in the 1960s took just a few seconds.[45]

With Langley's flush-flight deck, its navigational bridge was initially installed near the bow and under the deck. Visibility for the conning officer during maneuvers in close waters when flight operations were not occurring was a problem at times, but Langley developed a partial solution by installing a clothes locker-sized, cupola-shaped elevator that could be raised above the flight deck. After Langley, this problem was fully solved by the development of the island superstructure placed on the starboard side of all US carriers since then and moving the conning officer's bridge station there.[46]

*****

Captain William Moffett was appointed director of Naval Aviation in the Office of the Chief of Naval Operations in March

1921. After graduating from the Naval Academy in 1890, he served on surface ships and, after the Vera Cruz expedition in 1914, was awarded the Medal of Honor. As he tried in his new role to move Naval Aviation forward, he found he was totally enmeshed in bureaucracy. Naval Aviation responsibilities were divided among several bureau chiefs, and neither he nor the CNO could give orders to the chiefs. It is easy to see how this divided organization probably influenced relationships during World War I among Sims, Whiting, Sayles, Jackson, and Cone; until Naval Aviation was centralized, it would continue to prevent aviation from taking control of its own destiny. Moffett could not get aviation's needs met within the current Navy Department organization.

The solution lay in reorganizing the Department of the Navy, and on June 25, 1921, Congress created the Bureau of Aeronautics and centralized Naval Aviation under the new bureau. In July, Moffett was appointed the first chief of the Bureau of Aeronautics and promoted to rear admiral. Using his new powers, he controlled aviation purchasing and supervised the construction of aircraft and aviation-related ships. Although there were no aviators among naval leaders, he drew together enthusiastic junior aviators and began to build a coterie of Naval Aviation leaders for the future. BuAer would recommend aviator billets, but the Bureau of Navigation would make the final assignments. Moffett served as chief of BuAer for twelve years and died tragically on April 4, 1933, in the crash of the dirigible USS *Akron*. Moffett was an articulate and effective advocate for Naval Aviation. With the strong group of subordinates whom he recruited, he pushed the limits of airplanes, aircraft carriers, airship design and tactics. From the ground up, he built Naval Aviation into a powerful organization of aircraft carriers, naval air stations, long-range patrol bombers and dirigibles.[47]

Among the various personnel and offices moved into the new Bureau of Aeronautics was the Office of Aviation's Lieutenant Commander Kenneth Whiting, who transferred on September 1, 1921. With the conversion of *Jupiter* nearly completed and her commissioning scheduled for March 20, 1922, Whiting continued his campaign for aircraft carriers without interruption. As one of a group of naval officers testifying before Congress's Committee on Naval Affairs for construction of two new carriers—the USS *Lexington* (CV-2) and USS *Saratoga* (CV-3), Whiting said in January, 1922,

> The *Langley* when commissioned will provide our Navy with an experimental carrier which, while not ideal, will be sufficiently serviceable to conduct any development of the various types of aircraft...for those first are also lacking in our Navy, due to concentrating on [anti] submarine work during the War. The carriers will be successful, and an absolute necessity to any well-equipped navy in the future, there is not the slightest doubt in my mind. We are asking the Congress for the first properly designed carrier. It will take from three to four years to build it. Will they give it to us?[48]

The *properly designed* carriers Whiting wanted were first to begin to appear in November 1927, with the commissioning of *Lexington* and *Saratoga*. These had been laid down as cruisers, and they brought the thirty-three-knot speed of cruisers [enabling them to keep up with the fleet] and a flight deck much longer and wider than *Langley's*.[49]

Still ongoing were the carrier development efforts of other navies. Begun in 1918, the British Navy commissioned the HMS *Argus* in July 1923, the first carrier with a full-length flight deck and the first carrier to be planned and built as a carrier from the keel up. Japan built its first ship planned and built as a carrier, the *Hosyo*, and launched her in December 1922.[50]

*****

While Whiting was shepherding his proposal to convert *Jupiter* to the Navy's first aircraft carrier through the Department of the Navy and playing an instrumental role in obtaining funding from

Congress for the conversion, he also was fighting the battle to obtain authorization for this completely new type of ship at an important international conference. The Washington Naval Conference of 1922, held from November 12, 1921, to February 6, 1922, was all about preventing future wars by controlling the arms race, which many believed had helped fuel World War I. The Washington Naval Treaty produced by the conference was to have a major impact on the development of the aircraft carrier.[51]

Rear Admiral Jackson Tate documented the haggling of the great naval powers at the Washington Naval Conference over ships and tonnages. The high-ranking officers in the front seats fought for battleship and cruiser power, but in the back seats, a lieutenant commander named Kenneth Whiting, who would not be selected for promotion until after the conference, kept insisting to be heard for something called an aircraft carrier. No one cared much, but what he was asking for were ships that would replace the battleship as the backbone of the fleet and would thus change the whole paradigm of naval warfare. He finally got authority for an experimental carrier, and when the United States agreed to scrap her new battle cruisers, he fought to get the already laid-down keels of the first two, the *Saratoga* and *Lexington*, converted to airplane carriers.[52]

The treaty placed strict limits on the tonnages of battleships, cruisers, and carriers; each nation that signed the treaty now had total tonnage limits on carriers as well as an upper limit in the tonnage of each ship. The initial proposal was for a limit of 27,000 tons per carrier, with the proviso that carriers declared experimental could exceed 27,000 tons as long as their navy's total carrier tonnage was not exceeded. However, American naval advisors at the conference, mindful of the conversions of *Lexington* and *Saratoga* currently underway, got the individual carrier tonnage raised to 33,000 tons, plus 3,000 tons more for a ship being converted from another type of vessel. At the signing of the treaty, all the major navies were over-tonnage in battleships, but considerably under-tonnage in carriers. To address the treaty compliance issue and to take advantage of the extra 3,000 tons for conversions, many battleships and cruisers under construction or in service were converted to carriers.[53]

Both *Lexington* and *Saratoga* had been planned as cruisers, but after the United States ratified the Washington Naval Treaty of 1922 and agreed to limit its tonnage of battleships and cruisers, it was decided that both ships would be converted to aircraft carriers. The aviators got those keels for carriers and built the *Lexington* and *Saratoga* on them; they became our first real flattops. Until they were in action, Whiting, Griffin, Pride, and all the eager pioneers of Naval Aviation experimented on the Langley. As conversions, both were very close to the individual ship tonnage treaty limit. Both would be very fast, and at a planned top speed of 33 knots would be the Navy's first carriers able to keep up with the fleet. With flight decks 866 feet by 105 feet, 11 inches, they overcame the size limitations of *Langley* [and barely squeezed through the 110-foot-wide locks of the Panama Canal]. Other specifications were as follows: length—888 feet; beam—105 feet, 11 inches; draft—30 feet, 5 inches; displacement—37,000 tons; propulsion—180,000 horsepower, 4 shafts with 4 sets of turbo-electric drive motors; range—10,000 nautical miles at 10 knots; 2 elevators; complement—2,791 officers and men (including aviation crew); main battery—78 aircraft (one catapult); defensive armament—4 eight-inch guns, 12 five-inch guns.[54]

*****

In the middle of a Washington winter, Edna's mother, "Mrs. Dickie," visited the Whitings, and since Whiting had undergone his metamorphosis from academically lazy to academically serious, he was studying for his commander promotion examinations. He urged Edna and her mother to go to the movies, but it was snowing so hard that the two women could not get a cab. They later found out that the theater roof had collapsed. Whiting was notified of his promotion to the rank of commander on January 13, 1922, which was backdated to a date of rank of June 3, 1921, and he was transferred to Norfolk Navy Yard to fit out USS *Langley* and to serve as her executive officer after she was commissioned.[55]

*****

Whiting's initial estimate of four to five months for conversion became nearly two years, and on March 20, 1922, Whiting, reporting on board as her first executive officer, stood on the converted *Langley's* well deck—cluttered with air hoses; toolboxes; lumber; steel-plated, scaffolding, and debris—and commissioned her. The congressional authorization to fund her conversion was running out; rather than seek a new authorization, the Navy would follow an exception in the law for commissioned ships and use general repair funds to complete the job. Because *Langley* looked like an old-time Western-covered wagon after her conversion, Covered Wagon became her nickname. Her commanding officer was to be Captain Stafford H. R. "Stiffy" Doyle, who Pennoyer judged to be a fine officer, but a member of the battleship Gun Club who did not understand what the *Langley* was all about or the ideas Whiting and Chevalier were working toward. Though stationed only twenty-five miles away in Hampton Roads, Doyle did not attend the commissioning, so Whiting commissioned her as acting captain and thus became the first person to command a US Navy aircraft carrier. Because of construction delays, *Langley* had no masts on the day of her commissioning, so Whiting had to order her commissioning pennant nailed to a mop handle attached to the flight deck. Whiting remained as senior officer present afloat (SOPA) for several months until Doyle came aboard in June and assumed command.[56]

For Whiting, getting out of Washington after three years and becoming executive officer of the *Langley* was a dream come true. The pilots had already been working on takeoffs and landings on the turntable replica deck. The aviators and their families lived at the Pine Beach Hotel, which was supposed to be reserved for the families of submariners but had made room for the aviators. The hotel was a large frame building of mid-Victorian vintage. It had a large, circular ballroom with cupolas and gingerbread on the walls. All residents ate in the main dining room, served by Navy mess boys. Younger children attended the base school. There was swimming in the base pool and frequent picnic trips up the James River in summer when the air was heavy with honeysuckle—and alive with mosquitoes![57]

Langley moved to Pensacola for the winter of 1922–23. Edna followed and set up housekeeping on the Pensacola Bay shore, then a rural area. The Whitings had chickens, but the neighbors had cows, and it was common with Florida's open-range laws of those years to see Whiting chasing a cow on the beach by moonlight.[58]

The ship left Pensacola for Panama, but twenty-four hours later, it broke down and had to return to Pensacola for six weeks of repairs. Then Edna, who was pregnant, went to Larchmont to await the arrival of the Whitings' next child. Ken took leave and arrived in Larchmont on April 14, just in time to take Edna to Sloan's Hospital in New York City, where the baby was born on April 15, 1923. Some quality family time ensued.[59]

Although the Whitings could never afford to own a large sailboat on his Navy pay, the owners of large sailboats recognized the Whiting family's skill in piloting such boats and loaned them to the Whitings for racing and pleasure cruising. Clarkson Cowl had been loaning his two-masted schooner *Moira* to the Whitings every summer since 1913 as long as they raced her. A letter from Cowl congratulating the Whitings on the birth of their second daughter arrived on May 12, 1923. He made a suggestion, which the Whitings accepted, to name the baby Moira, for his sailboat. He asked Ken to write him in July, when Cowl's summer plans would be firmer, and he would know whether he could loan the schooner to the Whitings again for the summer of 1923.[60]

*****

Even after her commissioning, work on *Langley* progressed very slowly. Perhaps the biggest challenge, according to Whiting, had been that the conversion had the lowest priority in the yard, and he felt too much of the conversion money was going to the Navy Yard overhead and not to the ship.[61]

Whiting said the following:

> We thought she could be converted cheaply—that was a mistake, however. In any

event, she will have cost less when completely converted than any other ship we might have selected. We thought she could be converted quickly—that was another mistake. The war is over and labor, contractors and material men are taking a breathing spell. The recommendation for her conversion was made by the General Board of the Navy early in 1919. Congress appropriated the money in [July 11] 1919; she was promised for January 1921. She may be ready by July 1921.

She was not. *Jupiter*'s designation as a collier, AC, was changed to aircraft carrier, CV, on July 11, 1919; she went into the yard for conversion in March 1920 and was commissioned USS *Langley* (CV-1) on March 20, 1922, at Norfolk, Virginia.[62]

With a narrow deck, *Langley* was not large, but she would weigh less than *Jupiter* and have a slightly higher top speed. Fully loaded, she weighed 15,150 tons, 21 percent lighter than *Jupiter*; her svelte size earned her a top speed of 15.5 knots. Unfortunately, this was still not fast enough to sail with the fleet, but as the Navy's first carrier, she could and would be used as a laboratory for the exploration of the new naval warfare discipline of aircraft carrier operations. *Langley*'s primary weapons, her main battery, would be her aircraft; her guns would be for defense. Other post-conversion specifications of *Langley* were as follows: beam—65.5 feet; draft—24 feet; complement (crew and aviation personnel)—468 (*Jupiter* 163); main battery—36 aircraft; defensive armament—4 five-inch guns.[63]

Given the slowness of the Norfolk Navy Yard's conversion of *Langley*, she was not ready to leave the yard until almost six months after her commissioning. Whiting had served as senior officer present afloat for that time, but at this point, Doyle came aboard and took command. The ship proceeded down to the Hampton Roads Naval Base, where she was assigned dock space at the merchant ship end of the terminal. *Langley* was "unpopular, unlovely, unusual, and ugly," and no one at Hampton Roads was willing to admit that the unusual and ugly apparition was a warship.[64]

Under the supervision of her senior aviator, Whiting, *Langley* immediately began to carry out her assigned mission, to experiment with developing Naval Aviation. All new US Navy ships have shake-down cruises, where the ship and all her equipment are tested and her procedures worked out. Because she was the first aircraft carrier, the *Langley*'s shakedown cruise was much more complicated and extensive. Whiting developed a routine of daily conferences in the wardroom to settle all problems, both major and minor, and by leading many of the solutions, experiments, and innovations, Whiting continued to build his credentials as the father of the aircraft carrier.[65]

Launching and landing airplanes from a flight deck had never been done before, so aircraft carriers needed a new set of orders and procedures to manage flight operations. As a bugle call for announcing flight quarters, Whiting chose the old cavalry bugle call "Boots and Saddles." Procedures for new orders like "Rig the deck," "Pilots, man your planes," "White flag," and "Stand by to start engines" had to be developed.[66]

Taking off and landing an airplane on America's first commissioned aircraft carrier and being catapulted off a carrier were historic. Flying a Vought VE-7 Bluebird from *Langley*'s deck, Lieutenant Virgil C. Griffin made the first takeoff from an American carrier on October 17, 1922, and Lieutenant Commander Godfrey Chevalier made the first landing on October 26 in an Aeromarine 39B. In his "Notes," Pennoyer remembered that the first catapult launching of a seaplane was a flop, and it was his fault. From one of *Langley*'s two main deck-mounted catapults, Whiting himself made the world's first catapult launch of an aircraft from an aircraft carrier on November 18, piloting a Naval Aircraft Factor PT while *Langley* was at anchor in Virginia's York River. Led by Vice Admiral Emory Land, several high-ranking officers came down from Washington to witness the event. The plane was loaded on a car mounted on casters. At the end of the takeoff run, the airplane's hold-down straps, bolted to the deck by angle cleats, were to be stripped off by levers installed at the car's front end as it struck them. It was expected that the car and airplane would rear up sharply off the deck from the acceleration of the launch, but the amount was hard to calculate. If they reared up more than anticipated, the releasing levers would pass over the deck cleats without tripping. To prevent that possibility, the levers and cleats were made with the greatest possible overlap. Every possible static test on the rig, including jacking up the front end of the car to the limits of its strength, was tried. Despite the tests, the levers passed over the cleats without tripping as the airplane sailed off, leaving the bottom of both floats on deck strapped to the car. Whiting responded to frantic hand signals from the deck by landing the seaplane alongside, where it was picked up by the crane before sinking. The team covered its embarrassment by immediately altering the rig so the release system was at the rear of the car.[67]

A copy of *Langley's* Plan of the Day, dated February 1, 1923, and signed by Whiting as executive officer, gives some insight into the shipboard routine of an experimental aircraft carrier:

> The weather permitting, the ship will get underway at 9:00 A. M. tomorrow February 2, 1923, and will proceed out of the harbor for the purpose of flying planes off and on the ship.
>
> The tug Alleghany will accompany the ship and take station one hundred yards out and 200 yards astern of the starboard quarter, steaming at the same rate of speed as the Langley—about 6 knots.
>
> When [pilots are] flying off and on, both life boats will be lowered to rail and manned; the first or second motor sailing launch, depending upon which stack is in use will be lowered to the level of the poop deck, manned and equipped with grapnels, crash kits and six men in addition to the crew. The Boatswain will be in charge of this boat and will go in the boat.
>
> The Flight Surgeon will fly over the ship in a flying boat piloted by O. M. Darling, ACR, USN. This plane will maintain station 200 yards

behind and 200 feet above the plane which is flying off and on.

This seaplane will start from the Naval
Air Station upon a radio signal from the ship.
Boatswain Fehrer will go to the tug accompanied
by three men from the Fourth Division and a
crash kit.

In case of fog tomorrow the ship will not
get underway, but will stand by until noon; in
the event that the fog is cleared up by that time,
will proceed.

Steam will be kept on three boilers and
engines in maneuvering condition. In case plane
goes into the water, the first boat to get to it shall
at once attempt to rescue the aviator, at the same
time making a line fast to some strong point of the
plane, in order to hold the cockpit above water.
This line if possible should be passed around one
of the A frames or engine section, or a longeron
in the vicinity of the cockpit.[68]

The Navy began to stage eighteen years of annual Fleet Problems
in 1923. Fleet Problems involved mock battles, with one or more of
the forces designated to play the role of a European or Asian Navy
and with umpires assigned to grade the participants and determine
the winners and losers. These exercises, conducted from 1923 to
1940 and suspended during World War II, tested the Navy's evolving
doctrine and tactics for the use of carriers.[69]

Fleet Problem I was staged in February and March 1923, off the
coast of Panama, and as the first time an aircraft carrier participated
in a fleet problem, the *firsts* of the *Langley* were revolutionary in many
ways. The concept of the script was the Atlantic Fleet's first simulated
air assault on the Panama Canal to test its defenses. The *Langley* contributed both landplanes and seaplanes; the seaplanes were launched
and based at Porto Bello, and their refueling was conducted at Porto
Bello from a submarine. Pennoyer remembered the thrill of seeing

the submarine's conning tower break the surface at the precise second that the rendezvous was planned and the excitement of seeing the executive officer, an old friend and Naval Academy classmate, step on the deck.[70]

The main fuel tank in Pennoyer's airplane was under the pilot's seat, and the funnel with chamois for refilling had to be held between the pilot's knees. The submarine started pumping too fast, and Pennoyer's clothes became soaked with raw gasoline from the waist down. Pennoyer suffered "the torments of Hades" during the flight to and from the Canal locks, and when he landed at Porto Bello and ripped his clothes off, he saw "nothing but red meat from the waist down."[71]

Pennoyer closed his "Notes" with a lesson that a ship about to enter a sea battle should maneuver to place itself in the proper bearing relative to the wind before the enemy does, relearned for the launching of airplanes on *Langley* but as old as naval warfare itself. As Theodore Roosevelt wanted, this Naval Academy graduate was obviously using John Paul Jones as a standard to guide his thinking.

> Due to the slow speed of the *Langley* and necessity for heading into the wind during flight operations, it was vital that she never be caught with the enemy holding the weather vane. It was a revival of a basic tactic in fighting sailing ships dating long before John Paul Jones.[72]

One of the early innovations developed by Whiting, modified by advanced technology but still in use in today's aircraft carriers, was a landing signal officer, or LSO. Some writers explain it this way:

> To coach pilots in landing their planes on a carrier, Whiting used to stand in the Langley's aft port side netting to assess landings. One day, instead of just assessing, he began to coach pilots coming in for a landing. First, by grabbing white hats from nearby sailors so the pilots could see

his signals better and then replacing them with semaphore flags; he developed a system of signals to communicate to the pilots on short final approach the adjustments they needed to make in their glide path to land properly. Pilots found Whiting's flag and body language helpful and suggested an experienced pilot be assigned to occupy the position when Whiting was flying.[73]

Pennoyer explained the genesis of the landing signal officer in his "Notes" a little differently. Until late in 1924, all aircraft assigned to *Langley* were biplanes, and the pilot's visibility when landing them on the carrier's deck was bad. When the pilot flared the airplane by pulling up in his approach, the lower wings would mask the deck completely. On this first carrier, there was no "island" for a reference point, and the pilot had to land the plane on the deck blind. "When he judged that the plane was coming in too high or too low, Whiting would instinctively run out waving his arms. He provided at least a reference point that the pilot could see." Instead of signaling the pilot from wherever he was on the deck, in an obvious next step in this vital innovation, Whiting moved this activity to the *Langley's* aft portside netting, where the pilot could develop the habit as he made his final approach of checking a fixed point of reference to correct the attitude of his airplane. The landing-signal-officer concept, updated by technology, is still used on all US aircraft carriers.[74]

Another innovation incorporated by Whiting into the design plans for *Langley*, tried and subsequently eliminated, was a pigeon coop. Aircraft in those days had no means of distant communication, and pigeons had been carried aboard seaplanes since World War I. Carrier pigeons were also the only method of communication for a pilot whose airplane was forced down, and on any flight over fifty miles, to train the pigeons to fly back to the ship in case of a force-down a couple of pigeons were usually carried and released. Whiting installed a pigeon loft on the fantail under the flight deck, and a crew member was assigned there to feed, train, and breed the pigeons. The performance of the pigeons was normally perfect when the ship was docked or when only a few were released, but when the whole flock was released, they flew south and roosted in the cranes in the Norfolk shipyard. Based on the pigeon's erratic performance, Whiting eliminated the loft and the pigeons, and he converted the loft into the executive officer's quarters.[75]

A more humorous description of the homing pigeon innovation and the decision to eliminate it was that all escaped one day and flew back to Norfolk. The Navy discharged them for "dereliction of duty," and the pigeon coop was converted to quarters for the ship's first executive officer [Whiting]. After their discharge, some reported the addition of squab to the *Langley* mess menu.[76]

The pigeon coop and the landing-signal-officer innovation may have been linked in a way that naval aviator number 3, John Towers, who followed Whiting as Langley's executive officer, was probably not aware. Towers complained to his close friend Pierre de Grandmont, whom he later married, and said the following:

> The [executive officer's] cabin [high on the fantail, over which planes passed when landing] is the result of the efforts of two idiots... First, one who thought it would be a clever thing to carry homing pigeons on the ship and the other who, when the pigeon idea was at last given up, decided to convert the pigeon house into the Executive Officer's Quarters! I really live in a pigeon cote, complete with sitting room, bedroom and bath, all about the size of your hat.[77]

Of course, the "idiots" who made these two decisions were one in the same man, Kenneth Whiting. Having been so intimately involved from early on with developing the concept of an *experimental* aircraft carrier, Whiting had included the coop in the ship's plans because radio communications technology was not far enough advanced in the early 1920s to rely upon it. After the pigeons all flew away, and he decided to shut the coop down, the question became what to do with the space? With one of his other targets for experimentation being the development of the landing signal officer, Whiting was already spending time on the portside of the fantail observing and correcting aircraft landings. The coop had large ports facing aft (shown in a close-up picture of *Langley*'s stern on page 6 of Lee's fine article), which would allow anyone in the former coop space to simply raise his eyes, look out over the wake, and watch an airplane landing. Since Whiting had taken on the leadership of this innovation as a high priority for himself, he probably reasoned that this would be a perfect location for his quarters. Here, he had ready access to a ladder to take him above to the fantail and to the cabin's ports when he was not on the deck above. So he moved the executive officer's quarters to the former coop. When Towers became *Langley*'s executive officer on January 4, 1926, the landing-signal-officer system was already in place and experimentation on that innovation was complete. Thus, the executive officer no longer needed to focus on observing aircraft landings, and Towers could have exercised his authority and moved his cabin elsewhere.

Another innovation Whiting had built into *Langley*'s design plans was storage tanks of aviation gasoline. To prevent an explosion, sea water was added to the top of the gasoline in the tanks as the heavier gasoline was used. It was found that the carbon steel linings of tanks became progressively corroded with the salt water; the gasoline became contaminated; and slugs of water would sometimes come out with the gasoline. In a very time-consuming process, when the problem was first discovered, all the gasoline had to be chamoised into the airplanes. Meanwhile, an extensive search was conducted for an effective filter with the required flow capacity, to no avail, but in the meantime, the ship solved the problem by developing an effective mechanical filter.[78]

Another part of the design plan that became a problem of a different sort was a one-hundred-gallon tank between the flight and hangar decks for the storage of pure grain alcohol for cleaning aircraft instruments. To ensure the alcohol was not used for other purposes "peculiar to Naval Aviation," Pennoyer explained, the tank required an around-the-clock sentry. During *Langley*'s shakedown cruise, the ship received a letter from the Bureau of Construction and Repair requiring that the tank either be removed or that the grain alcohol be replaced with denatured alcohol. The ship's position was that this change was unthinkable, especially during Prohibition. Because Pennoyer was too junior to have any personal interest in the matter, Whiting asked him to draft a strongly worded appeal. When the Bureau withdrew the order in its reply, the entire ship celebrated.[79]

Whiting was credited with establishing many other basic tenets of carrier aviation, largely worked out during his first *Langley* tour. The Navy has always needed to protect its high-cost investment in the training of pilots, so Whiting was also responsible for initiating the assignment of escort destroyers to aircraft carriers as routine procedure. Their primary purpose was to act as plane guards to pick up pilots after crashes and forced landings. They took station on either quarter of the carrier. Providing an anti-submarine screen and as additional protection against attack from the air were subsequently added to the plane guard's responsibilities.[80]

He also suggested a ready room for assembly of pilots prior to flight, but non-aviator Captain Doyle said the pilots were already pampered enough and saw no need for it. After winning that battle with Doyle, Whiting equipped a room on *Langley* where pilots could wait for their next mission and be briefed on its details; every Navy carrier since then has had them.[81]

Another Whiting innovation had begun before *Langley* was commissioned; it was when Whiting and his design unit, headed by Pride and including Chevalier and Pennoyer, were using the Chambers Field turntable to develop arresting procedures by filming and grading every landing. Whiting insisted from the beginning of the conversion that the *Langley* have a large complete photography laboratory and darkroom because he planned to take both still and motion pictures of every landing and have them developed at sea. In the beginning, he had every landing on the carrier filmed with a hand-cranked motion-picture camera in both slow motion and normal speed to aid in the evaluation of landing techniques. After every crash, these movies were carefully studied to assist pilots in attaining and maintaining proficiency in the very difficult act of landing an airplane on a carrier. Such crashes were not infrequent, so the cost-conscious Whiting eventually ordered that only landings that appeared to be potential crashes were to be photographed. This final procedure for filming was thus adopted: (1) landing looks like a crash, (2) chief photographer begins cranking the camera, (3) crash siren sounds. Similar procedures are still followed on all carriers, and all landings are critiqued and graded.[82]

In his "Notes on USS *Langley*," Pennoyer tied the accident rate of landings on *Langley* to Whiting's innovation of filming every landing with a camera strategically located at the flight-deck level. Analyzing every landing was invaluable both for the pilots and Pennoyer's engineering efforts to perfect the arresting gear. Eventually, an accurate prediction of a coming crash could be made during an approach before the aircraft crossed the stern.[83]

Another use of the film was to edit out the pictures of major crashes and make a single, exciting crash film. Watching the crash film became a major source of humor for the pilots whose lives as naval aviators landing on carriers in that early era were quite stressful. To continue to be able to perform the feat required the relaxation of humor. One day, Pennoyer reported, the crash film had been shown to a new assistant secretary of the Navy. In the middle of the film, he shouted, "Stop it! Stop it! I can't stand such carnage!"[84]

During Whiting's tour as *Langley*'s first executive officer from 1922 to 1924, the book on perfect shipboard routine for carriers was written, and more than one of his fellow Navy officers gave Whiting credit for the authorship. Rear Admiral Tate described the *Langley* story as a tribute to Whiting, who "did most of her design, got building authorization and money, and wet-nursed her entire conversion. He developed Naval Aviation as we know it today." But in 1923, the Navy Department decided the *Langley* should return to Norfolk to prepare for a two-month publicity cruise up the Atlantic Coast.[85]

The Nisewaner and Walden Journal of Family Memories continues the story: While the Langley was in Norfolk, Edna stayed in Larchmont with her mother, "Mrs. Dickie." Edna's father, Charles, had died in July 1920, and "Mrs. Dickie" was now living alone in the large 98 Park Avenue house. Ken was able to get to Larchmont long enough for a cruise on the Moira with his brother Butts, but he returned to New York City, the first port of call, so the *Langley* could begin the publicity cruise. The purpose of the cruise was to show the public what Naval Aviation could do, and as the nation's first aircraft carrier steamed up the North River and anchored off Ninety-Sixth Street, Whiting said, "If John Paul Jones were to come aboard and take a squint, he would be content to lie forever undisturbed beneath the baroque curves of the Chapel of the Naval Academy at Annapolis." But he would be puzzled, Whiting continued, at this experimental ship his Navy had now and what it was doing—and all within the terms of the Washington Naval Treaty. With the ship anchored, the public swarmed over the ship, and the aviators flew off and on.[86]

The next port of call on the publicity tour was Gloucester, Massachusetts. Edna and the two Whiting daughters followed the ship and stayed at the Inn, a typical mid-Victorian structure replete with many old ladies who were charmed by baby Moira. Eddie rode back and forth to the ship in the twenty-four-foot ship's boat. Edna and Eddie lay in the nets that extended out from below the flight deck to get a better view of the planes taking off and landing. As planes landed, they could hear the clatter of metal slamming metal, as the fiddle bridges that held fore and aft wires and thwartship wires up slammed down.[87]

Many years later, Eddie remembered and wrote about another memory of the Gloucester port call, a party at the lavish home of John Hays Hammond Jr., the Father of Radio Control. Hammond held over eight hundred patents as a pioneer in the study of remote control and naval weapons. He was a lifelong protégé of both Thomas Edison and Alexander Graham Bell, and among his inventions was the variable pitch ship propeller, an amplifier for long-distance telephone lines and a radio-controlled torpedo. He built Hammond Castle as his home and laboratory on the rocky Gloucester Atlantic coast at 80 Hesperus Avenue.[88]

Eddie continued, "Hammond gave a party at his house, which had a tower with a special staircase running outside to the top and which provided an endless view of the harbor. Eight-year-old Eddie got into the spiked punch bowl and then went up to the top. On the way down, she got a little tipsy and came down by sitting alternatively on each step. Ken and Edna found her at the punch bowl, sipping a bit unsteadily."[89]

In the infancy of carrier operations, an operational problem that had begun with Captain Doyle's non-attendance at Langley's commissioning and his lack of interest in aviation and its challenges continued to manifest itself on the publicity cruise. The Nisewaner and Walden Journal of Family Memories documented the problem:

> Doyle went ashore and attended a few Chamber of Commerce meetings. Some of his speeches revealed his utter ignorance of the purposes and aims of *Langley* and Naval Aviation.

As a result, during the publicity cruise, Whiting began to lay the groundwork with friends in Washington for a law requiring aviator qualifications for any officers with command responsibility over aviation operations, carriers, and tenders. Whiting would continue his efforts to promote such a law when the Morrow Board met in 1925, and he could voice this important Naval Aviation initiative to a high-profile national board.[90]

While *Langley* was operating in the Pacific off Panama, Whiting suffered a more serious seaplane crash than when he and Orville Wright put a plane into an Ohio river. Flying a seaplane back to the ship, he had been knocked unconscious from a hard crash on the water. He came back to consciousness and swam to the surface, with some new bruises that eventually healed.[91]

The *Langley* returned to Norfolk, where the Whitings lived once again at the Pine Beach Hotel. Then *Langley* went back to Pensacola for the winter.[92] Unfortunately, and particularly in the American military with its practice of reassigning officers every two or three years, all good things end. Tate described Whiting's departure from *Langley*'s executive officer billet this way:

> Whiting, Pride, and Pennoyer made frequent trips to Washington with ideas for the slow

development of the battle cruiser hulls *Saratoga* and *Lexington*. They had notebooks full of many controversial ideas, advocating such things as heavier arresting gear, land-plane catapults, space available on board for aircraft overhaul, and so forth. The major item in Whiting's mind was the tactical use of aircraft, but that was an idea whose time was still a few years away... Then suddenly Whiting, Griffin, Pride, and Pennoyer were detached to Washington and finally to *Saratoga*...[Whiting's successor as executive officer was] Commander Warren G. Child, Naval Aviator #29, a nice person, but not much of a pilot. He possessed none of Whiting's fire, vision, or ideas about carriers.[93]

CHAPTER 9

BUILDING MORE CARRIERS AND FIGHTING THE BILLY MITCHELL WARS

Having been so immersed in acquiring and authorizing America's first three aircraft carriers, Whiting was ordered back to BuAer in July 1924, once again under Bureau Chief Moffett, as assistant chief of Bureau, and later, as head of the Aircraft Carriers Division. Given Whiting's dislike of Washington, Moffett promised him that he would not have to keep office hours and that this tour would not be as long as the previous one. In this tour, he was to help modify a lighter-than-air aircraft tender, USS *Wright*, into the Navy's first seaplane tender, to oversee the continuing development of the Navy's next two carriers—the USS *Lexington* (CV-2) and the USS *Saratoga* (CV-3)—and to play a major role in the Navy's war with Billy Mitchell before the Morrow Board and in the Mitchell court-martial.[1]

The *Wright* had been commissioned as AZ-1, a one-of-a-kind lighter-than-air aircraft tender, on December 16, 1921, during Whiting's first tour with BuAer. She was fitted with a unique balloon-well built into her hull and aft to enable her to experiment with kite balloons, which could become unstable and result on putting its pilot in danger, but after four months, those experiments ended, and the kite balloon was sent ashore.[2]

The *Wright's* characteristics were as follows: displacement—1,685 tons (full load); length—448 feet; beam—58 feet; draft—23 feet; speed—15.3 knots; complement—228 officers and men; aircraft—F5L and Curtiss NC-10 seaplanes; armament—2 five-inch guns, 2 three-inch guns, 2 machine guns.[3]

On December 2, 1926, the *Wright's* hull number was changed to AV-1, and she was declared the Navy's first heavier-than-air seaplane tender. Her first captain (later admiral) was Alfred W. Johnson, with collateral duties as commander, Aircraft Squadrons, Atlantic Fleet. Other captains (many of whom became admirals) were John Rodgers, Ernest J. King, Aubrey W. Fitch, Patrick N. L. Bellinger, and Marc Mitscher. One of the early pilots who served in *Wright* was Clifton A. F. "Ziggy" Sprague, who as an admiral with a carrier group with a call sign "Taffy 3" and with six light carriers, three destroyers, and four destroyer escorts stood off a Japanese task force of four battleships, eight cruisers, and eleven destroyers at Leyte Gulf in World War II in the October 25, 1944, Battle of Samar and protected the American beachhead at Leyte.[4]

The *Wright's* name was changed to USS *San Clemente* on February 1, 1945, to clear the name *Wright* for a new light aircraft carrier, USS *Wright* (CVL-49).[5]

The *Wright* must have been another labor of love for Whiting because it was named for Orville Wright, the man who taught him to fly and with whom he maintained a lifelong friendship. In her speech nominating Whiting to the Navy's Hall of Fame at NAS Pensacola, after his death, his daughter Eddie specifically mentioned Whiting's work in the development of the *Wright*. A December 17, 1925, letter from Rear Admiral G. S. Strickland, commander of Aircraft Squadrons, whose flag quarters were on the *Wright*, to Whiting at Buaer, documented discussions with Whiting about aircraft tender organization and how much independence the air squadrons attached to a seaplane tender should have.[6]

*****

The Navy's bureaucratic war with the US Army's Billy Mitchell actually began in early 1915, as war raged in Europe without the US, when then-Signal Corps Captain Mitchell garnered his first headline critical of the Army and the Navy. After Mitchell's lecture to a group of engineers, a Washington newspaper headlined SAYS FOE CAN TAKE US WHERE ARMY IS RAISED, and NOT SURE WE HAVE A NAVY.[7]

Later in 1915, now-Major Mitchell was transferred to the Signal Corps' Aviation Section and talked pilots in the section into taking him flying. Mitchell loved flying from the beginning and was good at it; he used his strong verbal skills and self-confidence to convince his volunteer teachers to continue his lessons and to allow him to solo when the time came. At the same time, he enrolled in a private flying school in Newport News, Virginia, at his own expense. As he continued to gain experience as a volunteer pilot, Mitchell concluded the US would enter the war in Europe at some point, and he "badgered his superiors" to send him to Europe as an observer to observe and report on French methods for manufacturing aircraft and training and organizing airmen; he sailed on March 17, 1917.[8]

In France, he began bombarding the War Department with suggestions taken from the French while continuing to take flying lessons from French pilots as a volunteer; after General Pershing arrived in France on June 13 with his headquarters staff, including aviators, he passed the test for the Army designation of junior military aviator. He continued his work as an aviation observer and reporter at a *furious* pace, for which he had to work with Pershing's aviation staff. Slowly, he worked his way into the headquarters, and though some fellow senior officers said he was "hostile and insubordinate," he eventually gained a position commanding the American First Army Air Service.[9]

On July 15, 1918, the German Army launched their last attack across the Marne, and Mitchell, flying low-level reconnaissance over the battlefield, discovered the strength and direction of the seventy-division offensive. Returning to First Army headquarters, he reported his observations to the staff. His report figured prominently in the First Army's St. Mihiel attack plan, and after writing the air support portion of the plan, he led the Air Service part of it. Pershing personally commended Mitchell for his work, and Mitchell, who had coordinated a force of almost 1,500 British, French, and Italian aircraft to support American ground forces, continued his fine work in the Meuse-Argonne offensive.[10]

Just before the November 11, 1918, Armistice, for his brilliant work, Mitchell was promoted to brigadier general and decorated with many medals, including the American Distinguished Service Cross and the French Legion of Honor. American aviator Henry H. "Hap" Arnold, future World War II Army Air Corps commander, said he was "the Prince of the Air."[11]

Mitchell returned from the war on top of the world, literally and figuratively, and convinced of the rectitude of his vision for the future of American aviation. He had fought bureaucratic battles to put himself in his high position and had led Army aviation to victory. He held the fervent belief that the British Royal Air Force, which had resulted from the merger of British Army and Navy Aviation, "is the best organized force of its kind in the world… If we could have the air organization in the US that the British have, we would be so far ahead of the rest of the world that there would be no comparison." Billy Mitchell took that conviction home with him and began a multiyear public campaign to convince his superiors and the entire country to enact it for America.[12]

When Mitchell reached Washington in March 1919, he was surprised to find that the government was hastily disbanding the Army and its Air Service. The new assignment for which Pershing had gotten him orders, director of Military Aeronautics, had been filled by someone else.[13]

He immediately started a seven-year campaign to strengthen the Air Service and merge Army and Navy Aviation on the British model. His campaign started with a three-hour meeting with the Navy's General Board, in which Mitchell argued that the Army should take the coastal defense mission from the Navy and that aviation had advanced to the point that an airplane could sink a battleship; when the battleship admirals on the Board disagreed, he proposed a series of bombing tests that would go on for several years to prove that he was correct.[14]

Mitchell then began a national four-year, 200,000-mile round of speeches in which he grew increasingly critical of national defense policy and of the Army and Navy Departments. Many of his ideas were prescient and even brilliant, but they were generally dismissed by a government that was pursuing a policy of disarmament.[15]

The Army responded by putting him on notice publicly as well as in writing henceforth to confine his ideas to the Department of the Army. Mitchell ignored these orders, appearing at twenty-seven major congressional hearings and numerous public forums over the next few years. The scope of his criticisms increasingly involved Naval Aviation, as he built his case to merge the aviation branches of both services. Although BuAer Chief Moffett and Mitchell agreed on the importance of building a strong air arm, Mitchell's criticism of Naval Aviation opened a long warfare between the two aviation leaders.[16]

The Billy Mitchell Wars reached a peak in the fall of 1925 when President Coolidge took two actions to stop the public conflict, the appointment of the Morrow Board, and the court-martial of Billy Mitchell; these two high-profile events were to overlap in the next few months.[17]

*****

Ken and Edna followed their usual practice and spent the month of July 1925 in Larchmont before President Coolidge appointed the Morrow Board. They frequently raced the *Moira* with Butts and others, and the girls stayed with "Mrs. Dickie" for the summer. The family returned to a large house on Woodley Road, west of Wisconsin Avenue in Washington, just in time for school and the start of the Morrow Board's hearings.[18]

During Whiting's second tour in BuAer, bureaucratic conflict with Army Aviation and its leaders like Billy Mitchell that had gone on since World War I came to a head. It did not surface as a separate issue but under the umbrella of general national concerns with commercial aviation and military aviation. Believing that Europe was getting ahead of the United States in commercial aviation and still smarting from the poor record of American aircraft production in the world war [partly because the decade-plus series of patent lawsuits before World War I between Glenn Curtiss, Alexander Graham Bell, and the Wright family limited the ability of American manufacturers to build airplanes, which forced the US Army and Navy to purchase many of their airplanes from French, British, and Italian manufacturers], President Calvin Coolidge appointed the Morrow Board, officially known as the President's Aircraft Board and named for its chair Dwight D. Morrow to investigate the concerns and make recommendations to address them. Also named to the board were Admiral F. F. Fletcher, a close friend of BuAer Chief William Moffett; Major General J. G. Harbord; Howard E. Coffin, Senator Hiram Bingham, Connecticut; Representative Carl Vinson, Georgia; Representative J. S. Parker, New York; Judge A. C. Denison; and Stanford Engineering Professor W. F. Durand. The board met for two and half months, starting September 27, 1925; one of the first witnesses heard was Billy Mitchell. Testifying on September 29 and 30, Mitchell offered to be sworn, but Morrow declined, asking him to speak informally. For most of his testimony, Mitchell chose to read from a book he had written, *Winged Defense*; he bored the board with a *singsong* recital of criticisms and ideas that were well-known.[19]

The board heard ninety-eight other witnesses, including several Cabinet secretaries, such as then secretary of Commerce Herbert Hoover, and national aviation leader Charles Lindbergh. Hoover and Lindbergh advocated strongly for the federal government to promote and regulate commercial air. The board recommended, and Congress passed the Air Commerce Act of 1926, which put the federal government in the business of promoting and regulating commercial aviation. The act was also credited with stilling the agitation and restoring calm to the national aviation environment.[20]

The national security portion of the Morrow Board's work involved an effort by some national leaders and members of the military, led by Brigadier General Billy Mitchell, to follow the precedent set by the British in 1918 and merge the aviation branches of the Army and Navy into one service. One of the witnesses who testified during the national security portion was Kenneth Whiting, who appeared before the board over a period of several days and accumulated almost fifty pages of testimony.[21]

Having met in France during the war when both had offices in Paris, Whiting and Mitchell were friends, shared some characteristics in common, agreed on their desire to advance aviation in their own services but were totally divided on the issue of merging Army and Naval Aviation. Born within two years of each other, they were both in their midforties. They both excelled physically from boyhood; Mitchell focused on polo and tennis and had proven his sense of balance and strength as a youth by climbing daily on the top of his family's greenhouse *and never falling through the glass*. Although they had not become pilots until their midthirties, they were both excellent at it. Perhaps their greatest difference was in their personalities. Sublimating his aviation specialty to the US Navy as a whole and his ego to the common good, Whiting was the consummate team player. Mitchell was brilliant, with an ego that drove him to believe that he was always right.[22]

Whiting began his Morrow Board testimony by reviewing his then-twenty years of naval service; then he explained the unrest in the relatively new Naval Aviation community and asserted that it could be quelled by the establishment of a definite policy and plan for Naval Aviation, including a system to manage the careers, assignments, and promotions of naval aviators.[23]

After identifying the problem and a general solution, instead of immediately moving to his preferred solution, Whiting laid out four options, then being proposed by various sources to address the unrest, including a unified air service, then being strongly advocated by Army Brigadier General Billy Mitchell, a Naval Aviation Corps supported by many young naval aviators, a plan first proposed by Whiting himself but since modified by a Navy Department committee appointed by the CNO, and a plan proposed by the Navy's Bureau of Navigation.[24]

After explaining the four options, Whiting moved into a description of the support each enjoyed within the Navy and his personal view of each one. All naval officers, he said, rejected a unified air service because policies for the assignment, regulation, pay, and promotion of naval aviators would be developed by an outside source and because new aviators would be loyal to the unified air service instead of to the Navy. Whiting said he was opposed to the unified air service not only because the Navy needed to manage the careers of naval aviators but because the mission and tactics of Naval Aviation differed from those of the Army and dictated many unique aspects of Naval Aviation training.[25]

Whiting asserted the following:

> Many younger naval aviators want a sep-
> arate aviation corps like the Marine Corps, but
> they haven't studied it carefully enough. They
> don't understand that you cannot have a corps,
> in which aviators would focus totally on aviation
> billets, and higher-level, surface, and carrier com-
> mand at the same time.[26]

Whiting went on to a detailed explanation of the Whiting Plan, first explaining that he was addressing the plan as modified by a CNO-appointed committee and recommended by the General Board. He said the committee's plan was premised on granting authority over all aspects of Naval Aviation, including training and assignments, to the Bureau of Aeronautics; the Bureau of Navigation, which now had final authority over aviator assignments, disagreed with moving authority over aviator assignments to BuAer. The Whiting Plan, he said, was based upon an analysis of the future needs of Naval Aviation manpower and the number of ships needed to produce a matrix by rank and age (taking into account attrition by accidents, resignations, courts-martials, and normal deaths) of the number of aviators needed to fill all aviation billets. An expanded Naval Academy would be the only source of naval aviators and would complete all aviator ground school training before graduation and flight training. To recognize that a career in Naval Aviation would require specific aviation knowledge and general knowledge as a general line officer and that the physical duties of more senior aviation command billets required younger officers, aviators would receive temporary promotions ahead of their surface contemporaries but would receive no pay increases until a promotion was made permanent. To manage this system of temporary promotions, new legislation requiring the modification of promotion examinations with more emphasis on the aviation specialization and less on other specialties like engineering would be necessary.[27]

The temporary promotion of naval aviators in the Whiting Plan before their contemporaries elicited considerable questioning from the board members about whether this would make naval aviators *greedy*, but Whiting defended this aspect of the plan by specifically describing how physically and mentally arduous aviation duty was, the higher level of accidents and deaths endured by aviators, and the impact on the aging of pilots from maintaining skill levels in aviation and surface duties. He reiterated that aviators would live life harder and faster than their contemporaries in other specialties and would not receive extra pay for their temporary promotions; thus, they would not be *greedy*. Whiting further justified the establishment of a unique plan for Naval Aviation by reminding the board that the Whiting Plan was based upon an extensive analysis of the current needs of aviation. He explained that upon his departure from the submarine service in 1914, he had performed a similar analysis of the then-current submarine officer development program, which had been based on each submarine captain developing his own officers and proposed the creation of a centralized system of submarine officer training and development. Just as that centralized system had been developed and adopted, other specialties like aviation needed to analyze their current needs and develop a plan to address them.[28]

Returning to the fourth option in his list of options, Whiting explained that the Bureau of Navigation plan would assign aviators back and forth—four years in an aviation billet, followed by four years in a surface billet. When a pilot returned to aviation, he would be commanding pilots more current in aviation than he was, and more senior pilots would need a four- to six-month aviation refresher course. In war, the US Navy's aviators would be handicapped by fighting against enemy aviators who had spent their entire careers in aviation.[29]

While taking advantage of a witness who probably possessed the longest and most extensive knowledge of aircraft carriers in the

1925 Navy, in its examination of Whiting, the board moved on to the characteristics and uses of this very new type of ship. Whiting affirmed that he had "been studying the question of carriers since entering aviation in 1914." He explained that carriers and tenders should only be commanded by aviators because when they operate on duty detached from the fleet, the commanding officer must decide when to launch planes and how to employ the carrier's aircraft. On the role of carriers in coastal defense, he said the best strategy for coastal defense was to keep the enemy away from your coast by going to him on the water and attacking him in his territory with carriers. He defended the current assignment of the coastal defense mission to the Navy by explaining its expertise and training in the support of coastal defense, including constantly developing and maintaining knowledge about the exact current location of all ships, friendly or otherwise; the location of submarines; and the probable locations of attacks. Were this mission to be reassigned to the Army, for which Billy Mitchell had advocated, it would have to train officers to perform these support roles and to develop a base of this information. He agreed that carrier decks were vulnerable to attack but asserted that they could be defended by the carrier's planes, and as the Army had well demonstrated, by the use of antiaircraft machine guns. If the Navy was going to have aircraft with the fleet, he said, it needed carriers; no other type of ship—battleships, destroyers, or tenders—could carry enough airplanes. On the current state of carrier aircraft development, because of the need to defend against German submarines during the war, the Navy had had to concentrate on anti-submarine scouting planes. But since the end of the war, the Navy developed good bombers, patrol, and observation planes, and the Army had done such a good job of pursuit plane development that the Navy used those Army pursuit planes. He educated the board on the Navy's three-year process of developing new airplanes, from pilot input through bid process to deploying them to the fleet, as well as the factors and the detailed steps the Navy followed to decide on the size of new carriers. To deal with the loss of trained pilots and growth needs for more, he agreed the Navy could use enlisted pilots as copilots, but primary pilots should be officers.[30]

Whiting discussed the causes of aviation crashes since the beginning of aviation some twenty years ago. In the early days, a lack of knowledge about aviation (how to get out of a spin, flying too low to recover from a mistake) and the use of unstable pusher-type airplanes were keys. The unique nature of military flying, such as formation flying and mission-necessitated risks, played roles. Material failures were a small factor. Finally, he compared the lower incidence of crashes by mail-service pilots to the higher rates of military pilots by explaining that the minimum experience requirement for mail-service pilots was five hundred flying hours while most Naval Aviation accidents occurred among pilots with less than two hundred hours.[31]

Whiting ended his testimony by returning to the ongoing Army-Navy disputes about airplanes sinking ships. He said that the Navy developed a meticulous statistical system to record the results of its experimentation in this area, and he asked that the Army adopt a similar system for comparison purposes.[32]

The final report of the Morrow Board, published on November 30, 1925, contained several conclusions and recommendations, for which Whiting had specifically advocated, on areas covered by his testimony. Perhaps most important, Mitchell's merger drive proved unsuccessful, and the board recommended that there should not be a separate, unified air service. To strengthen Naval Aviation, it said that a new position of assistant secretary for Air should be created to give Army Aviation more prestige; it recommended that the Army Air Service be renamed the Army Air Corps, equivalent to the Signal Corps or the Quartermaster Corps, that it be given special representation on the Army General Staff, and that a new position, assistant secretary of war for air, be created. F. Trubee Davison, principal organizer of the Great War's First Yale Unit of naval reserve aviators and a leader in Naval Aviation, was ultimately appointed the Army's assistant secretary of war for air and served from 1926 to 1932. With only one experimental carrier in commission and operating for three years and two more under conversion, the board drew the bold and prescient conclusion that the strength of the United States Navy was in aircraft carriers.[33]

The board recognized the unrest and dissatisfaction among aviation personnel of the Navy. Aviators felt their devotion to aviation has prejudiced their chances for promotion and opportunity for high command; they felt that the requirements for all officers to qualify in all branches ought not to be applied to aviators in full measure. In the board's response to this great Naval Aviation concern, it said the following:

> This is the most difficult question we have been called on to consider. The solution lies in the broad and generous recognition of Admiral Mahan's maxim that a naval officer should have a general knowledge of all branches of his profession and a specialized knowledge of one. Beyond that, special provision for promotion must be made for those officers who, through no fault of their own, have been confined solely to aviation duty, and junior officers in aviation who have not had required sea duty should have that duty before being examined for promotion.[34]

The board found that naval aviators objected to direct command of flying by nonflying officers and said it felt that this had arisen "largely through the fact that there are no officers in the higher ranks of the Navy with long experience in aviation. There appears to be justice in this contention, and we are recommending temporary advanced rank for naval aviators" so they could command aviation-related ships and activities. To keep their flying and associated aviation skills current, the board recommended that aviators assigned to general line duty to qualify for command should be dissociated from aviation to the minimum extent.[35]

The board concluded that every effort should be made to provide adequate aviation personnel, including the increased use of enlisted pilots and expansion of reserve training in aviation. These should make unnecessary the increase of the Naval Academy.[36]

So naval aviators could have the opportunity to present Naval Aviation problems to those responsible for shaping policies and handling naval personnel, the board recommended that naval aviators should be assigned to both the Office of the Chief of Naval Operations and the Bureau of Navigation. The men chosen must appreciate not only the special needs of aviation but the needs of the Navy as a whole.[37]

Finally, in an area very important to the independence of Naval Aviation and the protection of naval aviators from the inappropriate orders or judgments of senior officers not aviation-qualified, which Whiting had worked for several years to place in law and policy, the board recommended that selection for command or general line duty on aircraft carriers, seaplane tenders, naval air stations, and flying schools be confined to officers who, while otherwise qualified, were also naval aviators.[38]

Congress subsequently enacted this aviation command recommendation into law, which became a milestone in Naval Aviation's long campaign to take charge of its own destiny. Few people then realized how far into the future Whiting had been looking, and it was not until the US was well into World War II that President Roosevelt went a step further and issued an executive order that also required that all carrier task forces be commanded by aviators."[39]

The Morrow Board's recommendations on the merger proposal and the appointment of a naval aviation leader to the new assistant secretary of war for air position perhaps best demonstrate how well the Navy did in fending off Mitchell's merger campaign.

*****

During and since the war, Whiting had been involved either peripherally or centrally with the Navy's battles against the Army and its chief advocate, Billy Mitchell. They had begun with the Army's major objections to a plan Whiting wrote for the American and British Navies to bomb enemy submarine facilities in Holland and Germany by Navy seaplanes transported across the North Sea by fifty-foot lighters, by navy coastal stations like Killingholme and

Dunkerque [commanded by Whiting and Chevalier, respectively] and by Naval Aviation units like the Northern Bombing Group; the Army believed that the strategic bombardment of land targets was their exclusive mission. Mitchell had been one of the major spokesmen for the Army in these conflicts, and as the author and American executor of the Killingholme plan, Whiting played a major role for the Navy. As a result of these battles on a Navy ship "returning from Europe in February 1919, Mitchell had bombarded the ship's company with calls to merge Army and Navy Aviation Forces." Since the Royal Flying Corps and the Royal Naval Air Service was merged on April 1, 1918, in the name of efficiency, Mitchell's arguments probably included that act by the British government as a precedent and rationale for performing the same merger with the aviation branches of America's Army and Navy.[40]

Believing he might convince senior Navy leaders like CNO Benson, who were considering eliminating Naval Aviation to become allies in his drive to unify all military aviation, Mitchell met with assistant Navy secretary Franklin Roosevelt and the General Board on April 3, 1919, to discuss aviation. Mitchell urged the development of Naval Aviation because of the growing obsolescence of the surface fleet. His assurances that the Army could design a bomb to sink a battleship and his proposal that Army and Navy Aviation should be unified into one national air service were met with cool hostility. Naval aviators feared that land-based aviators in a unified independent air force would no more understand the requirements of sea-based aviators than ground forces commanders understood the capabilities of air power, and they vigorously resisted any alliance with Mitchell. Rebuffed by the Navy, Army chief of Air Service Mitchell organized a set of large public tests to prove that an airplane could sink a battleship. In a series of meetings to negotiate the details of the tests, Mitchell represented the Army while Captain Alfred Johnson, commander of the Atlantic Fleet Air Detachment, with Whiting as his special assistant, represented the Navy. The tests occurred in June and July 1921, off the Virginia Capes. Mitchell and his Army pilots sank three German ships captured during the war, a destroyer, an armored light cruiser, and a battleship, the *Ostfriesland.*

They also sank two aging US battleships—the *New Jersey* and the *Virginia*—but the Navy claimed that Mitchell cheated by exceeding the agreed-upon parameters of the test.[41]

The Army picked up Mitchell's aviation merger cause over the next few years, and in numerous instances, including testimony before the Morrow Board and others, congressional committees and in published reports, Army and Navy antagonists, including Mitchell and Whiting, debated the aviation merger and revisited the old World War I controversies.[42]

In his lengthy testimony, Whiting was the star witness for the Navy before the Morrow Board. He delighted all Navy partisans in his rebuttal to cross-examination by Congressman Frank Reid, the board counsel. Giving Naval Aviation a platform to grow and using the Morrow Board as a megaphone to communicate his ideas about Naval Aviation to a much wider audience, Whiting presented an organization plan that would allow officers to specialize in aviation while maintaining their competence as regular line officers. He called for more carriers, faster carriers, and more airplanes, and in the years to come, much of his plan was adopted by the Navy. As it turned out, Britain's April 1, 1918, merger of the Royal Navy's Aviation Arm and the Royal Flying Corps, which Mitchell had used as a precedent, was to result in limiting Britain's continuing Naval Aviation innovation, losing its dominant international position in Naval Aviation and ceding the Royal Navy's position as the world's Naval Aviation leader to the US Navy by the end of World War II. Although Whiting and the Bureau of Aeronautics could not have seen this reversal coming in 1925, Whiting did use the great differences between the Navy's World War I anti-submarine mission and the Army's bombardment mission to explain why the proposed merger would not work. The offensive warfare mission of carriers made it necessary to train naval aviators differently from Army aviators, and the gap between the two missions was simply too great to be blended. He used the ongoing *Lexington* and *Saratoga* construction, which he was currently spearheading, to explain why a unified air service would not know how to use carriers.[43]

Summing up his testimony before the Morrow Board, Kenneth Whiting was chosen by BuAer Chief Moffett to work with the board.

In his lengthy testimony, he demonstrated comprehensive knowledge and experience in the many areas covered by the questions of the board members. The effectiveness of his answers is demonstrated by the related conclusions and recommendations contained in the board's final report; the board's conclusions and recommendations in a high percentage of the issues agreed with the positions for which Whiting advocated.

Whiting's work before the Morrow Board demonstrated a strong grasp of the broad range of subjects and issues discussed, a great improvement over his academic work at the Naval Academy. The Whiting Plan he presented demonstrated an ability to conduct research and to develop a complex plan based on that research. His explanation of the plan and his answers about other topics showed an ability to steer a sensitive course between advocating the positions of Naval Aviation and the larger Navy while trying when he could to strengthen the Navy's badly strained relations with its sister service, the Army. At the time when the Morrow Board did its work, the issues between the Army and the Navy was planted during the world war and had festered in the seven or eight years since then. The role Whiting was asked to play during the Morrow Board's work required a knowledgeable advocacy of the positions of Naval Aviation and the US Navy, but also where it was possible to soften the acrimony between the two services. He attempted to present issues comprehensively and fairly, and this was probably a significant factor in the popularity he enjoyed within the Navy. Examples of this work within the Navy included his efforts to represent the diverse positions and opinions of the Navy's officers, committees, and bureaus. For example, he first explained the four current positions on quelling the dissent in Naval Aviation before identifying his own preference and advocating for it. He explained a committee's position before identifying opposition to the committee's position by other parts of the Navy bureaucracy and his own personal position.

As he tried to represent all the different positions taken by parts of the Navy's bureaucracy, he took advantage of opportunities like highlighting the effectiveness of Army antiaircraft fire and the quality of the Army's pursuit planes. When he was forced to choose between advancing a position of his service—the Navy versus the Army—he represented the Navy. He used complex coastal defense information-gathering processes that the Navy developed and for which it trained its officers to explain his opposition to the proposal, first broached by Mitchell in his April 1919 meeting with the General Board, of transferring that mission to the Army. At the end of his testimony, he took a parting shot at the Army in the ongoing internecine warfare over bombing and sinking battleships by asking the Morrow Board to strengthen the comparability of the effectiveness of the work of both services by recommending that the Army adopt the same statistical analysis methodology developed by the Navy in its bombing tests.

Gaining bureau status for the Bureau of Aeronautics in 1921 paid dividends for Naval Aviation by better enabling the Navy to defend itself against the furious attacks by Billy Mitchell-led Army partisans and their efforts to merge Army and Naval Aviation. In the end, the fleet closed ranks around its flyers and House Bill 8533, the merger bill filed in Congress on January 28, 1926, was defeated by a unified Navy.[44]

At the same time, as the Morrow Board was conducting its investigation, in multiple bomb tests, Mitchell proved several times that an airplane could sink a battleship, but in doing so, he violated the rules of engagement previously negotiated by Johnson and Whiting and agreed to by the secretaries of the Army and Navy. As Mitchell continued to publicly criticize the Army and Navy for being insufficiently farsighted regarding airpower, his relations with his superiors continued to sour. He crossed a line when he publicly ascribed the cause of some recent military aviation crashes and deaths to "the incompetency, criminal negligence, and almost treasonable administration of the national defense by the Navy and War Departments." All this caused major ruptures in congressional support for the Navy and its budgets as well as in the relations between the Army and the Navy. For this, the Army court-martialed Mitchell, charging him with violation of Article 96 of the Articles of War, "Conduct of a nature to bring discredit upon the military service." The court-martial convened on October 28, a month before the Morrow Board finished its work.[45]

At the behest of BuAer Chief Moffett, who obviously felt he had to defend the Navy and Naval Aviation against Mitchell's attacks then and to send the message that they would not be tolerated in the future, Whiting was assigned to special additional duty by the secretary of the Navy to attend the trial, to assist the trial judge advocate in formulating questions, and to testify against Mitchell. In his testimony, Whiting refuted Mitchell's longtime assertion that Naval Aviation was behind the air service of the Army and of other countries. He defended the Navy's role in the battleship bombing tests and fought attempts to reveal classified information. He insisted that most naval aviators wanted more autonomy for Naval Aviation within the Navy, not full independence or a merger with the Army and predicted a much more important role for aviation in the Navy's warfighting strategy in the future. After hearing seven weeks of testimony from ninety-nine witnesses, the court-martial board found Mitchell guilty and sentenced him to be suspended for five years without pay or allowances.[46]

Because of Mitchell's outstanding record in World War I, President Coolidge restored all his allowances and half of his base pay. But in the end, Mitchell resigned from the Army on February 1, 1926. He passed away on February 19, 1936. Over fifteen years after his resignation, the events of World War II proved to many that Mitchell had been correct in much of what he said, and since World War II played out in many of the ways Mitchell predicted, President Harry Truman and Congress posthumously restored him to the rank of major general and struck a special medal for him. Today, he is considered to be the Father of the United States Air Force.[47]

Although many of Billy Mitchell's ideas and predictions have been proven correct by events which occurred after his death, there can be little doubt that the US Navy was the victor in the Billy Mitchell wars and that the 1920s vision of officers like Moffett and Whiting of the organizational place of Naval Aviation and its role and importance within the Navy's warfighting doctrine has come true.

*****

It is interesting to expand the earlier discussion about the impact of courts-martial and reprimands on the careers of Whiting, Ellyson, Nimitz, Eisenhower, and Patton by including the Billy Mitchell case. In the Army, after World War I, Brigadier General Billy Mitchell was publicly outspoken over several years about several proposals and ideas that some of the Army's leadership found unacceptable. At the same time, Lieutenant Colonel George Patton and Major Dwight Eisenhower began to write articles in the Army's *Infantry Magazine* about the need to develop tanks and how such new weapons should be used. Patton and Eisenhower wanted to mass tanks on future battlefields to envelop the enemy and drive into his rear, destroying his logistics and command and control. The infantry-minded generals who set policy in the Army in the 1920s wanted to have tanks, but they wanted to divide them up among infantry units and use them to support small infantry units or give up the powerful mobility factor they brought to the battlefield by actually digging them in and using them for artillery. Patton and Eisenhower both received official reprimands for speaking out and writing in military publications about tanks and, in order to save their military careers, then stopped their efforts (until the eve of World War II twenty years later when the Army realized their leadership was critically needed because it was far behind countries like Germany and Russia in tank development and doctrine). Mitchell, on the other hand, refused to back down when ordered to do so by the conservative generals who set policy for the Army and, after being court-martialed, resigned over his punishment. No such restraints were put on Kenneth Whiting, however, in his advocacy of aircraft carriers, and despite the concerns of the Navy's battleship admirals, the Gun Club, Whiting was able to push for aircraft carrier development and to keep the Navy apace with the navies of other countries, like Japan and Britain. A key difference, however, between Mitchell and Whiting was that Mitchell went outside the service in his campaigns, and in the end, it cost him his career; Whiting conducted his campaign for carriers under Moffett's protection and within the confines of the Navy, except when Moffett specifically authorized him to act outside the bounds of the Navy. Perhaps another key difference lay in their very different personalities and styles. Whiting was a consummate team player, and all knew that with him, the Navy came first over Naval Aviation. Mitchell, on the other hand, led from his ego and placed first priority on his personal agenda over that of the Army and the Navy.[48]

*****

After playing a leading role in the creation of the Navy's first aircraft carrier, planning the second and third, *Lexington* and *Saratoga*, and coordinating the process of gaining congressional authorization and funding for their construction, on September 20, 1926, Whiting was ordered to the American Brown-Boveri Electric Company in Camden, New Jersey, to oversee construction of *Saratoga*. It was here that he began a love affair with the ship that went on for years. Both ships were laid down as battlecruisers in 1921, but their construction was delayed while the Navy obtained approval at the Washington Naval Conference to convert them to aircraft carriers and made the decision to convert them both. After her conversion, *Saratoga* was commissioned on November 16, 1927. After her commissioning as the second American aircraft carrier, *Saratoga* achieved a top speed in her sea trials in 1928 of 34.59 knots [1.59 knots greater than the specification under which she was constructed]. Her other initial specifications included the following: displacement—33,000 tons; length—880 feet; beam—106 feet; draft—24 feet, 1 1/2 inches; range—10,000 nautical miles at 10 knots; complement—2,122 officers and men; propulsion—16 boilers, geared turbines, electric drive, 4 propellers; armament—91 aircraft; defensive armament—4 dual eight-inch guns, 12 single five-inch guns. Visually identical to her sister ship *Lexington*, *Saratoga*'s funnel was painted with a large black vertical stripe to help pilots recognize her. Her first air officer and future World War II carrier task force leader Marc A. Mitscher landed the first aircraft on her deck on January 11, 1928.[49]

After the Whitings spent their usual month of July 1926 in Larchmont, the family moved to Morristown, New Jersey, close to Ken's work on *Saratoga* in Camden. The months fitting out *Saratoga* were happy ones for Whiting, and the results of many years work and a long fight for funds for carriers were about to be realized in *Saratoga* and *Lexington*. Lexington was also building in Boston and "Spuds" Ellyson was to be her executive officer.[50]

After a year at Morristown, the Whitings' lease ran out, and they were forced to rent another house in Haddonfield, New Jersey. Edna believed that the less one owned in the Navy, the better. Their family possessions at this time were one large trunk of silver, linen, pictures, bits of china and glassware, a great stack of brass ashtrays, and a 1924 four-door Dodge sedan. Trips to Larchmont were now fourteen-hour safaris over narrow Jersey roads, across the Dyckman Street ferry, and through the heart of New York City. According to first daughter Eddie, "These trips always ended with Ken and Edna maintaining a stony silence."[51]

Having completed *Saratoga's* construction and fitting out, Whiting was assigned as her executive officer on November 16, 1927. Captain Harry Yarnell was in command, but Whiting was the first one to conn her when he took her down the river after commissioning. In January 1928, the Saratoga was ready for sea, and joining the rest of the fleet in Long Beach, California, she headed to Panama. Whiting's tour of duty as her executive officer was characterized by continuing development of carriers as a weapon for the projection of American sea power.[52]

Whiting injured his back on January 31, 1928, on *Saratoga's* voyage to Panama, when he had flown and landed a seaplane in the Pacific. He was standing on top of the wing trying to reach a hook being lowered to hoist the plane aboard when a large wave slammed the plane against the ship; Whiting fell twelve to fifteen feet onto a pontoon, landing flat on his back. The plane was hoisted aboard with Whiting lying motionless on the pontoon. The ship's flight surgeon ordered him to bed for several days of rest.[53]

Edna sailed for Panama with Eddie and Moira early in February 1928 on the SS *Santa Maria*. As she was joined by her brother Frank who lost his wife, "Mrs. Dickie" was no longer alone in the Larchmont house. Ken met them on the dock when the *Santa Maria* arrived, and he made arrangements for them to stay in Cristobal with Jack [later Rear Admiral] and Hilda Tate.[54]

In 1928, the Early Birds of Aviation, an international group of early aviators, was created, and Whiting became a charter member. To recognize the December 17, 1903, date of the Wright brothers' first Kitty Hawk flight and to exclude the large number of aviators who became pilots during World War I, candidates were required to have soloed before December 17, 1916. The charter class included 598 American and international pilots, and more were added when later research identified others who met the criterion.[55]

The *Saratoga* went to Bremerton for overhaul in fall 1928. This was the first of two years for the Whiting family following the *Saratoga*, with no permanent place to live. In Bremerton, Edna and the girls stayed in the Kitsop Inn; then they moved to Long Beach, and then Panama. The annual fleet problem was to be carried out in Panama. In the middle of the fleet problem, the crew was to get liberty there, and then the rest of the fleet problem was to be concluded. All this was to take two months, so Edna decided to take the girls to Panama to arrive in time for liberty. In January 1929, they sailed on a freighter that called on ten Central American ports in 19 days, loading coffee at each one.[56]

In January 1929, *Saratoga* sailed through the canal to participate in her first annual fleet exercise, Fleet Problem IX, a simulated attack and defense of the Panama Canal. Getting through the canal's 110-foot-wide locks was hard since her 106-foot beam made her one of the largest ships ever to go through.[57]

The performance of the *Saratoga* and her sister carrier, the *Lexington*, in the 1929 Fleet Problem IX were auguries of the future. Using the cover of darkness and bad weather to prevent the opposing force from becoming aware of their presence, the *Saratoga* launched a force of 69 planes. They arrived on target without interference, and the canal was theoretically destroyed. Twelve years before the Japanese attack on Pearl Harbor, the ruse enabled the *Saratoga* to predict the future dominant place of the fast carrier in the fleet.[58]

*****

Ken returned to Cristobal, and he and the family took passage on the SS *Friedland* back through the canal on a pleasant 12-hour voyage.[59]

After a brief stay in Balboa, Edna and the girls sailed for Long Beach on the SS *President Cleveland*. After *Saratoga* and Whiting reached Long Beach, they got the news of longtime friend and Annapolis roommate "Spuds" Ellyson's death. He flew from Norfolk to Annapolis to visit his sick daughter. With Chevalier and Ellyson gone, Whiting was grateful he still had Pete Mitscher, "Squash" Griffin, and George Murray close at hand to continue to train new naval officers how to use these big new carriers and their planes.[60]

Whiting's tour as executive officer of *Saratoga* ended on May 28, 1929, and he received word of his promotion to captain on August 16, with a date of rank of July 1, 1929.[61]

Whiting ordered that no farewell gifts be given to him at the conclusion of his executive officer tour in *Saratoga*, but the crew gave him a new sword. The officers gave the *Saratoga* plank owner [a member of the crew of a Navy ship at its commissioning is called a "plank owner" of the ship] Whiting a small duffel bag containing a miniature ditty box made from a plank of the flight deck, with gold wings inlaid on top, an egg, and a card imprinted "To a good egg."[62]

Whiting was now a forty-eight-year-old, middle-aged naval officer who had served as executive officer of two of the Navy's first six aircraft carriers. His annual flight physicals show him down 10 pounds to 146 pounds from his days as a submarine captain in the Philippines. His resting pulse was 60, but after a minute of sustained exercise, his pulse rose to 88. He smoked a pack a day of cigarettes and drank moderately.[63]

His vision had changed in 1928 when he failed one of two color tests (he passed the other). The Navy restricted him to day flying only for a year, but then the Bureau of Medicine and Surgery waived this requirement. He had also been fitted for reading glasses of 1.75 power the same year.[64]

*****

In September 1929, Whiting moved to a new assignment, appropriate for his new rank, chief of staff and aide to the commander, Air Squadrons, Battle Fleet. The flag of Admiral Henry Butler Jr., commander, Air Squadrons, Battle Fleet, flew on the *Saratoga*, so Whiting still worked in *Saratoga*, but in the quarters occupied by Butler's staff instead of with the ship's officers and crew. From December 1922, all US Navy ships were part of the United States Fleet, divided into a smaller Atlantic presence (Scouting Fleet) and a larger Pacific presence (Battle Fleet). Newer battleships, all aircraft carriers, a light cruiser squadron, and several destroyer squadrons were assigned to the Battle Fleet, based in Pearl Harbor, Hawaii. All Battle Fleet aircraft squadrons were assigned to the commander, Aircraft Squadrons, Battle Fleet, but the squadrons could be divided among the carriers and tenders of the Battle Fleet.[65]

The family stayed at the Breakers Hotel on the ocean in Long Beach while Edna looked for a place to live. She still had the family on a strict budget, and she found the hotel a budget breaker. They moved to the Commodore Apartments on Ocean Avenue, a duplex opening on to a court, on a high bluff overlooking the beach. The pounding of the Pacific surf was ever present. The girls enrolled at Ms. Porter's School for Girls—Eddie in the sixth grade and Moira in nursery school.[66]

Moira's memories began about this time, and she remembered her father initiating rough play with her. She felt this was probably part of her father's wish for boys who could assume the sons of the Cincinnati mantle. She particularly remembered a pillow fight with him when she was five or six years old. Her bed had a brass or iron bedstead, and she chipped a tooth on it during the fight.[67]

Ken had Moira chin herself on his thumbs when she was very little, then graduated through his forearm to a bar in the backyard. She had to learn how to swim early, and she was expected to do it well. Moira remembered her father putting his hands on his hips when he was standing up, fingers out, and one little finger stuck out from the side of his hand. Her mother explained that he had caught it on somebody's football jersey, either in practice or in a game, and pulled it way down.[68]

In summer 1929, Admiral Butler moved his flag to Coronado, and the Whiting family settled in a house on C. Avenue. Both girls got whooping cough, and the family hung a quarantine sign on the door. Moira followed whooping cough with mumps.[69]

Edna did not like the West Coast and longed to go back to the house in Larchmont. In the fall, Edna went back to Larchmont because Mrs. Dickie was sick. She left Ken and teenager Eddie to fend for themselves. Perhaps remembering the last time Ken did all the family packing, before leaving, she packed all the silver herself and had everything ready for moving. Eddie cooked for her father. Her repertoire consisted of eggs, bacon, lamb chops, creamed carrots, and peas. After a week, Ken invited a heterogeneous group of 25 to Sunday night supper; the menu was elegant and prepared on board ship. Flatware had to be borrowed because Edna had locked the trunk and took the key. The guests stayed until the wee hours. Eddie wondered why Ken wanted the party. The answer was soon apparent. Reciprocating invitations for dinner from all soon came. No more lamb chops.[70]

Early in 1930, the *Saratoga* headed east once again, via the Panama Canal, and Admiral Butler prepared to embark his flag on the ship. However, Whiting did not enjoy the chief of staff billet, perhaps because he preferred the independence of command, and alternatives to continuing as chief of staff came. First, he received a temporary assignment to lead the first mass flight of Navy planes on a sortie over Washington, DC; New York City; and New England, demonstrating what planes from a carrier could do. The May 1930 event included 139 planes from seven squadrons, the largest air armada to complete 1,000 miles of formation flight and the longest formation flight to that time. Another record it achieved was that the flight experienced only one major accident, a broken strut. The event received much attention in the newspapers, which met the overall goal of raising the visibility of Naval Aviation. Before leaving the chief of staff billet, he made arrangements to reunite with his daughters and Edna in Larchmont for their normal annual leave during the month of July.[71]

Further evidence of the Navy's recognition of Kenneth Whiting during the 1920s as an early leader in the field of Naval Aviation and aircraft carriers is provided by many of his assignments. Shortly after his return from World War I, he was appointed on September 27, 1919, to a board to consider changes to two ships that had been designated as aircraft tenders. Upon his return to BuAer for his second assignment there, on September 18, 1924, Admiral Moffett wrote that his primary duties would be "with all plans and alterations of aircraft carriers and their equipment, built, building, or contemplated. You will be liaison officer of the Bureau of Aeronautics with other bureaus and departments in all matters pertaining to aircraft carriers." He was assigned to travel to the Naval Academy and the Naval War College to deliver lectures on the subject of aircraft carriers on February 27, 1925, and August 10, 1926. He reported to the chief of the Bureau of Engineering for an October 20, 1926, conference to determine the most satisfactory means and methods of illuminating the flight decks of aircraft carriers. In good company, Whiting and Marc Mitscher were ordered to attend a BuAer conference on aircraft carrier characteristics. He appeared as a witness for BuAer before a BuNav board to consider Naval aeronautical policy on early May 1927.[72]

CHAPTER 10

COMMAND AT HAMPTON ROADS
AND NORFOLK CASTS A SHADOW
OVER WHITING'S CAREER

After nearly a year in the Pacific Battle Fleet staff billet, Whiting received orders to take command of the Naval Operating Base Hampton Roads, Virginia, effective August 4, 1930. On October 4, he received additional orders to take concurrent command of NAS Norfolk. These facilities provided support for Naval Aviation activities and the ships of the Atlantic Scouting Force. In addition, NAS Norfolk was much involved in experimental work, with which Whiting had considerable experience.[1]

October 27 was Navy Day (first organized by the Navy League of the United States on October 27, 1922, birthday of then-deceased naval enthusiast and former assistant secretary of the Navy and President Theodore Roosevelt), which provided an opportunity for major naval installations and ships to invite the public to a public relations event with static displays, tours, and aviation demonstrations. Whiting and his staff and pilots planned a full day, complete with an aerial dog fight, sky writing, stunt flying, parachute jumps, and bombing demonstrations. If they were able to obtain sufficient airplanes, they planned to add two simulated races, one for fighting planes and one for bombing and fighting planes. In case a sufficient number of airplanes were not available, they left the last two events off the printed program.[2]

As it turned out, approximately 30,000 people visited the Naval Operating Base that day; 5,000 of whom were at the Naval Air Station to see the air activities. A sufficient number of planes were available, and the two races were conducted. The two races were flown over a triangular course, part of which went over some of the 5,000 civilians.[3]

Rear Admiral Guy H. Burrage, the commandant of the Fifth Naval District, headquartered on the air station, walked around the area in the rear of the crowds to get some idea of the success of the day and to gather ideas for future improvements. (Burrage had recently requested that Whiting be assigned an additional duty on his staff as aide for aeronautics, and may have been miffed that Whiting had not copied him when he notified BuNav of his Larchmont leave address for the month of July. But Whiting apologized to Burrage in writing, started his new assignment, and the Navy Day activities were underway.) Burrage was surprised to see three planes, one after the other, flying low. He decided that they were racing or simulating a race that did not appear on the Navy Day program. He watched the three planes one after another bank and make a turn. Concerned about the altitude of the racers and their compliance with the Navy's flying rules, he spoke with Whiting that day and asked him to investigate the matter.[4]

Whiting conducted an investigation and provided Burrage a written report dated November 14. It included statements from his executive officer, Lieutenant Commander H. T. Bartlett (put on restriction by Admiral Gleaves in 1916 for destroying government property after he crashed an airplane), the three pilots (among the most skillful pilots in the Navy and whose flying experience totaled well over 30 years), Lieutenant T. D. Guinn, Lieutenant S. H. Ingersoll, and CAP Fred Wallace, and the planners of the races—Lieutenant Commander K. McGinnis and Lieutenant A. M. Pride. The reports were in substantial agreement, and Whiting attached a summary document. The reports stated that the Navy Department-approved rules for participation in races by naval aircraft required a

KENNETH WHITING

minimum altitude of 100 feet and that the airplanes in these races were flown at altitudes no lower than 150 feet. The reports also asserted that, in the event of engine failure of any of the planes, to protect the spectators, the pilot could have landed at adjacent flying fields or a golf course, neither of which were in use for the day. (Lieutenant Ingersoll's report added that the route of the race only skirted the grounds of the naval air station and thus the route was not over the naval air station or the crowd.) They stated that similar races had been conducted at NAS Norfolk and NAS Anacostia in the past that the Navy had participated in similar races at other sites, and that safety rules for races had always been followed. In Whiting's summary document, he mentioned a similar November 25, 1920, Thanksgiving Day race sponsored by the Aero Club of America which he had observed while on temporary additional duty at Mitchell Field in Mineola, New York.[5]

Finally, Whiting wrote the following:

> The race [and all events] were authorized by me as Commanding Officer...there was no willful or intentional disregard of safety orders as issued by the Navy Department or the Department of Commerce...[and] as the pilots who took part in this race were carrying out orders received from higher authority, they are not guilty of any offense.[6]

Upon receiving Whiting's report, non-aviator Burrage wrote to Rear Admiral Frank B. Upham, chief of the Bureau of Navigation on November 15 and said the following:

> I was standing approximately 1,000 feet from the nearest building. The lower wing dipped so low that it appeared to almost touch the buildings. The optical delusion [sic] was due to the building over which it banked being in line with the nearest building to me, about nine

hundred feet beyond the nearest building. The
height of the quarters, approximately forty feet,
gave my eye a definite scale to estimate the height
of the flying. After flattening out they passed over
the nearest building to me at approximately the
height of the building; forty feet over the building
or approximately eighty feet above the ground.
They then passed at approximately this same
height over the heads of the crowd of 5,000.[7]

Burrage went on to cite the Bureau of Aeronautics Manual,
which established a minimum altitude of 2,000 feet for Navy aircraft
to fly over populated areas, crowds, or gatherings at public places
unless authorized by proper authority or in case of an emergency.
Also prohibited was placing an aircraft in any position where a power
plant failure would add to the danger incurred. He said the pilots
flying in the race violated both the minimum height and the pow-
er-plant-failure provisions.[8]

Then Burrage stated that "the episode of the low flying was
reported to the Commanding Officer of the Air Station [Whiting].
He took upon himself full responsibility. Later, I inquired and found
nothing had been done to his subordinates who were involved."
Burrage then went on to cite Navy court-martial precedents for vio-
lations of these rules. He asked Upham to advise him "as to the Navy
Department's policy concerning disciplinary action for violation of
flying rules by naval personnel such as is contained in this report."
Finally, he added, "It is my opinion that something beyond minor
disciplinary action is desirable for the good of the service." Whiting's
report and Burrage's communications and questions found their way
from BuNav Chief Upham to the office of the secretary of the Navy.[9]

To add to our understanding of this process, the fate of a captain who has been a major spokesman in the decade-long battle for
the aircraft carrier between Naval Aviation and the Navy's battleship
admirals was in the hands of two of those battleship admirals who
had served closely together during a part of their careers. Burrage had
served on battleships for seven years, the last four as commanding

officer of the USS *Nebraska* from 1915 to 1919. Upham served in battleships *Oregon*, *New Jersey*, *Nebraska*, and commanded Battleship Division 3; his first year in *Nebraska*, he served as executive officer to Upham, Nebraska's captain. Upham also commanded NAS Pensacola in 1927–1928 and graduated from the short-lived, 1922–1930, Naval Aviation Observer course, designed to create senior officers who had soloed and were familiar with flying an airplane. But it is hard to imagine that one-year in aviation overcoming Upham's loyalty to battleships and to a man with whom he had served closely as his first captain in *Nebraska*. Was this an opportunity for battleship admirals to exact a measure of bureaucratic revenge in the battle?[10]

As a result of the NAS Norfolk air-racing incident, Whiting received a letter of admonition from secretary of the Navy Charles F. Adams. This letter and copies of all related documents were stamped "Finished Discipline File" and "Selection Board Jacket" and entered into this file and jacket by the Bureau of Navigation on November 28, 1930. The cover sheet on the communication from Secretary Adams read, "Admonition, regarding policy of the department regarding disciplinary action for violation of flight rules."

In addition to the official, typed documents, dropped in the file was a short handwritten statement on Burrage's Fifth Naval District Commandant's Office stationery, which said, "The crowd was not kept back to the red line but advanced beyond the dotted red line."[11]

Provisions pertinent to letters of admonition in the Navy's Manual for Court-Martial state that they are part of the Navy's Article 15 disciplinary authority and that, while a naval officer receiving such a letter may submit a statement in response, a letter of admonition from the secretary of the Navy may not be appealed. No statement in response from Whiting was included with the documentation of the event.[12]

The result of the letter of admonition was that Whiting bore total responsibility for the actions of all his officers. He could have taken the position that he had been in command of NAS Norfolk barely three weeks on Navy Day, that the officers involved had planned it all, and that he had not been involved. Acting on that position, he could have used his command authority to prefer charges against all his involved subordinates and probably walked away with his career untainted. But while other officers might act in that way, that would not have been congruent with the style of leadership Kenneth Whiting displayed during his entire career. It would also not have reflected the truth as he saw it. He and his officers complied with all the Navy's special rules for air races, and in his judgment as the senior naval aviator in command, neither he nor they had done anything wrong. The Nisewaner and Walden Journal of Family Memories document that Whiting was well aware of the damage the letter of admonition would have on his career, and he probably knew it very early in the process. As the last decade of his career rolled out, his supporters at the Bureau of Aeronautics were able to minimize the damage to his assignments done by the letter of admonition. Where it was probably to hurt him was the next time he was considered for promotion. But when Whiting watched as some of the officers who had been involved in the air race incident were promoted to flag rank, he must have taken some satisfaction from protecting their careers from a disciplinary taint. Pride retired as a full admiral while Ingersoll ended his career as a vice admiral.[13]

Using this incident as an example, senior non-aviators not understanding aviation nor listening to its aviators, the Navy seems to have changed little from its 1915 battles with young aviators like Whiting and Mustin (although CNO Benson had reversed the negative action Bristol had taken against Mustin) in the investigation boards of the Pensacola crashes or of punishing a younger aviator Bartlett for suffering a crash and damaging government property by restricting him to quarters. Upham and Secretary Adams took the word of non-aviator Burrage, who admitted he was 1,900 feet away and who had estimated the altitude of the aircraft, over the signed, written statements of seven aviators with close to fifty years of experience in reading altitude gauges and headed by a qualified naval aviator who obviously believed that he had the authority as the senior naval aviator in command to authorize the simulated race under the law passed in 1925 upon the Morrow Board's recommendation. What are the chances that, at the same time, seven altitude gauges were all incorrect or that seven aviators misread their gauges? Or is there a greater chance of former *Nebraska* executive officer Upham following the lead of his former *Nebraska* captain Burrage in this matter? The coming of World War II would change the way the Navy listened to those at the tip of its aviation spear, its pilots, but it would be too late for the one who carried all the responsibility for what may have been an incorrect decision on the Navy's part in the NAS Norfolk air-racing incident.

Burrage retired as a vice admiral in 1931 at the end of his tour as commandant, Fifth Naval District, but the poison of the air race investigation that he had initiated and of Whiting's letter of admonition that had resulted from it continued to affect Whiting's personnel jacket for the rest of his Navy career.[14]

*****

The Hampton Roads billet required Whiting to entertain important people, such as the nationally popular radio comedy team of Amos and Andy and the well-known aviator Amelia Earhart. In addition, because of the federal government's promotion of aviation and Norfolk's geographic position on the East Coast, the station was a jumping off point for transatlantic flights. Because of these responsibilities, the billet's staffing was enhanced with a chauffeur and a full complement of cooks and messboys. Well-known aviator Amelia Earhart dropped into the field for a speaking engagement in September 1930. Depression-era maintenance of the field was notoriously poor, with many holes, mud puddles, and little grass. As she was landing, Earhart skidded in a mud puddle and her red Lockheed Vega turned upside down. Her head was gashed, but the Navy doctors took care of her gash and the Whitings housed her. She made her speech and then left, leaving Whiting to get her broken plane to her in New York. But she did write a bread-and-butter note to Edna thanking the Whitings for their hospitality and assistance.[15]

Two years at NOB Hampton Roads were punctuated with Edna's monthly trips to Larchmont to see her mother, Mrs. Dickie, who had suffered a stroke and was confined to a chair. During Edna's trips, Ken would take Eddie "ship visiting" because the big quarters were too quiet for him, and he sought the warmth of Navy companionship.[16]

Ken's father, Eliot, died on February 6, 1932, and his mother, Daisy, came to visit for a month. She announced that she would like to drink some beer and play some poker. Ken replied, "Yes, Mama," and arranged a game. Even though she had not played the game in fifty years and was not familiar with some the game's new variations, Ken's mother, who had demonstrated her competence many times over the years, was the only winner.[17]

*****

In late winter 1932, the nation was shocked by the March 1 kidnapping of Charles A. Lindbergh Jr., the baby son of Charles Lindbergh, the famous Lone Eagle. The search was on, led by Colonel H. Norman Schwartzkopf, the chief of the New Jersey State Police and the father of Gulf War Commanding General H. Norman Schwartzkopf.[18]

Having brought Lindbergh and his airplane the *Spirit of Saint Louis* back from Europe after his famous 1927 transatlantic flight, Burrage knew him, and he asked Whiting to do what he could to assist in the kidnapping case. From his Hampton Roads office, Whiting arranged a meeting between John Hughes Curtis, a prominent Norfolk boat builder, and Lindbergh about information Curtis said he had about the kidnapping. Of all the clues Lindbergh received, the Curtis clue was the only one he felt might be true because Curtis knew the carefully guarded secret that the baby had a piece of flannel sewed with blue thread inside his shirt. Whiting made arrangements for Curtis to fly to Hopewell, New Jersey, Lindbergh's home. The meeting produced a plan for the baby to be brought on a Curtis yacht to a rendezvous at sea off Cape Hatteras by the kidnapper or his agent to return the infant. Whiting had Navy aircraft scout the area and provided one other important support for the anxious Lindbergh, who neither smoked nor drank alcohol. But he loved chocolate cake, and during the tense time, Whiting, whose cook made the family a chocolate cake every week, provided half a cake in a shoe box every Sunday.[19]

The plan called for a Gloucester fisherman to sail Curtis's sailboat from Boston to the Cape, leaving at a certain time and arriving at a certain time, but with his knowledge of sailing, Whiting warned Lindbergh that it was a hoax because you could not sail that far in the time set in the plan. But Lindbergh felt, hoax or not, that he had to follow the plan because of Curtis's knowledge about the flannel and the thread.[20]

The rendezvous failed, and a Navy search found no Gloucester fisherman-manned sailboat for miles around the Cape. Lindbergh returned to Hopewell, and Curtis was arrested and charged with obstruction of justice. Whiting testified at Curtis's trial. He was convicted and fined $1,000, but some felt he was really convicted for perpetrating a hoax.[21]

Meanwhile, the baby was found dead near the Lindbergh house. Bruno Richard Hauptman was arrested for capital murder, tried, convicted, and executed for the crime.[22]

Whiting remained in command at NOB Hampton Roads and NAS Norfolk for nearly two years, relinquishing command on June 16, 1932.[23]

By the time Whiting relinquished these two commands, Edna and her daughters were in the habit of supporting Whiting in his Navy career in very special ways. Edna taught her daughters always to serve him, lay out his clothes, even to turning the socks partly inside out so it would be easier for him to put them on. Be sure there was a clean handkerchief in his breast pocket and one in his left hip pocket, cigarettes, and matches in his coat pocket, wallet in his right hip pocket, and so forth. I don't think he was helpless, just absent-minded... For sure, he always had lots on his mind and great responsibilities. Thus, did she protect him from *failing inspection*, so to speak, and make sure he always had what he needed to face the day.[24]

CHAPTER 11

MOFFETT FIGHTS TO
REMOVE THE SHADOW

Whiting served in a variety of submarine and aviation billets over nearly thirty years, and now the Navy offered
him the chance to return to the classroom and to the
Rhode Island area, where he had addressed the many challenges of
USS *Seal*/G-1 20 years before, for a year of postgraduate instruction
at the Naval War College in Newport, Rhode Island. He attended
there from June 30, 1932, until May 26, 1933, and while there,
he also received instruction at the Naval Torpedo Station. Whiting's
class included good minds like the twelve captains who eventually
retired as admirals, including James Richardson, William F. Halsey,
Wilson Brown, W. S. Pye, and Ernest J. King. Whiting enjoyed the
war games at the Naval War College working with toy ships on a
large table.[1]

Each year, during the interwar period, the Naval War College
class studied the US's Rainbow War Plans, with plans for war with
different countries identified by specific colors, and each class
expanded and modified the Rainbow Plans. War Plan Orange, with
Japan, addressed the advanced base problem, how to seize and use
islands to overcome the distances of the vast Pacific Ocean to reach
Japan in order to attack her. The Class of 1933 decided that the
fleet must work toward an economic blockade of the Japanese home

islands. The island path that was considered went from Truk in the Caroline Islands to Guam, Saipan, and Tinian in the Marianas. The final target would be Okinawa in the Ryukyu chain, which the class anticipated would complete the blockade of Japan's trade; then the Japanese home islands would be bombed from Okinawa and the Navy's carriers. Without much thought given to an invasion, it was assumed that this strategy would force Japan's surrender.[2]

During Whiting's War College year, the family lived at 81 Kay Street in Newport, in a house that had been owned by Rear Admiral Stephen B. Luce, the founding president of the War College. Luce lived in the house during Whiting's *Seal* tour but had passed away by the time Whiting returned to Newport. Moira attended private school nearby, and Eddie boarded at the Mary C. Wheeler School in Providence. Whiting took his dog Scamp, a terrier that he had acquired in Norfolk.[3]

On April 4, 1933, an event occurred off the coast of New Jersey that was to have a significant impact on the rest of Whiting's career. Rear Admiral William Moffett, head of BuAer for twelve years and a mentor of Whiting's, died in the crash of the Navy dirigible *Akron*. Deaths from *Akron*'s crash included seventy-three of the airship's seventy-six crew and passengers, the largest loss of life in any airship crash and twice that of the Hindenburg's thirty-five deaths four years later. Selected to replace Moffett at BuAer, Ernest King left the class early.[4]

Graduation from the Naval War College opened the door for Whiting to head larger units ashore and ship commands afloat, and on June 15, 1933, he took his first ship command, USS *Langley* (CV-1). Having crossed the Atlantic Ocean in *Neptune* as commanding officer of the First Aeronautic Detachment, having had much to do with retrofitting the other collier *Jupiter* to become the carrier *Langley*, and having served as *Langley*'s first executive officer, Whiting knew the ship well and was delighted with the new billet.[5]

The *Langley* was based in Coronado, and for the first time ever, the family traveled there as a group. When the car was totally packed in Larchmont and everyone squeezed in, Uncle Frank snorted, "Gypsies!" Baggage overflowed from the trunk into the back seat, where it was piled high to make a platform for the dog Scamp. Eddie and Moira were squashed into the other half of the back seat. On the floor was a gallon jug of ice for Scamp, a quart thermos of water for the family, and a jug of whiskey for Ken. Edna drove first for what became a harrowing trip. During one of his stints behind the wheel, Ken hit a cow in Arkansas. In Pecos, Texas, Edna and Ken stopped speaking, and Eddie and Ken met his old friend Jimmy Dean, who was traveling east, in Pecos's hotel grill. Jimmy's wife was absent and also not speaking to him.[6]

Whiting enjoyed *Langley* because once again, he was working with the operating Navy, but his command of *Langley* was short. The Navy was building more aircraft carriers and wanted to take advantage of Whiting's experience and knowledge about construct-ing them and preparing them for service. After only six months commanding *Langley*, he assumed command on January 1, 1934, in Newport News, Virginia, of the Navy's newly constructed fourth carrier, USS *Ranger* (CV-4), to fit her out for service in the fleet. To comply with the Washington Naval Treaty gross-tonnage limit for carriers of 135,000 tons because the tonnage of *Lexington* and *Saratoga* took up over half that displacement and because *Ranger* was the first American carrier built from the keel up, *Ranger* had been built as a smaller carrier of 14,500 tons. In three months, he had *Ranger* ready for the fleet, and the Navy again transferred him. On April 9, 1934, he was assigned to the Newport News Shipbuilding and Drydock Company as superintending instructor and naval inspector to assist in developing plans and specifications for two more new carriers, the USS *Yorktown* (CV-5) and USS *Enterprise* (CV-6). In planning *Yorktown* and *Enterprise*, the Navy and Whiting were guided by the experience of *Lexington* and *Saratoga* in Fleet Problem XIV. Greater emphasis was placed on the design for each ship than on maximizing the number of carriers the Navy was building. The airpower and ability of each carrier to operate independently was to be increased. Thus *Yorktown* and *Enterprise*, though 40 percent smaller than *Lexington* and *Saratoga*, could steam as fast and launch as many aircraft as *Lexington* and *Saratoga*. Much of their decrease in displacement was accounted for by a reduction in armor; changed

Navy doctrine now called for more escort ships to protect carriers, so they would not need as much armor.[7]

Some of those changes also came as a result of *Yorktown* and *Enterprise* being built under a different American president than *Lexington* and *Saratoga*. New president [and former assistant secretary of the Navy] Franklin Roosevelt wanted to spend more on shipbuilding to provide more jobs for unemployed workers than had his more conservative predecessor Herbert Hoover. In building his Navy, Roosevelt also wanted American tonnage levels to reach closer to the limits of the Washington Naval Treaty than had Hoover.[8]

By now, over the last fifteen years, Whiting played major roles in advocating and gaining approval for planning and constructing, fitting out, or serving as executive officer for all six carriers the United Stated Navy had built. But he had only commanded the first carrier, the *Langley*, designated from the beginning as experimental because of her slow speed and small size. Since his two-year command of Hampton Roads Naval Operating Base and before his year at the Naval War College, his command of *Langley*, his fitting out of *Ranger*, and his time leading the planning for *Yorktown* and *Enterprise*, the Bureau of Aeronautics had been working to overcome the letter of admonition that Admirals Burrage and Upham had recommended Navy Secretary Adams to sign and advocating for Whiting to command a real fleet carrier, USS *Saratoga*. Within a year after the NAS Norfolk air racing letter of admonition and while Whiting was still in command there, BuAer notified BuNav that it was renewing the recommendation that Whiting relieve Captain F. R. McCrary as commanding officer of *Saratoga*. To support the recommendation, BuAer prepared a seven-page document arguing that Whiting was qualified to command *Saratoga*, and the document included a paper detailing his Naval Aviation service to that time and his almost fourteen years of service afloat.[9]

Addressed to Admiral Upham, still chief of the Bureau of Navigation (Whiting's nemesis Admiral Burrage had retired), the Bureau of Aeronautics document argued that Whiting was considered better fitted than any other officer available, owing to his long experience in Aviation and to his particular experience in connection with the construction of the present carriers, duty in connection with them, their fitting out, etc... The fact that this officer has not had independent command at sea recently is due to the fact that his services in the Bureau of Aeronautics at the time of the acrimonious discussion going on in Congress and in connection with the Morrow Board, and further because his knowledge and experience was needed by this Bureau in connection with the design of the aircraft carriers *Lexington* and *Saratoga*.[10]

The document continued BuAer's uphill battle with BuNav over Whiting's future assignments against the backdrop of his recent letter of admonition.

Captain Whiting was Executive Officer of the *Langley* and of the *Saratoga*. His experience as Executive Officer of these ships would surely be enough to make him capable of commanding the ship as far as handling her goes, whereas for performing the far more important functions of an aircraft carrier, namely, handling the operations of aircraft, he would be more competent than any other officer could be who was sent to Pensacola to qualify as an Observer. This experience cannot be acquired during a short course of training at the Flight School, but requires close association with aircraft operations over a considerable period of time and under various conditions which arise in Fleet exercises... The substance of the report and recommendations of the Morrow Board stressed the point that the Commanding

Officers of aviation units should be experienced
in aircraft operations... There is attached hereto
a summary of the record of Captain Whiting,
which in my opinion shows that he is eminently
fitted to command an aircraft carrier.[11]

It took two and half years for the BuAer document to achieve
its intended purpose, but during that time, BuNav sent Whiting to
the Naval War College, briefly assigned him to command *Langley*,
had him fit out *Ranger*, and finally ordered him to plan *Yorktown* and
Enterprise. But the term of Upham's assignment as chief of BuNav
ended in August 1933, which removed the Upham-to-Burrage loyalty factor, and BuAer was finally able to achieve its goal, placing
Whiting in command of *Saratoga*. On June 12, 1934, in New York
City Whiting took command of USS *Saratoga* (CV-3), the most
important and up-to-date ship of his career. Having played a major
role in her planning and construction and having served as her first
executive officer several years previously, Whiting knew *Saratoga* well,
and he was proud and pleased but wary. After the change of command, Whiting commented, "Now I've got the bull by the tail."[12]

Two bull-by-the-tail incidents occurred while the *Saratoga*,
whose beam was just a few feet less than the width of the Panama
Canal locks, was going through the canal. It was always a harrowing
transit, but a westward trip through the canal in 1934 was particularly so. The Panama Canal pilot seemed to be losing control of
the ship, and finally, as she came out of one of the locks, he did lose
control. Fearing that one of her propellers was about to be damaged,
Whiting relieved the pilot and with the skill of a master straight-
ened her out and took her the rest of the way through. In another
similar incident, Whiting feared the pilot was about to run the ship
aground, and he again relieved that pilot.[13]

During Whiting's command tour in *Saratoga*, she participated
in Fleet Problem XVI. This involved five separate exercises, all totally
unrelated, spread over the Pacific from the Aleutians to Midway and
Hawaii. The major air operations occurred during the third phase of
the problem. The ship did well in fleet competition winning several

Navy *E*'s [the *E* stands for "excellence"], but the fleet competition was marred by a series of plane and personnel casualties. When his plane crashed into the sea and sank just after takeoff, Lieutenant (junior grade) Mathis Beally Wyatt died on May 11, 1935.[14]

Edna again packed the car and became a ship follower for a year. *Saratoga*'s home port was Long Beach, California, where the family lived during Whiting's command tour from June 1934 through July 1935, in the Villa Riviera, a sixteen-story apartment building with an ocean front.[15]

Located at 800 East Ocean Boulevard, Long Beach, the building opened in 1929 as the second-tallest in the region and won the grand prize at an international architectural contest for its Tudor Gothic design. It is known for its fierce-looking gargoyles, which occupy both sides of bay windows overlooking the city and the ocean in the top-floor, penthouse suites. The building was originally opened as a residential stock cooperative, but vacancies grew during the Depression, and it became known as the Home of Admirals, when senior naval officers with guaranteed salaries were able to rent many apartments there.[16]

From a window high on the top floor, where the building swayed, Ken could see *Saratoga* riding at anchor. Whiting often spent the wee hours of the night sitting on the Villa Riviera's ledge by the gargoyles outside his window. Perched high above the Pacific, he observed the stars and pondered questions—like, Where do we go from here? and How far can man go in the air—to outer space? From a man who led the US Navy's revolution from battleships to aircraft carriers, such thinking is not only imaginable but believable.[17]

Moira remembered one night, or early morning, her father took her to a window of the Villa Riviera apartment, showed her the constellations, and told her about the universe. He was in awe of it all.[18]

But Whiting did more than think and teach his daughters astronomy on the Villa Riviera's roof ledge. Whiting's second daughter, Moira, was considered to be as *gutsy* as her father; she inherited her love of risk from him. While living at the Villa Riviera, when she was ten years old, she went out on the ledge that surrounded the roof. She went all the way around and bragged to her father about her exploit. Later, the family observed that the seat of Ken's blue uniform trousers was covered with white plaster dust, and the family lore is that he had tried to duplicate his daughter's exploit by going all the way around but was too large for the ledge.[19]

More fun on Whiting's part occurred during fleet maneuvers, held in the Pacific waters surrounding the Hawaiian Islands. Captain A. B. "Cookie" Cook, a classmate who commanded *Lexington*, invited Aubrey "Jake" Fitch and Whiting to dinner at the Royal Hawaiian Hotel. Because he was very meticulous, Cookie prescribed tuxedos as the uniform; the three met and dined in style. Cookie was upset with Fitch and Whiting because they declined wine for dinner and settled for beer. As the evening progressed, Whiting joined some younger men and continued the party. Finally, he decided to go to bed in his room, fourth floor, room 407. He unlocked the door and started to walk in, then quickly backed out to the screams of a distraught young lady. He went right to the front desk and demanded to know why a woman was in his room. A careful check ensued, and Whiting was assured that he was not registered in the hotel. Whiting produced his key as proof, but the clerk refused to back down—right room, wrong hotel.[20]

During his year commanding *Saratoga*, Whiting became beloved by his crew and famous for his many escapades. Returning aboard late one night at Guantanamo, Whiting called the officer of the deck's attention to a list to starboard. While the OD was checking, Whiting disappeared off the starboard gangway into dark waters. The crew searched with great excitement but to no avail, in the midst of which, Whiting appeared on the port gangway. He had swum under the ship, which drew twenty-four feet, one and half inches of water at her keel, and now said he was satisfied that she was not in the mud.[21]

Although he had been promised a two-year tour commanding *Saratoga*, a bigger Navy plan to increase the number of experienced senior naval aviators intervened. Many senior officers were selected to attend a special course at NAS Pensacola to get those senior officers aviator wings; some aviators, like Towers, called those selected as "Johnny-Come-Latelys." One of those Johnny-Come-Latelys was William F. Halsey, later to become "Bull" Halsey, who earned an important award going through the senior aviator's course at Pensacola. The "Royal Order of the Jackass" was awarded to Halsey for trying to land with his wheels up! But Halsey earned his wings, and in the Navy's rush to complete the second half of the plan, to get the new aviators command time in carriers, Whiting's command tour on *Saratoga* was curtailed to a one-year tour, and he was ordered to turn command over to Halsey.[22]

Halsey just completed the senior aviators' course when he received his urgent orders to get to Santa Monica, California, to take command of *Saratoga*. The orders were so urgent that, at the change-of-command ceremony on July 5, 1935, Halsey's personal gear had not caught up to him, and he had to borrow a pair of Navy blues from Whiting. The uniform was so tight that the buttons were strained.[23]

In the middle of Whiting's *Saratoga* command tour, the fifty-three-year-old's vision had improved to 20/15 in both eyes. Although the improvement lasted for two years, it was not to be permanent. Instead, as Whiting went through his fifties, his health began decline.[24]

Leaving *Saratoga* was sad for Whiting. He had fathered her from drawing board to command, and he had grown with her. Had he known when he walked across her gangway for the last time that his carrier days were over, he would have been even sadder.[25]

CHAPTER 12

COMMAND ASHORE IN BEAUTIFUL HAWAII

Having completed a tour afloat in command of the *Saratoga*, Whiting received orders to a shore billet on May 27, 1935, and assumed command of Aircraft Squadrons and Fleet Air Base in Pearl Harbor, Hawaii. This would be the fourth naval air station Whiting had led since Pensacola Naval Air Station twenty years before.[1]

After Whiting turned over command of *Saratoga* to Halsey, the Whiting family returned to Long Beach, where Edna finished packing the silver trunk, brass ashtrays, and a few other meager belongings. They sailed for the Hawaiian Islands on the Matson Lines' SS *Lurline*. Whiting had never traveled by commercial steamer before, and Edna had to keep explaining to him that everything had to be paid for in advance.[2]

The base was on Ford Island in the middle of Pearl Harbor. There were three sets of quarters—one for the commanding officer, one for the executive officer, one for the station doctor, and a large, empty set of bachelor officers' quarters, which were said to be haunted.[3]

Soon Whiting found a wide range of needs at the station and worked to address them. They had bombs for their planes, but the bombs had no fuses; after many letters from Whiting, the fuses arrived. There were a number of chief petty officers and their families on Ford Island but no school. Soon a school was built, and Whiting had it painted red—the chiefs' children had a little red schoolhouse.[4]

When Whiting took command, working hours at NAS Pearl Harbor were 7:00 a.m. to 1:00 p.m., but that soon changed. Whiting also got more planes. More planes meant more personnel, and more personnel meant more quarters. The deserted old harbor came to life with the arrival of aviation cadets.[5]

Building on recommendations he had first made while working at the Department of the Navy between 1919 and 1920 that Johnston Island be surveyed and a photographic survey be made of the chain of islands from Oahu to Midway, Kure, and Wake Island, Whiting continued to address the advanced base problem during his Pearl Harbor command. He directed improvements at French Frigate Shoals, Johnston Island, and Pearl and Hermes Reef so they could be used as bases for seaplanes. He also completed photographic surveys of Kingman Reef, Palmyra, Howland, Baker Islands, Phoenix group, Britain's Jarvis Union group, American Samoa, Christmas, Washington, and Fanning Islands.[6]

Soon after their arrival in Hawaii, the Whitings were invited to a party with mostly civilians. A small wizened man of Chinese ancestry asked twenty-year-old Eddie if she would like to meet her cousins. Then he introduced two of his daughters, Mary and Elizabeth Au Fong. Their father laughed and asked, "Can't you see the family resemblance?" Eddie agreed. Albert Au Fong was right. Mary and Elizabeth were cousins, and except for their coloring, Eddie and Elizabeth looked a great deal alike. Albert's mother had been a Whiting, so she was the common ancestor.[7]

By fall 1936, the whole Whiting family was well entrenched. Eddie and Moira were taking hula lessons, and Eddie had her own star boat to race. But Edna began to pay a price for Hawaii's distance from Larchmont. She was called home for the first time when her uncle Frank died on March 14, 1936. Late in October came word that Edna's mother was dying, but there was a shipping strike, and no ships were sailing from Honolulu. Pan American started their clipper service, and Edna made a reservation, but when the day of the reservation came, headwinds were predicted and all baggage, company officials, and Edna were left behind. Edna finally sailed on the Coast Guard cutter *Itasca*, which was going east for overhaul. Edna's last order to then-twenty-one-year-old Eddie was, "We are having a party for Ernie King. You'll have to take care of it." But in her frazzled state of mind, she forgot to give Eddie the guest list.[8]

After the first year of Whiting's planned two-year tour as commander of NAS Pearl Harbor, he received a letter from Rear Admiral A. B. Cook, now BuAer chief, dated August 23, 1936. Cook said that the bureau was doing the routine work of preparing the slate of new assignments for the next year. Whiting was slotted in as commander, Carrier Division 2, providing the Bureau of Navigation would approve the creation of the billet and the detail of a captain for the assignment, which would normally require a rear admiral. Cook said there was no one senior to Whiting who was qualified for the post.[9]

Whiting's health began to decline in 1936, with an incident on June 18, 1936, on a Hawaiian dock in which he had become weak and had fallen down. He remained conscious, but the incident was troubling. Then Whiting's flight physical at age fifty-five on December 31, 1936, noted some other health concerns. The flight surgeon found a hernia on his right side and recommended its surgical repair. He confirmed the five missing teeth, on both sides, which Whiting had probably lost in his athletic youth, and reported the rest of his teeth were in poor condition. He noted fine tremors of his tongue and a trace of albumin in his urine. When kidneys become damaged, they begin to leak proteins into the urine, and albumin is an easier one to leak. Albumin in the urine may be a sign of significant kidney disease, or its presence may just be the harmless result of vigorous exercise. Still, none of these concerns took Whiting off flight status.[10]

But command of Carrier Division 2 was not to come to Whiting because, in the meantime, the Navy decided to reorganize its patrol aviation assets in the Pacific. Effective October 1, 1937, the Aircraft Base and Scouting Force, Pacific, was reestablished. With the change, five patrol wings were created as separate administrative commands over their assigned squadrons. Rear Admiral Ernest

J. King was placed in command of Aircraft Base and Scouting Force, Pacific, based in San Diego. As a result, after over two years in command at Pearl Harbor, Whiting was held in the Pearl Harbor billet and received an additional assignment in September 1937 to commission and command one of the five patrol wings, Patrol Wing 2, Aircraft Base and Scouting Force. The wing included five organic squadrons—VP-1, VP-4, VP-6, VP-8, and VP-10. Whiting commissioned the new wing at Fleet Air Base Pearl Harbor on October 1, 1937, and maintained this command until June 3, 1938.[11]

The squadrons flew the new consolidated PBY Catalina, whose missions were anti-submarine warfare, long-range maritime reconnaissance, and search and rescue. Introduced in 1937, the PBYs had the following characteristics: crew—10; length—64 feet; wingspan—104 feet; height—21 feet; power plant—2 Pratt and Whitney twin wasp radial engines, 1,200 horsepower each; maximum speed—196 mph; cruising speed—124 mph; range—2,520 miles; ceiling—18,200 feet; armament—3 thirty-caliber machine guns, 2 fifty-caliber machines guns, 2,000 pounds of bombs plus two torpedoes, or depth charges.[12]

King visited the Pearl Harbor Base on an inspection trip, and for an advanced base exercise, he and Whiting flew some of the seaplanes to French Frigate Shoals, an atoll about 500 miles west of Pearl Harbor; the exercise would take a while, so they set up tents and settled into an environment of sand, surf, and "gooney birds." The Navy was still working on the same War Plan Orange advanced base problem that King and Whiting worked on at the Naval War College—how to overcome the vastness of the Pacific Ocean and seize and hold advanced bases to enable them to reach the Japanese mainland. The planes at French Frigate Shoals were due back soon after Edna's departure, but when that return date arrived, Eddie received an official wire from her father. "The King is coming. Hurray! Hurray! Get up for breakfast."[13]

But Whiting and several others had been left behind at French Frigate Shoals to recover a top secret Norden bombsight from a PBY that had sunk. Eddie met future Navy Commander-in-Chief King in an official car, which had been bought by Whiting for ten dollars from the previous commanding officer. But he had soon discovered termites in the doors and removed them.[14]

In addition to King, his chief of staff Charles Alan "Baldy" Pownall and his wife, Mary, were staying at the Whiting quarters. Pownall and his wife helped Eddie with the King party, and Eddie was grateful for the assistance. As the party began and Edna was half-way to the West Coast on her way home, word arrived that Edna's mother had passed away. As the guests arrived, Whiting's executive officer Henry Mullinix brought word from French Frigate Shoals that both the PBY and the bombsight had been lost; King, who was known for being an angry man, was most displeased. A quote from one of his daughters had made the rounds in the Navy. "He is the most even-tempered man I know. He is always in a rage." It helped considerably that Eddie arranged gambling at the Army Air Corps Officers Club at Luke Field; King was among the guests who had won quite a bit from the Army officers at the roulette table.[15]

After Whiting returned from French Frigate Shoals and King returned to the West Coast, life settled down. The shipping strike was still on, and some things were hard to obtain. Thanksgiving was coming, and with Edna still on her Larchmont trip, Whiting ordered Eddie to prepare a Thanksgiving dinner for all the new aviation cadets. It was to be a typical New England Thanksgiving—turkey and all the trimming—but because of the strike, turkey was hard to find. After a long search, Eddie found a huge, mean-looking bird on the hoof at the native market. For the next couple of years, four of the cadets who helped eat that bird were invited back for Thanksgiving dinner at the Whitings.[16]

Moira remembered her father bringing her some very beautiful strings of seashells, light aqua in color, and very delicate, from French Frigate Shoals. He also brought back a turtle "big as our dining room table," and put her in a dog pen. She had a harpoon scar in her shell. When he judged the turtle had recuperated enough to return to its natural habitat, Whiting took her down to the main dock and let her go.[17]

Edna returned via Pan Am clipper shortly before Christmas, and she resumed her role in charge of the Whiting household. Eddie returned to being her assistant, and life in the islands became much more pleasant. Edna was an avid sightseer, and there were endless trips—a hike up to Sacred Falls, a jaunt to the big island of Hawaii, a visit to the crater of the volcano Kilauea, and a trip to the city of refuge on the Kona coast of Hawaii. When they were not traveling, Whiting had acquired two S-boats for the station and joined the yacht club. The family sailed every weekend.[18]

The S-boat was designed by Nathanael Greene Herreshoff in 1919; it is fast in light winds due to its large sail area and handles well in a strong breeze due to its full load keel and curved mast. At 27 1/2 feet long; a beam of 7 feet, 2 inches; a displacement of 6,750 pounds; and a draft of 4.75 feet, it is best sailed with a crew of four or five. Herreshoff built S-boats between 1919 and 1941, and the Navy built two in Hawaii.[19]

*****

While in command at Pearl Harbor, Whiting had the opportunity to work again with Amelia Earhart in January and February 1937. Due to Earhart's becoming the first woman to complete a solo flight of the Atlantic in 1932 and other high-profile aviation activities, her fame had grown considerably since their last contact in 1930. In correspondence from W. T. Miller, airways superintendent at the US Department of Commerce, dated January 29 and February 1, 1937, he was asked to provide support to Earhart on her planned east-to-west, around-the-world flight. The Miller letters were part of a larger chain of confidential correspondence, dated January 15 and January 28, 1937, originating with Earhart's husband George Palmer Putnam, a wealthy and well-known backer of Earhart's aviation activities, which contained a statement of Putnam's gratitude "for the commander-in-chief's intimation that he will be pleased to render such assistance as may be practical."[20]

Putnam was corresponding with Miller and Captain A. C. Pickens, chief of staff, US Fleet, in San Pedro, California. His support requests to Pickens included a voyage by the Pearl Harbor-based US Coast Guard Cutter Duane to Howland Island, with personnel and equipment to construct an emergency landing field there, gasoline, two mechanics, a meteorologist, radio navigational assistance to Earhart from Howland, and ultimately transporting these personnel and equipment back to Honolulu. Putnam also requested that another naval vessel be stationed during the flight between Honolulu and Howland, or "even better, southwesterly of Howland on the general course to Lae and British Guinea."[21]

Miller's letters to Whiting repeated Putnam's request for the services of two mechanics from Pearl Harbor, adding that they should be familiar with the Pratt and Whitney R-985 Wasp H engines installed in Earhart's Lockheed Model 10 Electra aircraft and carry a complete set of tools for the Wasp engine. Miller also informed Whiting that the Duane would be carrying a run-in-cylinder assembly and a full set of spark plugs for Earhart's plane. In case Whiting had any doubt about providing the requested support, Miller mentioned that "Commander Marc Mitscher advised me yesterday that the chief of Naval Operations has approved the temporary loan of two mechanics from your station." The two mechanics, Miller continued, will be members of the Department of the Interior's Expeditionary Force embarked on the Cutter Duane and "will be paid for by the Department of the Interior."[22]

Earhart began her west to east, around-the-world flight from the West Coast and landed at Luke Army airfield at Schofield Barracks. Early on March 20, 1937, Whiting was at Luke Field to see her take off for Howland Island, the next leg of her trip. The Navy advised her to take off to the north but to be prepared for crosswinds as she rose. The Army advised her to take off to the south. Her plane was fully loaded, and when it was fully loaded, her copilot Fred Noonan had always assumed the controls. But this time, Earhart decided she would take the Army's advice, take off to the south, and fly the plane herself. At midfield, the plane ground looped and upended on its nose. As she walked away from the broken plane, she said to Whiting, "Every time I see you, I get into trouble!"[23]

A copy of a March 18, 1937, picture from the *Larchmont Times*, Whiting's hometown newspaper, contains likenesses of Earhart, Hawaii Army Air Corps commander Brigadier General Barton Yount, Hawaii Luke Field commander Colonel R. C. Hammond, and Whiting, the cutline of which said that it may have been the last picture of Earhart taken before her March 20 crash.[24]

Less than a year later, Earhart was once again trying to fly around the world but, this time, in an easterly direction. She and her navigator, Fred Noonan, took off from Lae Airfield, New Guinea, at midnight GMT on July 2, 1937. Their destination was Howland Island, which Whiting had surveyed, with ten feet elevation, 6,500 feet by 1,600 feet and 2,556 miles east of Lae. With the Coast Guard cutter *Itasca* docked at Howland to provide radio and navigational support, they established radio contact but were never able to find the island. *Itasca* began a search; Whiting sent a patrol plane to search for them, and the Navy sent the *Lexington* to join in the search. She was never found, and the disappearance of Earhart and her copilot Noonan became one of the most famous mysteries in the Pacific Ocean.[25]

In addition to Whiting's work in support of the Earhart flights, his activities and those of his NAS Pearl Harbor command included interservice work with the Army in Hawaii. On May 11, 1937, he received a letter of commendation for Patrol Wing 2 from Admiral King, commander, Aircraft Base Force. King's letter quoted liberally from a letter he had received from the commanding general, Eighteenth Composite Wing, US Army Air Corps, who commended the commanding officer and all officers and enlisted personnel of the Pearl Harbor Fleet Air Base for their fine work in recent concurrent exercises. It congratulated Whiting on the loyal and efficient force under his command. King directed that the letter be filed in Whiting's personnel jacket and that it be included by Whiting in the fitness reports of all the officers involved.[26]

Whiting commanded Pearl Harbor Fleet Air Base for over two years, and on September 25, 1937, he received orders relieving him of that billet but leaving him in command of Patrol Wing 2.[27]

*****

The year 1938 was not to be a good year for Whiting's health. His problems could not have come at a worse time because it was to be the year chosen by President Roosevelt and Congress to begin pre-

paring for the anticipated war with Japan by launching a shipbuilding program and identifying the officers who would lead the Navy
if war came. The confluence of those factors would eventually affect
his Navy career. The year began with his annual flight physical on
January 4, in which the scar from the repaired hernia on his right side
was noted and some previously detected problems had worsened.
His weight had fallen to 142 pounds, and with a resting pulse of 80
and a resting blood pressure of 130/95, the flight surgeons reported
a finding of slight hypertension. In addition, the tremor previously
noted in his tongue had spread to his eyes and fingers. Nevertheless,
Whiting's vision was still 20/20 in both eyes (although he missed one
letter on the 20/20 line with his right eye and four with his left eye),
and the Navy did not find that his flying status was affected, yet.[28]

Whiting had now completed over two years in a shore billet as
commander, Aircraft Squadrons and Fleet Air Base, Pearl Harbor,
and nearly six months in command of Patrol Wing 2. It was time
for the Navy to consider his next assignment, which would normally
be duty afloat. On February 14, 1938, he wrote the chief of the
Bureau of Navigation, with a copy to his friend and chief of BuAer
Cook, and submitted three requests, in order of preference. First,
he requested duty afloat in command of Carrier Division 2, which
Cook had discussed previously with him. If this billet was not possible, he requested to remain in command of Patrol Wing 2. Finally,
if neither of his first two requests were available and he must go to
shore duty, he requested command of Naval Air Station San Diego.[29]

Cook responded on March 4 with the answer of both bureaus. In
response to his recommendation that Whiting be assigned to command
Carrier Division 2, he reported that the chief of Naval Operations and
the Chief of the Bureau of Navigation had disapproved it because the
billet was properly a flag officer billet, because Whiting had already
commanded a carrier, and because other aviator captains were due for
their first carrier commands; Cook thus recommended that Whiting
remain in command of Patrol Wing 2 until about January 1, 1939,
and the Bureau of Navigation soon concurred.[30]

*****

All the Pacific Fleet would rendezvous in Pearl Harbor for the annual fleet exercises, and Pearl Harbor would fill with battle-ships, cruisers, and destroyers. The battleships would tie up on the Ford Island piers. In April–May 1938, Fleet Problem XIX was no exception.[31]

As an operating unit of the Pacific Fleet, Patrol Wing 2 took part in Fleet Problem XIX. Simulated PBY strikes on the carrier USS *Ranger* achieved 80 percent damage. Then PBY Catalina patrol planes from Whiting's Patrol Wing 2, as well as other Catalinas commanded by Rear Admiral Charles Blakely, were tasked with providing reconnaissance of the seas around Pearl Harbor, looking for an enemy force twenty-four hours per day. But there were not enough planes, so Whiting concentrated Patrol Wing 2's assets to the north-west and northeast [the direction from which the eventual December 7, 1941, Japanese attack on Oahu would come]. Even though the normally great Hawaiian weather was notably bad, they had great success. After thirteen-hour searches, minimal rest, bad storms, zero visibility, and a predawn launch, one Catalina slammed into the Oahu surf, and another just disappeared. Others were damaged try-ing to take off, and others were forced down. Several planes were lost with all aboard. During a night flight, one taxied into the dock, and when the crash alarm sounded, Whiting jumped into his car and sped to the dock. Before anyone else moved, he dived through the water to the submerged airplane to save the crew but was only able to enter the aircraft through the cockpit hatches and save the two pilots. Pacific Fleet Chief Admiral Bloch cancelled operations so all ships could search for downed Catalinas; a total of eleven men died. Disappointment and anger went all the way to the White House.[32]

The loss of life caused a great hue and cry in the local press, and it triggered an open letter to Senator Gerald Nye in Washington. Because the letter's authors had not witnessed the incident firsthand, the letter included some inaccuracies, but it still caused an investi-gation. Whiting survived the investigation and was commended on his handling of Patrol Wing 2 and for his geographic concentration of Catalina assets in the face of insufficient aircraft. The after-action report adopted many of his suggestions for the defense of the island.[33]

CHAPTER 13

AS THE NAVY PREPARES FOR WAR, WHITING FIGHTS HIS OWN BATTLES

At the same time, as Fleet Problem XIX was developing, President Roosevelt, in an effort to prepare the United States for a war that was predicted by many, asked Congress for new legislation to expand the size of the US Navy, both in numbers of ships and in numbers of officers to man them. On May 7, 1938, Congress passed the Naval Expansion Act, which provided a 20 percent increase in active naval vessels, including authorizing 40,000 tons for new aircraft carriers. New carriers laid down in 1939 and 1941, respectively, were the Navy's seventh, USS *Hornet* CV-8, and eighth, USS *Essex* CV-9. These were the Navy's first aircraft carriers in whose construction Kenneth Whiting had not been involved.[1]

After dealing with the ship need, Congress considered and passed H. R. 9997, an act of June 23, 1938, to regulate the distribution, promotion, and retirement of officers of the line of the Navy. H. R. 9997 established a merit system for the promotion and retention of Navy officers. It established a system of selection boards that would review all officers by rank every year and determine who was best fitted for promotion, fitted, and not fitted. Those best fitted would be placed on the promotion list and promoted as Congress authorized and funded the promotions. Those fitted would be kept in grade and be eligible for consideration by the next years' board, and those not fitted would be removed from the service. Officers would be eligible to go before the promotion board two times, and those not accepted as best fitted at least once would be mandatorily retired on the next June 30. The selection boards were to be given all records of the officers except medical records. Nine rear admirals were to serve each year on the board for rear admiral, captain, and commander promotion, and no one could serve two years in a row (this would ensure that every officer would be reviewed by eighteen rear admirals during his two years of eligibility). A yes vote of at least six of the nine rear admirals would be required for selection as best fitted. Officers under consideration were specifically authorized by the legislation to forward a written communication to the board that stated their case for selection, and selection boards were required to state the reasons specific officers were not selected. The law also put an overall cap on the total number of naval officers of 5.5 percent of the number of enlisted men on active duty and raised the number of admirals the Navy could have from 58 to 70.[2]

Before this law, although promotions were partially limited during the Depression, no limit had been placed on the number of pass-overs for promotion an officer could accrue. For example, before 1935, George Van Deurs, who retired after World War II as a rear admiral, was passed over three times for promotion from lieutenant (junior grade) to full lieutenant. He was kept on active duty and finally promoted with the help of more senior officers like John Towers.[3]

The first selection boards created by H. R. 9997 convened in late fall 1938. The nine admirals appointed to serve on it included eight Gun Club mainliners, like Claude Bloch, Bill Tarrant, Walton Sexton, John Wainwright, Cyrus Cole, and Arthur Fairfield. Aviator Kenneth Whiting was one of the captains considered for promotion to rear admiral. Perhaps because of his personal modesty or because he thought the writing was on the wall from his 1930 letter of admonition in the NAS Norfolk air-racing incident, he made no effort to take advantage of the provision of H. R. 9997 allowing a candidate to submit supportive material. Unlike what some of his competitors did, he submitted no letters of recommendation or personal material in support of his candidacy. No letters from admirals still living with whom he had worked, like Ernest King, Harry Yarnell, and Hutchinson Cone, were found in the 1938 file. The results from the selection board for promotion of captains to rear admiral were as follows:

	Considered	Selected Percentage
All line officers	269	35 percent
Aviators	42	50 percent

Captains selected for promotion to rear admiral by the 1938 board were as follows:

- Arthur Bristol, commander of Patrol Wing 2, NAS Pearl Harbor (who had succeeded Whiting in this billet less than six months before)
- Leigh Noyes
- W. L. Calhoun
- J. M. Smeallie
- R. L. Ghormley
- Russell Wilson
- W. A. Glassford
- Frank Jack Fletcher
- N. F. Drasmel[4]

Kenneth Whiting's name was not on the list of selectees. For eight years, his selection board jacket had contained the poisonous 1930 letter of admonition from the Norfolk NAS air-racing incident, and it probably caused his nonselection when the 1938 selection board passed him over for rear admiral. In their votes, the eight Gun Club admirals may have been affected by loyalty to their fellow Gun Club admirals Burrage and Upham, now retired.[5]

In the absence of the legally required letter of explanation found in the files stating the reason for his nonselection, the Nisewaner and

Walden Journal of Family Memories attempted to provide an explanation of Whiting's being passed over.

> His career was really coming to an end. He had known since NOB Norfolk in 1930 that he would never make admiral and had kind of given up. But at least he could see carriers coming along, and the Navy beginning to see the light.[6]

Despite the NAS Norfolk letter of admonition, Moffett and the Bureau of Aeronautics fought for him. But Admiral Upham in BuNav had been able to fend off the Bureau of Aeronautics' desire to place him in command of *Saratoga* until Upham was relieved from his billet as BuNav bureau chief in 1933. Whiting had been sent to the Naval War College [designed to prepare officers for higher rank], commanded USS *Langley*, fitted out USS *Ranger*, helped develop plans for the *Yorktown* and *Enterprise*, commanded USS *Saratoga*, commanded NAS Pearl Harbor, and commanded Patrol Wing 2. It is hard to believe that the Bureau of Aeronautics would have entrusted Whiting with the growing responsibilities of those billets if it were not supportive of his continuing career advancement, but with Moffett's death in 1933, Whiting may have lost his strongest advocate. BuAer's support was strong enough during the 1930s to get Whiting placed in billets of growing responsibility but not strong enough without Moffett to overcome the probable damage to his career of the letter of admonition and get him promoted.[7]

Despite his daughters' opinions that he thought his career was over and that he had given up, Whiting held at his core the strong principle of "Don't quit." It is hard to imagine his giving up at any time.[8]

Another possibility is that his candidacy for promotion was affected by his physical condition. Although his flying status had not yet been affected, some negative findings had already begun to appear in his flight physicals. By the provisions of H. R. 9997, the selection board was not allowed to see his medical records, but it is conceivable that in the Navy's close senior officer community, a rumor of his growing health issues reached them. It is also conceivable that some of his peers had begun to note his tremors or heard about the incident on the Hawaii dock in 1936.

Coming hard on the heels of being passed over, the now fifty-seven-year-old Whiting took a flight physical on December 28, 1938, and in addition to eye, tongue, and finger tremors, the Navy's doctors found a major new weakness—his distance vision had declined. Both Whiting's eyes tested at 6/20, with his right eye correctable to 17/20 and the left to 20/20. These new negative findings caused the flight surgeons and the head of the Bureau of Medicine and Surgery, Dr. Ross McIntyre, to delay a decision on his flight status until March 6, 1939, when he ruled Whiting physically qualified for duty as a pilot provided he wore glasses and only flew with a copilot.[9]

On March 10, Whiting received an even stricter directive (with no explanation of its strictness) from BuNav [still functioning as the Navy's personnel office] Chief Chester Nimitz, which said, "You will not only fully indoctrinate…this copilot…but will turn over control of the airplane to him in all situations wherein your defects interfere with safe and effective control of the airplane."[10]

With its first group of aviators and those attending flight school late in their careers reaching an age where some deterioration in visual acuity is normal, impositions by the Navy of limitations on flying status were fairly common during the 1930s.

After ten years on flight status, Captain Richmond Kelly Turner's annual flight physical in December 1937 revealed the absence of adequate visual acuity. In February 1938, the Bureau of Navigation officially informed Turner that he was "qualified for duty involving flying only when accompanied by a copilot." The deficit was not an unusual one for a man turning fifty-three. What was unusual in Turner's case, though, was his decision to give up his flying status in response to the limitation.[11]

From the time Halsey went through flight school at Pensacola in his early fifties, the same condition—"qualified for duty involving flight only when accompanied by a copilot"—was affixed to his records.[12]

In a more extreme case, at the age of forty-eight Towers was diagnosed in 1933 with a cataract in his right eye by the Navy's doctors, but rather than approve an operation (because the cataract was not *mature* yet), the solution of then-senior doctors Rear Admiral and Surgeon General Percival Rossiter and Captain Ross McIntyre, the Navy's chief of ophthalmology and President Roosevelt's private physician, was to try to force Towers to retire. After the Navy tried to take him completely off flight status and recommended that a retirement board review his status, Towers went outside the Navy and had a civilian doctor perform the surgery. He achieved enough improvement in vision for the Navy to put him back on flight status with several conditions. He could only fly with a copilot, and he had to wear a special contact lens. But the Navy's senior doctors were not through with him. Rossiter became enraged that Towers had circumvented the Navy's system, and he found an ally in McIntyre. Together, the two doctors waged a campaign of retribution against Towers for several years with mandatory reexaminations and threats to his flight status and career, and Towers had to mount a long defense with many letters written on his behalf.[13]

It is not hard to imagine the toxic climate created in the Navy's medical community by the multiyear battle between Towers and the senior doctors about Towers's vision. Could that toxic climate have affected the doctor's view of Towers's fellow senior aviator Whiting's flight qualifications?

Another possible factor in Whiting's first pass-over was that perhaps his strongest supporter in the Navy had been Medal of Honor winner and Vice Admiral William Moffett. He was chief of BuAer from 1921 until 1933, had selected Whiting twice to serve in that bureau, and more importantly, had placed him in many positions to lead the Navy in the development of its first six carriers and in representing the Navy in the Morrow Board hearings and the Billy Mitchell court-martial. But Moffett died in the crash of the dirigible *Akron* in 1933 during Whiting's Naval War College year; we will probably never know the complete impact of the loss of Moffett's strong voice on Whiting's career.[14]

Whiting himself shed light on the impact of the first pass-over on his personal psyche in a letter, dated April 10, 1939, to his good friend BuAer Chief Cook.

> You can't realize it, because it has never hap-
> pened to you, but the pass-over, when it becomes
> a fact, is more than an ordinary jolt. It shakes
> your confidence in yourself for the time being.
> Makes you feel that everybody else must feel
> likewise.[15]

Whiting was informed that the Navy planned to relieve him of command of Patrol Wing 2 in January 1939, but he received his pass-over, and that date had come and gone. With the pass-over, the picture for Whiting's next assignment had changed, and Whiting continued with the primary purpose of his letter to Cook, to continue discussing his next billet.

> Thank you for your continued and consid-
> erate efforts to find me a job. One reason why
> it has been so difficult, probably, is because I
> couldn't make up my mind whether just to mark
> time in some place that might be preferable for
> personal reasons, or to try something where I
> really could be useful.[16]

Where he could really be useful, Whiting said, was a billet which would draw on his long experience in building and developing air stations and bases in places like Pensacola, France, Norfolk, Hawaii, and potential places in the Pacific islands. His experience looking at potential Pacific islands had begun in his first BuAer tour in 1919, when he surveyed all the small western Hawaiian islands as an important way to begin to address the advanced base problem. Twenty years before his pass-over, he had begun learning all he could about those outlying islands, about the physical aspects of the places in which the Navy would have to operate in case of war, and about operating them as advanced bases. He continued to study those islands during the four-year stint of his Hawaiian command, and he asserted his belief that he knew as much or more about those islands than anyone in the service. He said that his information and background could be useful to the Navy Department on preliminary planning for those Pacific islands and in coordinating and speeding up the work. His suggestion, he concluded, was that the Navy let him make some use of the information that he had spent nearly twenty-five years collecting and to give him special duty in operations or in the bureau in connection with the preliminary plans for the Pacific Air Bases and, in particular, coordinating the work with the other interested bureaus.[17]

*****

Almost four years in Hawaii was the longest Whiting had spent anywhere in the Navy, and it gave Moira a chance to go to one school, Punahou, for four years in a row. She boarded there during the week since it was too far from Pearl Harbor for a daily trip. She also was finally able to make some friends at the school. During the summers, she visited her roommate for two years, Pat Williams, on the Big Island and spent much of the time high in the mountains rounding up cattle for branding. Moira had also become an accomplished hula dancer, and before the family left Honolulu, she was invited to be a guest dancer before an audience at the Royal Hawaiian—complete with her proud father.[18]

Edna was pleased with Punahou and thought Moira was safe, but Moira was now sixteen and had grown into a charming young woman. Edna did not know she was slipping out and going motorcycle riding with one of the aviation cadets.[19]

Given his athleticism and manual dexterity, Whiting was also a natural with a carving knife. After sailing on Saturdays, the family would come home for supper, usually chicken with gravy and stuffing, mashed potatoes, and salad, left ready for the family by Haruko, the cook, and Mary, the Chinese maid. There would also be a couple of invited guests, aviation cadets whom Whiting was teaching to sail. From one little roast chicken, Whiting found enough meat to feed six or seven people. Despite his hand tremors, Eddie and Moira remembered very well his carving the bird with his little, very sharp fowl knife, standing at the head of the table cutting slices so neatly and severing wings and thighs so easily.[20]

In January 1939, Eddie's engagement was announced to Lieutenant (junior grade) Terrell Andrew Nisewaner, a Class of 1932 Annapolis graduate and a Navy destroyerman, whom she met in 1935. She wanted to go home to Larchmont to get married in Saint John's Episcopal Church, where her parents had been married.[21]

CHAPTER 14

A NEW WORLD WAR WITHOUT A FRONT-LINE ROLE FOR WHITING

Because of the pass-over, the bloom was essentially off Whiting's Navy career. So he applied for a transfer to get home to New York for Eddie's wedding and on June 1, 1939, received orders to the Third Naval District in New York City as general inspector of Naval Aircraft, Eastern Division. Eddie's fiancé was en route to the East Coast aboard USS *Sirius*, and Eddie was to leave Hawaii before the family to go to Larchmont to open the house. Eddie sailed May 18, the night of the first blackout of the islands; Hawaii was practicing for the real thing. The family left in June with much fanfare for the always popular Whiting, who had made many friends both in and out of the service.[1]

Eddie and Andy were married in Larchmont on July 12, 1939, at Saint John's Episcopal Church, as planned, and Eddie moved to Annapolis.[2]

Two days after his daughter's wedding, Whiting reported to the Third Naval District office in New York City. In this billet, he made speeches and traveled through the northeast to factories that supplied parts and engines on contract for the Navy's airplanes. The US government was ramping up its contracting for airplanes, in preparation for the war many believed was coming. Rather than doing this under the same bureaucratic system within the government that had been used in World War I and derided by the Morrow Board, but which some in Roosevelt's administration preferred, Roosevelt chose to build what would become World War II's "arsenal for democracy" on a private, cost-plus-contracting model. Led by corporate executives like automobile magnate William Knudsen and shipbuilder Henry J. Kaiser, the system worked extremely well and did turn the country into the arsenal for democracy for airplanes, tanks, ships, and other war implements.[3]

*****

Hitler invaded Poland on September 1, 1939, and World War II began in Europe. The Japanese had been conquering and occupying parts of China since 1931. Of the major powers, only the United States was still not declared belligerent, but it was engaging in anti-Nazi U-boat operations in the Atlantic without a formal declaration of war and negotiating with the Japanese to limit their acquisition of raw war materials in the Far East.[4]

Since his flight physical in December 1938, fifty-eight-year-old Whiting's health had deteriorated further, and the flight physical and annual physical examination he took on September 18, 1939, at the Brooklyn Naval Hospital confirmed the decline. His weight had fallen to 140 pounds, and his slight hypertension had continued with a resting pulse of 81 and a blood pressure of 140/88. His visual acuity in his right eye had declined further to 4/20, correctable to 20/20; his left eye was unchanged at 6/20 correctable to 20/20. Continuing findings included the fine tremors of his fingers, tongue, and eyes, albuminuria, and color blindness. His oral health had also declined, and the findings now included a heavy buildup of hardened plaque, which could lead to more tooth decay and gum disease, and periodontoclasia, the destruction of periodontal tissues and gums and the loosening of secondary teeth caused by the breakdown and absorption of the supporting bone. Bacteria had developed, caused cavities, and contributed to his gum disease. He had also developed severe prostatitis.[5]

Based on these findings, the doctors who performed his annual physical examination found him unfit to perform all the duties of his grade at sea, but the flight surgeons who oversaw his flight physical found him physically qualified to fly with a copilot. When the reports reached Dr. McIntyre at the Bureau of Medicine and Surgery on October 25, he disapproved the findings and ordered Whiting to be hospitalized for a study and report of a Board of Medical Survey as to his physical qualifications for all the duties of his rank. With the upcoming convening of the 1939 rear admiral selection board, the Bureau of Navigation added to the order with the requirement that the Board of Medical Survey report reach that office by November 15.[6]

Whiting was hospitalized at the Brooklyn Naval Hospital from November 3 to November 22 in compliance with Dr. McIntyre's order. In addition to carrying out the Board of Medical Survey, Whiting received treatment for some of his medical issues. His prostatitis was treated and cured. No tremors of consequence were noted in his neurological examination. His repeated passing one test of color blindness and failing another was confirmed. Three more teeth were extracted; his heavy plaque was cleaned; and some cavities were filled.[7]

At the completion of his hospitalization, the Board of Medical Survey found Whiting fit once again to perform all his duties at sea, and the Bureau of Medicine and Surgery and the Bureau of Navigation approved.[8]

The 1939 rear admiral selection board, which would give Whiting his second crack at selection for promotion, convened on November 22. Despite his reticence about self-promotion, this time he took advantage of the provision in the new promotion law allowing candidates to make a personal statement. He submitted a five-page statement, dated November 20, 1939, and apparently written in the hospital, to make sure the board was aware of his many accomplishments over his nearly forty years of service. The letter is also important because it is the only existing report written by Whiting detailing his personal perspective on what he considered to be the highlights of his Navy career.[9]

He began with a summary of his 6 years of submarine service, which had occurred 25 years before and was therefore likely to have been forgotten. In keeping with the modest aspect of his personality and his long held belief that his triumph was not significant; he did not mention that he was the first to successfully escape from a sunken submarine. He did, however, relate that he taught himself to dive to a depth of 80 feet with a breastplate and helmet in the recovery of torpedoes. He also taught the crews of *Shark* and *Porpoise* to do it, and when the dry-dock *Dewey* sank in 1910, he and his men used their diving skills to raise her. He mentioned his patent for putting exercise heads on torpedoes to make them recoverable and reusable.[10]

Instead of reviewing all the challenges presented by *Seal*, which he had conquered while in command; he only included two of them. Covering the first time a submarine was given a deep submergence test voluntarily with the crew on board and him in command, he reported *Seal* had achieved a depth of 256 feet. He also discussed the battery explosion on the *Seal*, the cause of which he had suggested was lack of good ventilation. He concluded by saying that he had also written a letter to Admiral Stirling, pointing out the danger of the new Edison battery. The battery later blew up and caused several deaths.[11]

He reminded the selection board that, as he left the submarine service in 1914, he had written in some detail urging a standard system of training in submarines. Admiral Stirling had given him credit for his suggestions in the foreword to his first regulations issued at the new submarine school in New London.[12]

Whiting began the documentation of the aviation portion of his career with flight training under Orville Wright. Upon returning to a naval billet, he arrived at Pensacola and found he was the senior officer present, with 5 or 6 line officers, a civil engineer, a warrant machinist, and a Marine captain in charge of all buildings. Under written orders from secretary of the Navy Daniels, he had taken over the Pensacola Navy Yard from the Marines and established the present Naval Air School. After he was relieved as SOP by Lieutenant Commander H. C. Mustin, he remained as second in command and started the first catapult school, firing the students from the catapult in the order of their entering aviation. He reported his suggestion to Lieutenant Commander Mustin to develop a retarding gear for airplanes, but not his construction of the gear on a coal barge with H. C. Richardson nor the initial efforts to perfect it which he led.[13]

In the entry about taking the first aviation unit to sea during the winter of 1916–1917 under Admiral Gleaves on the USS *Seattle*, he mentioned the catapult, which he convinced the conservative admiral and captain to allow him to install on the USS *Seattle* and conduct experiments to correct its problems. However, he did not review the trials he led to correct the problems and the successes that resulted.[14]

He summarized his experience in command of the First Aeronautical Detachment in World War I, which is important because it is the only written explanation from his own perspective to the concerns expressed later by some writers that he exceeded his authority in the package he negotiated with the French. Upon the entry of the United States into World War I, he said, he was given command of the First Aeronautical Detachment and took it to France, arriving just before General Pershing. Admiral Dubon, French Minister of Marine, immediately suggested that the Navy establish fourteen seaplane stations and three lighter-than-air stations on the French seacoast. After a hurried inspection of Dubon's proposed sites, he agreed to establish three stations, at Saint-Naziere, at Dunkerque, near the port of Bordeaux, and a school for bombing and machine-gun training at Moutchic. He referred the other stations to the Navy Department via a courier, Captain B. L. Smith, USMC. Whiting did not feel, he said, that he "could agree to such a large order as my rank at the time was lieutenant." When this request was received in the United States, the Navy Department realized how large an effort was desired by the French, and Commander H. I. Cone was sent over to take charge of the work; Commander Thomas T. Craven was sent to assist him, and Whiting became Cone's assistant in all heavier-than-air matters.[15]

Cone and Whiting visited the larger British seaplane stations, and after conferring with the British Admiralty, they inspected four sites for seaplane stations in Ireland and one in Scotland. Cone and

Whiting recommended all the Irish stations be built but not the Scottish one; the Irish stations were all eventually built and manned.[16]

Next, Whiting listed that he was ordered to return to the US on a secret mission to prepare for air raids on Wilhelmshaven, Cuxhaven, and Kiel using newly-designed lighters to transport the bombing planes across the English Channel but failed to mention that he wrote the proposal. Upon his return, he took command of the station at Killingholme and worked to prepare his command for the mission, which was never accomplished due to defective propellers and radiators.[17]

Having witnessed the British development of aircraft carriers and previously obtaining information from the French on their plans for carriers, Whiting arranged for Chevalier to visit the British carriers two months before the armistice to get all possible information on carrier operations.[18]

After the World War I Armistice and his return to his first assignment at the Department of the Navy in Washington under Captains Irwin, Craven, and Moffett, Whiting detailed a lengthy list of his many successful appearances for the three captains before the General Board as assistant director for Aviation, in which he recommended the following:

- conversion of the *Jupiter* to a carrier (took this through Conversion and Repair, Engineering, General Board, House and Senate Naval Affairs Committees);
- development of a retarding gear for carriers and put in direct charge of development, achieving success in time to install the equipment on *Langley*;
- two and a half years improving the retarding gear and many other devices required on a carrier;
- commissioned Langley as acting captain;
- suggested the turntable catapult and instrumental on installing catapults on light cruisers and battleships;
- at Admiral Moffett's request, led the conversion of the *Saratoga* and *Lexington* to carriers;

- fitted out *Saratoga*, then served as executive officer one and a half years and commanding officer one year;
- took *Saratoga* away from the pilot in the Panama Canal, the first time to prevent running aground and then to protect the port propeller from damage;
- at the request of Commander Aircraft Battle Force, ran *Saratoga* through the fleet (all ships dark) at 29–30 knots between Cape Canaveral and Jupiter Inlet;
- reported a series of strong operational statistics in long-range battle practice merit rate, the rates of landing squadrons, and oil consumption in comparison to *Lexington* during his command year on *Saratoga*;[19]
- In a major contribution, Whiting wrote, "I fought the battle of 'Billy Mitchell' and feel that Captain M. G. Cook, USN, and I did as much if not more than anyone else in preventing General Mitchell taking Naval Aviation out of the Navy";[20]
- Whiting then summarized his work from 1919 to 1939 to address War Plan Orange's advanced base problem by surveying many islands west of Oahu in the Hawaiian islands and making physical improvements to some for use as seaplane bases;[21]
- Whiting ended by modestly understating the role he played in the construction of the Navy's first six aircraft carriers and first seaplane tender: "I assisted in the design of the *Langley, Saratoga, Lexington, Ranger, Yorktown, Enterprise,* and *Wright,* and I think in all cases improved their design."[22]

He also had Rear Admiral Craven, with whom he had worked several times in his career, submit a letter to the board, dated November 17, 1939. In his letter, Craven said the following:

> Whiting's distinguished service during the World's War is a matter of record but his efforts after the conclusion of hostilities toward putting aviation afloat have received only slight recog-

nition. Realizing that aviation must have ships from which it might develop usefulness Whiting's efforts were of great assistance in procuring the *Wright* and the *Langley* (the latter over the strong objections of the Division of Operations). This officer was instrumental in the introduction of the catapult.

The efforts of this officer at a time when the Navy abandoned the aviation establishment built hastily for the purpose of war in Europe and constructed a permanent service on broad lines of service merit retention and reward. His long experience and familiarity with Naval Aviation mark him as worthy of retention.[23]

While Whiting's case was strengthened by Craven's letter, letters of support from other admirals like Ernest King, Harry Yarnell, and Hutchinson Cone would have added to that strength. Given his concerns about the 1930 letter of admonition, it is a bit surprising that he did not seek more letters from the many admirals with whom he had worked during his thirty-five-year career. Perhaps being in the hospital by medical order prevented him from the round of contacts that would have been necessary to ask for these personal favors.

With much of Europe under Nazi domination and the Japanese continuing to maraud in China, the selection board selected twelve captains for promotion to rear admiral:

- Aubrey "Jake" Fitch
- John Towers (passed over, like Whiting, in 1938, but got an automatic selection in 1939)
- F. L. Reichmuth
- Isaac C. Kidd
- R. M. Brainard
- S. A. Taffinder
- Alexander Sharp
- R. A. Heskold

- Raymond A. Spruance
- H. K. Hewitt
- F. X. Gygax
- C. A. Dunn[24]

Once again, with the 1930 letter of admonition still in his promotion jacket, Whiting was not selected for promotion to rear admiral. Although others were selected on their second review, under the new officer selection law H. R. 9997, either mounting a persuasive campaign for support or being the beneficiary of special action by others seem to have been necessary.

There was an exception—that is, political involvement. Whiting had advocated forcefully and effectively, within the confines of his Navy, for concepts and policies that he believed would be good for the Navy. But, unlike others, he had a strong, modest predisposition that seemed to prevent him from using his contacts and powers of persuasion to advocate for himself. An earlier example came at the end of World War I when friends of his requested his early return from Europe because of trauma in the Whiting family; his friends specifically stated that Whiting was not aware of the request.

Towers advocated strongly for himself in his battle with the Navy over his visual acuity, even going outside the Navy to have cataract surgery. After being passed over for promotion to rear admiral by the 1938 selection board, Towers was invited to the White House to see President Roosevelt. Like Whiting and others, Towers worked with Roosevelt when Roosevelt served as assistant secretary of the Navy in the 1920s. Roosevelt began the meeting by noting the pass over, and Towers confirmed it. Roosevelt said that he had a plan to overturn the selection board's action. He was going to appoint Towers to the then-vacant position of chief of the Bureau of Aeronautics, which carried an automatic promotion to rear admiral. Thus Towers, who retired after World War II as a full admiral, was able to overcome his pass-over and was promoted twice more.[25]

Another who may have received political help in getting over the barrier to admiral rank was Wilson Brown. Brown, a non-aviator, served in the White House as naval aide to two presidents, including

Franklin Roosevelt. In the middle of his tour as Roosevelt's naval aide in 1936, Brown was promoted to rear admiral.

Another example of strongly advocating for himself came from John S. McCain, grandfather of Senator John McCain. McCain was passed over for promotion to rear admiral in December 1939 for the first time by the same selection board that passed Whiting over for the second time. In comparison to Whiting's five-page career summary and the letter from Admiral Craven, in his second opportunity to be selected, McCain successfully sought strong letters of support from senior Admirals King, William D. Leahy, and Thomas Washington. This strategy was effective and resulted in the December 1940 selection board giving him enough votes to elevate him to rear admiral rank.[26]

As the selection board was meeting, Whiting was given another flight physical on November 28. His weight and blood pressure had not changed, but his pulse had dropped three beats per minute. His teeth and gums were noted to be in good repair. This flight surgeon still noted a fine tremor of his fingers and eyelids, but said it had improved; instead of a deterioration of Whiting's nerves, he said he suspected it was caused by a chronic kidney infection. The visual acuity of his right eye was 5/20, correctable to 20/20, and of his left eye 6/20, correctable to 20/15. This physical found Whiting qualified to perform all the duties of his grade at sea and for flying an aircraft, with a copilot.[27]

On December 5, Dr. McIntyre at BuMed disapproved the recommendation and found Whiting not physically qualified to control an aircraft.[28]

For once advocating for himself, Whiting reached out for help to his longtime friend and protégé Mitscher at BuAer in a letter on December 14, and Mitscher responded in a letter on December 19 with a list of actions he had taken on Whiting's behalf. Mitscher was able to delay any action by BuNav on McIntyre's decision. He got BuAer's chief Towers to speak with Nimitz at BuNav, and together, the two bureau chiefs convinced McIntyre to change his decision and approve Whiting to fly with a copilot. But McIntyre wanted Whiting to fly to Washington immediately, so he could speak personally with him before changing his decision.[29]

Whiting traveled to Washington on January 3, 1940, and submitted to a special flight physical for reassignment to flight status by McIntyre's flight surgeons at the Navy Department Dispensary. His weight had fallen to 138 pounds, but his pulse and blood pressure had not changed. With a change in the scale, Whiting's visual acuity in both eyes was now 20/200 correctable to 20/20, and the tremors in his fingers were found to be due to normal tension in the fingers. The next day, McIntyre approved the findings that Whiting could fly on his present assignment with a copilot because his condition has not become worse since the November 28, 1939, examination. But he added another limitation with the phrase *on his present assignment*; McIntyre placed an even shorter leash on Whiting's flight status and the only airplanes he could personally test would be those with a copilot seat, so no fighters like the new Hellcats or Corsairs for Whiting. On January 8, BuNav Chief Nimitz approved.[30]

Having been passed over twice for promotion, following the provisions of H. R. 9997, the Bureau of Navigation began the process to transfer Whiting to the retired list on June 30, 1940. However, with the possibility of a war looming and the Navy evaluating officers approaching retirement for retention on active duty, the Bureau did document on May 20 that they considered Whiting physically qualified for recall to active duty after moving to the retired list. The Bureau of Aeronautics facilitated Whiting's postretirement recall when Towers signed a communication that "the services of this officer are urgently needed to continue as general inspector of naval aircraft, Eastern District, New York, New York." Whiting responded, "It is requested that I be recalled to active duty upon retirement on June 30, 1940. I understand the Bureau of Aeronautics desires my services." With a war looming and after the two pass-overs and the mandatory retirement, it is easy to suspect how satisfied Whiting felt when he typed the last sentence. It is also easy to suspect that, as he typed it, Whiting also thought of all the other times in his career when BuAer had desired his services to advance Naval Aviation or to defend it from political attacks. When he received Whiting's request, with war looming and most aircraft factories located in Third Naval District, Towers overlooked McIntyre's on-his-present-assignment limitation and appended a handwritten note to his last communication "orders to active duty *involving flying* after retirement in present billet own consent."[31]

As Hitler continued to conquer European countries and as Roosevelt continued to use the Navy to protect convoys of vital lend-lease war supplies to Britain from the Nazi U-boat threat and diplomacy and embargoes of vital war supplies to try to force Japan out of China, Kenneth Whiting continued to manage the testing of new airplanes. One can only imagine the frustration of this career Navy man who had once been a warrior, but from a seventy-five-year perspective, it is also logical to suspect that Whiting's lifelong reticence to advocate for himself caused him to suffer his declining health in silence. As Towers's aggressively bypassing the Navy's doctors and obtaining civilian medical help may have helped keep him on active duty during the 1930s, either accessing the Navy's medical community sooner, or bypassing it might have prevented some of the decline in Whiting's health.

One possible reason that Whiting did not access the Navy's medical community and self-identify for some of his physical problems was the possibility of his triggering the very negative response from the medical community that he was hoping to avoid. One way of avoiding such a negative response would have been to seek attention surreptitiously from a Navy doctor as the author's father did in his Norfolk boot camp when his arches fell. In boot camp in the first months of World War II, he went to the dispensary *in the dead of night* [he always said] and had them tape his feet, ankles, and calves without putting it on his medical records to prevent the Navy from possibly discharging him. Although his arches bothered him and he wore orthotic arch supports for the rest of his life, he served on active duty on two Pacific Fleet ships until the end of World War II, many more years of reserve service, and earned a pension upon his retirement.

Now retired but recalled to active duty, the frequency of Whiting's flight physicals declined. The records reflect that he took the last one on October 15, 1941. In a man who was always described as fit, his weight of 137 pounds represented a decline of almost 12 percent from his peak weight during his career. Neither his pulse or blood pressure had changed, but his visual acuity in both his eyes had improved, with his right eye at 20/40, correctable to 15/20, and his left eye 20/100, correctable to 20/20. The condition of his teeth had improved with the help of the Navy's dentists, but with eight of them missing, he no longer met the requirements for a commission in the Navy. Dentures were recommended, but Whiting did not have them made until February 20, 1943. It is easy to speculate about a connection between his continuing dental problems and the declines in weight he had experienced over the last few years.[32]

For a naval aviator in the declining years of his career who had had to deal with the negative findings of the flight surgeons to remain on flying status, the documents from his flight physicals in the last five years of his career and life show a total of 608 hours flying naval aircraft, an average of just over 120 hours per year. For comparison, in the 23 years from 1914, when he had earned his wings, through 1937, Whiting averaged just over 100 hours flying per year. For all his flying years, 1914 to the end of his career, his flying hours totaled 3,000. In his last squadron-level flying billet on USS *Seattle* in 1917, Whiting flew nearly every day and polished his flying skills by making 126 takeoffs and landings in five months.[33]

But Whiting's two decades of peacetime flying ended when the Japanese bombed Pearl Harbor on December 7, 1941, from six aircraft carriers, the type of ship that Whiting had spent the last 25 years building and developing for his country. Even as Whiting sat on the sidelines as he had done in the last three quarters of the Navy-Army football game in 1904, he must have dreamed of what he could do—would do—if only he were given the chance. Franklin Roosevelt had pushed the envelope of peace for nearly a year in the Atlantic and the Far East, but after Pearl Harbor, Roosevelt told Congress that a state of war existed and asked Congress for a declaration. The United States declared war on Japan on December 8, 1941.[34]

*****

And with America's Pacific Fleet in ruins, resting in the mud of Pearl Harbor's floor, newly-appointed Navy commander in chief, United States Fleet (COMINCH, soon to become COMINCH-CNO) Ernest King and Pacific Fleet Commander Chester Nimitz had to be both aggressive and careful how they used the few aircraft carriers they had left in an ocean that was fast becoming a Japanese lake. Four carriers in the Pacific (of a US Navy total of seven) had escaped Pearl Harbor. Five Essex-class carriers, upgrades from previous classes, were under construction, but it would be a long time before these were ready to fight. "Meanwhile, younger, more aggressive and savvier aviation flag officers were needed to make the best use of the precious carrier inventory that existed. Unfortunately, there were not enough prepared to take charge."[35]

King was putting pressure on all the Pacific carrier admirals to employ their assets more aggressively. With the Navy on the strategic defensive, he ordered that Nimitz's Pacific Fleet take the tactical offensive in the Central Pacific in hit-and-run raids against Wake and Marcus Islands, the Marshalls, the Gilberts, and the Bismarck Archipelago. He also strongly supported Roosevelt's desire to raid Tokyo, which became the Doolittle Raid. He based these strikes on the Mahanian doctrine of going on the offense to dictate to the enemy and for morale and public relations reasons. To go on the offense, you need more aggressive leaders who, like the Army's George Patton, may have been closeted in peacetime. Instead, the Navy's promotion system had given King and Nimitz aging non-aviators like Wilson Brown and Frank Jack Fletcher, who commanded Carrier Task Force number 11 and 17, respectively, and for whom King had little enthusiasm. A presidential executive order that was issued further in the war requiring commanders of carrier task forces to be aviators was not yet in effect.[36]

For example, when Task Force 11s (which was organized around *Lexington*), commander Wilson Brown communicated his desperate need for reprovisioning, King responded, "Carry on as long as you have enough hardtack, beans, and corn willie. What the hell are you worried about?" And when King suspected Fletcher was avoiding a strike on Japanese transports, he goaded him, "Your [message] is not entirely understood if it means you are retiring from enemy vicinity in order to refuel." Only inspiring and relentless fighter Halsey fit the ideal profile, but overreliance on the only carrier admiral who met the ideal profile came with a terrible cost. After the stress of continuously leading carrier strikes across the Pacific for six months, Halsey returned to Pearl Harbor just before the critical upcoming Battle of Midway with shingles, a serious skin condition that cause unbearable itching and made it nearly impossible to sleep. Navy doctors ordered him first to the hospital in Hawaii, then home to the West Coast, and finally to take six weeks of medical leave in the States. Nimitz had to replace Halsey with non-aviator Raymond Spruance; the only other carrier admiral at Midway, Frank Jack Fletcher was also a non-aviator. King and Nimitz needed more aggressive Halseys [during the first six months of the war]—more rear admirals qualified as aviators and by surface experience—but they didn't have them.[37]

Meanwhile, Nimitz was providing guidance at the other end of the continuum of aggression and cautiousness. While King pushed for more aggressive use of carriers during the first six months in the Pacific, Nimitz was sending messages interlaced with more caution. In a letter of instruction to Fletcher and Spruance in his Operations Plan 29-42 for the upcoming Battle of Midway, he directed them to be guided by the principle of calculated risk, which they were to interpret to mean "the avoidance of exposure of your force to attack by superior enemy forces without prospect of inflicting, as a result of such exposure, greater damage to the enemy."

After sinking four Japanese carriers (losing only one American carrier, the *Yorktown*) and achieving what became known as the Miracle of Midway, non-aviator Spruance followed that guidance and came under criticism from many of his young pilots for withdrawing his carrier force instead of aggressively pursuing his wounded enemy. But Nimitz supported Spruance's judgment; he had eliminated the core of the Japanese Naval Aviation strength in the Pacific and applied well the principle of calculated risk.[38]

Even with Roosevelt's future presidential order requiring carrier groups to be commanded by aviators, with non-aviator admirals like Fletcher and Brown, the United States Navy could have used an aggressive aviator admiral Kenneth Whiting in the Pacific in the first six months of World War II. After that, with a greater number of qualified aviator admirals identified and promoted, the urgent need for Whiting in command of a carrier group would have diminished.

An example of an alternative for more substantive use of Whiting was provided by another more senior officer. Rear Admiral Joseph "Bull" Reeves, who retired in 1936, was recalled to active duty on May 13, 1940, advanced to vice admiral on the retired list, and served in the office of the secretary of the Navy from May 21, 1940 until 1946, when he retired a second time after a total of fifty-four years of service.[39]

*****

The Whitings moved into the Andresen's old house at 98 Park Avenue in Larchmont, which Edna had inherited. Edna and Moira settled in at Larchmont, with Edna glad to be home at last. Ken and Edna returned to sailing.[40]

By now, Whiting was a sad, lonesome man. He hated to ride the commuter trains every day into his office at Third Naval District in New York City. In the middle of America's biggest war, even though he was on the retired list [as others were], it is hard to believe that he could not have asked Navy COMINCH-CNO King, for whom he had worked in his last billet in Hawaii, for an assignment closer to his skill set, like designing and building the many carriers that were coming down the weighs. Did his personal modesty intervene again?[41]

He longed to go to sea again but instead was inspecting aircraft and making speeches. As one of Orville Wright's few living students, he sat beside his old instructor pilot and was one of the speakers at the August 19, 1940, dedication of the Wright Brothers Monument in Dayton, Ohio.[42]

If Whiting could not go to the Pacific himself to lead carrier groups, he had the sure knowledge that, like Moses and the Promised Land, he had left in his wake some of the admirals who were doing that. These leaders

> had spent time with him in the early years
> and had lived through all-night bull sessions

about carriers and planes and how best to use them. One of these was Marc "Pete" Mitscher who served under Whiting several times, and had been in on those bull sessions. Pete became the man who learned how to use carriers task forces as deadly weapons, and thereby did as much as anyone to win World War II. Others were W. F. "Horse" Pennoyer and A. M. Pride.[43]

Moira was a high school student at Rye Country Day School then, and she remembered long talks, frequently at happy hour, with her father.

Nothing about God from him, except for his deep awe of a respect for life in all its forms. He was always curious, about the ants in Grandma's backyard, about the gooney birds at French Frigate Shoals, about that sea turtle, our chickens on Pensacola Bay, the sky and its constellations, the mysteries of physics, just the wonder of it all... I remember having long talks with him...about world history, war, our country, the Constitution... Ant [Eddie] was married and no longer in the household, so I sort of had my turn at him.[44]

He...helped make me a patriot, with a deep and passionate love of my country, and an awed understanding of its place in human history... He left me with a good sense of the need for a strong military, especially after the troubles his Navy had after World War I, getting the money from Congress to prepare for the Japanese. There was no doubt that we'd have to fight them some time, in the Pacific, and we sure would need carriers to do it. He was a Yankee, after all, a Son of the Cincinnati, with the idea of liberty well built in, and a clear knowledge that freedom isn't free, it has to be earned by each succeeding genera-tion, and the Constitution is the only glue that holds the Republic together…the importance of a limited, federal government, and a limit to handouts by it.[45]

He [also] taught me, as he said, not to be "a tease," being promiscuous with guys but not letting them do anything. To be fair, I guess, in behavior with men, and indeed, to be fair in everything I did. Objective, seeing both sides? [punctuation is correct][46]

Moira also remembered some of the things her father said, some serious and some funny. He was a reader and a thinker, she remem-bered, and one of his favorite authors, for light reading, was a raunchy and funny author named Thorne Smith. When she was acting up as a young kid, he would make her feel small and ashamed by compar-ing her to her best self: "Be yourself, daughter!" When she danced the hula at the Royal Hawaiian, in a white cellophane skirt, bra, and a crimson carnation lei, he may have been thinking about sailing when he urged, "Set up your backstays!" When he wanted something done and neither Eddie nor Moira was doing it, he'd say, "I'll get Jimmy to do it," which is why Eddie named her second James. Going back to his submarine days, he used to say "Back to battery" when he or anyone was getting better after being ill or tired or not doing some-thing right. Disparaging Army pilots, he used to say this to his Navy fliers, "If you get lost, follow a railroad track, but be sure to stay to one side or the other because the Army will be coming right down the middle!"[47]

Whiting had Moira memorize some songs and poems that he found particularly meaningful or fun. One was "The Wreck of the Julia Plante: A Legend of Lac St. Pierre," the French Canadian poem by William Henry Drummond, that includes "For de win' she blow lak hurricane, Bimeby she blow some more" and "You can't get drown on Lac St. Pierre so long as you stay on shore." Others included several stanzas of the "Rubaiyat" of Omar Khayyam and a little poem called "The Idealist," about a louse that longed to dwell in the head of a queen.[48]

For their humor value, Whiting had her learn the words to "Abdul Abulbul Amir," including the following:

> The sons of the Prophet are brave men and bold and quite unaccustomed to fear,
> But the bravest by far in the ranks of the Shah was Abdul Abulbul Amir.
> Then this bold Mameluke drew his trusty skibouk with a cry of Allah-Akbar! And with murderous intent, he ferociously went for Ivan Skavinsky Skavar.

> Finally, of course, Moira had to learn several verses of the "Armored Cruiser Song:"

> Away, away with sword and drum.[49]

Eddie's husband, Andy, was off to war, and she came home to Larchmont with the apple of his grandfather's eye, her baby son, named Ken Whiting Nisewaner but called Danny. Ken spent many long hours gazing at maps, following the war. He was sure it was not being run right and longed to command a carrier or an island base. He was proud of Pete Mitscher but doubtful of Bill, now called Bull Halsey. Ken thought he talked too much.[50]

CHAPTER 15

A NOTABLE LIFE AND CAREER OF ACHIEVEMENT SUDDENLY INTERRUPTED

J ust before Eddie's second son, Jimmy, was born, Whiting received orders on February 19, 1943, to take command of NAS New York, New York, located at Floyd Bennett Field on Jamaica Bay near the southwest tip of Long Island. Defending the sea lanes around the important port of New York against attacks from German U-boats mirrored his World War I service in France and England and was a step in the right direction for him. Ken took command, and the Whitings began the process of moving from their house in Larchmont into quarters at Floyd Bennett.[1]

The weekend after April 15, 1943, Moira's twentieth birthday, she drove from Sarah Lawrence College in Bronxville, where she was enrolled in her sophomore year, to Floyd Bennett to spend two days with her father. He took her to the officer's club, where she got *goggle-eyed* on martinis, and on Sunday afternoon, after more cocktails, Moira and Ken went to Coney Island. On Monday morning, Moira said goodbye to her father and drove to Sarah Lawrence and then to Larchmont. On Tuesday, April 20, Whiting flew from Floyd Bennett to Washington, DC, to visit the Navy Department, to urge carrier assignments for some of his young pilots who were ready for a step up after doing ferry and test flying, and to see old friends and Naval Academy classmates like the current chief of the Bureau of Aeronautics, Rear Admiral John S. "Slew" McCain Sr. Whiting planned to return on Friday to be home for his and Edna's thirty-first anniversary, Saturday, April 24.[2]

While in Washington, he stayed at the home of his nephew Whiting Willauer, who worked for the State Department and was a former ambassador to Guatemala. He was the eldest child of Whiting's younger sister, Virginia, who had died after a cancer operation in France on March 3, 1939.[3]

Whiting had begun to feel ill a couple of days previously but carried on a full program of work until April 23. Willauer had not seen his uncle in eight months, and they met early in the evening of April 22. Willauer was startled by his uncle's poor appearance, in particular, his marked facial pallor. Although Willauer thought that "he looked like hell," the two went for cocktails and returned to Willauer's home for dinner. They went to bed about midnight.[4]

On Friday morning, April 23, Whiting failed to rise for work. He fell twice trying to get to the bathroom and sustained minor bruises over his arms and legs. Willauer's wife noticed that Whiting had the same gray facial pallor and was irrational at times and feverish. She called Edna that morning and told her about Whiting's illness. It was agreed to call a civilian doctor, who came about noon. He made an initial diagnosis of *either grippe or pneumonia* and prescribed codeine and aspirin capsules.[5]

Whiting grew steadily worse as the day went on, with his face becoming grayer, his breathing increasing, and his temperature rising. At eight thirty that evening, he was taken by ambulance to the Naval Hospital at Bethesda. On admission, his temperature was 105 degrees and his breathing was abnormally rapid.[6]

Edna tried all day to make arrangements to fly from Floyd Bennett to Washington to be with her husband. After dark, Edna and Moira drove to the field through a cold, foggy, rainy night. Edna continued calling people at the station, trying to arrange in a wartime environment for that Washington flight.[7]

As the evening wore on, the Bethesda doctors noted that Whiting was mildly confused, irrelevant at times, restless, and drowsy. They prescribed an oxygen tent, a chest X-ray, urinalysis, sputum typing, and a continuous watch.[8]

By 10:45 p.m., a purple or red rash had appeared on the backs of Whiting's hands, forearms, the upper part of his abdomen, and chest. His breathing was still rapid, and he seemed confused mentally. The doctors identified three possible diagnoses: meningococcal septicemia, Rocky Mountain spotted fever, and typhus. His blood culture showed a marked reduction in white cell count and bodies occurring in pairs within the remaining white cells that resembled bacteria.[9]

By 11:10 p.m., Whiting was sinking progressively into deep shock. The skin over his whole body was cold and gray, except for the purple and red rash. The veins in his extremities were collapsing, and he complained of not getting enough air under the oxygen tent. His blood pressure was very low, and it was difficult to obtain a drop of blood from his finger.[10]

The group of doctors treating Whiting now agreed that the diagnosis was meningococcemia with Waterhouse-Friderichsen syndrome or bleeding into the adrenal glands commonly caused by severe bacterial meningitis infection leading to massive blood invasion, organ failure, and shock, with widespread purple and red rash. They prescribed two units of plasma, another blood culture, and Sulfadiazine intravenously.[11]

After these treatments were administered, Whiting died at 1:50 a.m. on April 24, 1943, Edna and Kenneth's thirty-first anniversary. Although treatable with more advanced drugs now with a survival rate of 40–45 percent, the sulfa drugs of the time were not sufficient to treat meningitis.[12]

About 2:00 a.m. the Willauers called the Whiting quarters and said Ken had passed away at Bethesda. Nineteen hours had passed from the onset of symptoms until Whiting's death. Edna and Moira fell apart completely, but they called Ken's brother Butts to get him to come help. He arrived at noon, about the same time that a florist delivered a dozen red roses from Ken for their anniversary.[13]

Only the Nisewaner and Walden Journal of Family Memories can tell the sad story of the effect on the three Whiting women of sudden, unexpected death of the man they knew as the Skipper, who his younger daughter, Moira, described as "a god, mysterious, distant, unknowable. In one household, there were the three gals—my Ma, Ant, and me. And DADDY."[14]

That evening, Beetle McGurk, one of the young pilots Moira had been dating, who was on Ken's list to try to arrange for sea duty and who was later killed attempting a landing on the *Enterprise*, came over to visit her. Moira and Beetle went for a walk, taking Whiting's twelve-year-old dog Scamp, who was deaf and couldn't see well. Scamp had been given to Whiting when he commanded NAS Norfolk in 1930. It was still gray and very foggy, and Moira and Beetle walked along a seawall that bordered Jamaica Bay. They stopped to talk with a sentry who was on duty there, and when they turned around, there was no Scamp. They never found him and suspected he walked off the seawall into the Bay and drowned.[15]

By then, Edna and Butts were making funeral plans, but first, Edna wanted someone at Bethesda to tell her why her chum died. Bethesda's first guess was Rocky Mountain spotted fever, but Edna wanted an autopsy to be sure. The autopsy was performed, and the final cause of death reported by Bethesda was that Whiting had had pneumonia when he arrived at Bethesda, but that he then had a heart attack. Although the medical personnel who treated Whiting at Bethesda said meningitis and all their medical records reflected that, when the Navy's public affairs personnel became involved, the answers changed. All the official Navy public statements, as well as the cause of death reported in the press, repeated the false cause of death.[16]

A lengthy April 29, 1943, article in the *Larchmont Times* headlined "CAPT. WHITING DIES SUDDENLY IN BETHESDA, MD," with the subheadline "Lifelong Larchmont Resident Had Distinguished Naval Career," reported the cause of death in the lead paragraph as pneumonia.[17]

Whiting's body was to be put in a casket, to be selected by his nephew, and then to be flown to Larchmont for the funeral. Edna and Butts planned the funeral, which would, of course, include the Navy Hymn and be held at Saint John's Episcopal Church. The Rev.

Francis J. H. Coffin would officiate, and he would be assisted by Lieutenant Edward Reighard, chaplain at NAS New York.[18]

The funeral was fairly simple; it was the burial that was complicated. Whiting had always said he wanted to be cremated and his ashes spread at a location that had given him so much pleasure for 45 years of sailing in Long Island Sound. The deepest part of the sound, at 114 feet, had been the starting line for all the races in which he had sailed the *Moira*. It was the C-1 buoy at Execution Light. Ever the leader of fun and humor, Whiting said he wanted to be there so he could call out the guys who were over the starting line at the gun.[19]

Edna was committed to do this last thing for her chum, which meant cremation, arranging for a boat, setting up the date, getting the state's permission, and lots more details. For days, she carried in her purse a little piece of paper, with the latitude and longitude of the C-1 buoy, 40.88N, 73.73W.[20]

Whiting's casket arrived on Monday, April 26, and stood in the parlor across from the living room, unopened, until the funeral on Tuesday. Two hours before they had to leave for Saint John's for the funeral, Eddie and Moira were sitting on the front steps in black coats and dresses. As they sat there, a beautiful cock pheasant, which they had never seen in the neighborhood before, walked up the front path toward them. Then it turned off to the left and went toward the nearby house where Ken's mother Daisy was living. The sisters agreed that it must have had something to do with their father.[21]

For Whiting's funeral on April 27, 1943, the Navy assembled a distinguished group of honorary pallbearers. They were led by the undersecretary of the Navy, the Honorable James V. Forrestal. Forrestal was a World War I naval aviator, who was later appointed to the post of secretary of the Navy and then served as the nation's first secretary of Defense. After his death, the Navy named the aircraft carrier USS *Forrestal* after him.[22]

Forrestal was joined by the assistant secretary of the Navy for Air, the Honorable Artemus L. Gates. Receiving pilot training as a member of the prestigious First Yale Unit, Gates went on to serve as a naval aviator in the First World War. After his discharge, he climbed the ranks of the private sector. He returned to public service when he served as the Navy's first assistant secretary for Air. During World War II, he served briefly as undersecretary of the Navy before completing his career as a private sector executive.[23]

The senior naval officer in the pallbearer delegation was Vice Admiral T. T. Craven, who as director of Naval Aviation in 1919 ordered the conversion of the *Jupiter* to become the *Langley* and assigned Whiting to shepherd his decision through the approval process. He retired from active duty in 1937 but was recalled to active duty at the start of World War II and assigned to be superintendent of the New York Maritime Academy at Fort Schuyler, New York, from which he retired again in 1946.[24]

Three more admirals served as honorary pallbearers. Rear Admiral J. H. Newton served as a capable administrator of several Pacific Ocean areas and retired as a vice admiral. Rear Admiral John S. McCain Sr. was director of the Bureau of Aeronautics at the time of the funeral but was to return to the Pacific to command carrier task forces and groups and be promoted posthumously to full admiral. Rear Admiral George Murray—naval aviator number 22, who was trained to fly in 1914–1915 at Pensacola when Whiting was senior officer present—had already commanded the USS *Enterprise* during the Doolittle Raid and the Battle of Midway; he retired as a full admiral. Another Whiting classmate was Captain R. C. MacFall, who was credited by Fleet Admiral Chester Nimitz with the creation of the circular tactical formation for carrier groups that was so successful in World War II.[25]

Captain E. O. McDonnell, who retired as a vice admiral, had already won the Medal of Honor at Vera Cruz in 1914, begun pilot training with Orville Wright just before Whiting, and trained the First Yale Unit as pilots. Captain William Baggaley was another 1905 Naval Academy classmate, and Captain Homer Wick had commanded a USS *Saratoga* aircraft squadron in 1929.[26]

Rounding out the pallbearer group were Lieutenant Commander Harry Guggenheim, a former US ambassador to Cuba, whose family foundation had funded many aeronautical advances, including financing the equipment used to operate the first regularly scheduled American airline and funding Robert Goddard's liquid fueled rocketry and space flight experiments on which the subsequent development of rocketry and jet propulsion was based, and Commander Samuel Gordon of the Navy's Civil Engineering Corps.[27]

After the funeral, the family reached the C-1 buoy on a Coast Guard boat, with a Navy chaplain, the board for the urn with a flag over it, a bugler for Taps, and airplanes from NAS Floyd Bennett circling in the distance for the flyover. The burial went off without a hitch, except for one unplanned addition. As the seamen were upending the board,

> two big sailboats, one white and one black, both on a reach under full sail and going like blazes, passed each other in the ship channel next to the buoy, one going to New York harbor, the other East up the Sound. We could hear the rush of the water on their leeward rails. With the planes going overhead at the same time, it was a very eerie moment. And Taps was unforgettable.[28]

The day after his burial, airplanes from Floyd Bennett spread flowers over the C-1 buoy. Afterward, there was a ceremony at the station, when the speaker said the following:

> This is a thumbnail sketch of a great captain. First of all, he was Navy. He embodied the characteristics which John Paul Jones listed in his Qualifications for Navy Officers. He was a gentleman of liberal education, refined manners, punctilious courtesy, and the nicest sense of personal honor. His superiors loved him because, while oblivious of his own rank, he was respectful of theirs... At family parties, the captain would always take his mother's arm as they left the dining table. But when his younger brother was promoted to rear admiral over him, the captain fell back and tried to give the place of honor to the

man of senior naval rank. [But the brother, Rear Admiral F. E. M. "Pete" Whiting, said that Ken was still his big brother and refused to take the place of honor. Their mother, Daisy, loved it.][29]

For nearly thirty-five years, Captain Whiting has worked for the advancement of the aviation in the Navy. With a high regard for achievement, he had maintained a modest spirit, having walked with kings he did not lose the common touch. The officers and crew have always felt that the captain was their friend.[30]

I wish I could share the incidents that show his deep consideration and affection for the men of this station, which he so briefly commanded. However, I am sure he would not like it because he is a modest man.[31]

The day I reported at this station, the captain talked to me at length about the death of one of our pilots and the pitiable sight of the little, young mourning widow at the memorial services in the hanger. The captain could not forget the pathetic little figure, and a month later, her grief was still his. This is a Whiting trait.[32]

Amidst her great sorrow of the last few days, Mrs. Whiting's first concern has been for the wife of our pilot who met with an accident on Monday. Each time I have seen her, the captain's wife has first of all inquired for news of the ensign's wife and yesterday in spite of the confusion in Larchmont before the funeral, she telephoned the florists to send orders for some of the captain's flowers by wire to St. Louis for the funeral of our pilot.[33]

The flowers and testimonies of his many friends at the funeral service yesterday was the greatest tribute I have ever seen paid to a man.

> In addition to the banks of flowers sent from our
> station, more flowers arrived than the church
> could hold. Nearby florists lacked enough flow-
> ers to fill the many orders they had.[34]

*****

Although at times Whiting enjoyed some of the privileges
of wealth as a base or station commander, with large quarters and
staff, as a captain in the US Navy, he had not achieved any personal
wealth. As an excellent sailor, he captained large, borrowed sailboats
and touched wealth, but it was not his.

His final will showed that. Dated February 6, 1936, on a one-
page Navy form, it listed his home of record as 98 Park Avenue,
Larchmont, New York, which his wife had inherited from her parents. It listed his wife, Edna May Whiting, as his first beneficiary and
next of kin. It listed his next beneficiaries as his two daughters, Edna
and Moira. His final contingent beneficiaries he listed as his brothers, Butler and F. E. M., and sister, Mrs. Phillip Reed (Virginia, who
had passed away in March, 1939).[35]

*****

Sixty-five years after these events took place, with the help
of Eddie and Moira's Journal of Family Memories, we can correct
the wartime record. In the middle of a huge war and faced with
the importance of maintaining civilian and Navy morale, the press
was informed that Whiting's cause of death was pneumonia, which
caused a heart attack.[36]

According to the Whiting family, Kenneth Whiting's real cause
of death was meningococcal septicemia or meningitis.[37]

> Meningitis is a swelling of the membranes
> of the brain and spinal cord. It can be due to a
> viral, fungal, or bacterial infection. The symp-
> toms, which usually occur within a week of expo-

213

sure, are a distinct skin rash, fever, headache, and feeling ill. Meningococcal bacteria reproduce in the bloodstream and release poisons (septicemia). As the infection progresses, blood vessels become damaged, which can cause a faint skin rash that looks like tiny pinpricks. The spots may be pink, red, or purple. As the infection spreads, the rash becomes more obvious and the spots may turn dark red or deep purple and resemble large bruises.[38]

When discussing the meningitis and its symptoms, Tilly Walden, daughter of Moira Whiting and granddaughter of Kenneth, commented, "Oh, that awful rash!" Even though Tilly was born twelve years after her grandfather died, the description of the rash had passed down through family lore.[39]

Moira captured the emotional toll of Kenneth Whiting's death on his family.

For my poor mother, there was nothing in life any more. You've never seen a sadder person. For me, there were years ahead, marked by the trauma of his death, that affected everything in my life. I was well into my 40s before I really got a handle on it. I don't know how deeply it affected my sister, though I know it did, and she never forgot [how Daddy died].[40]

CHAPTER 16

THE KENNETH WHITING PERSONA

Kenneth Whiting lived from 1881 to 1943 and passed away nearly eighty years ago. In writing a biography of a deceased person, with no one living today who can describe him or his personality with firsthand knowledge, the challenge for an author is to collect all the available facts about the subject, to find third-person descriptions of his persona from family, friends who knew him, and researchers who have written about him or who have posted pictures of him, and consolidate them into some meaningful whole.

The reader has now read the author's findings, the facts about Kenneth Whiting's life and the descriptions of his personality. From all those sources, below is the author's attempt to describe the persona of Kenneth Whiting. What was Kenneth Whiting like as a person?

Kenneth Whiting was a natural leader, who led from the front and by example. The more difficult the task he was asking his men to do, the more likely he was to do it first. From escaping a submerged submarine through a torpedo tube to piloting an airplane being catapulted for the first time from the deck of a carrier, Kenneth Whiting put himself first in line.

Although the Naval Academy *honor concept* was not adopted until 1953, long after Whiting's Navy career ended, had Whiting been alive then it is easy to predict his support for the *honor concept*. Pertinent parts of the concept say, "Midshipmen are persons of integrity. We stand for what is right. We tell the truth and ensure that the full truth is known.

We do not lie." He told the truth to his flight surgeons, even at a cost to himself, as his health began to decline near the end of his career. One cannot read the written statements he made about the 1930 NAS Norfolk air race without believing he would have supported the code. The man who recommended that he receive some discipline left the door open for Whiting to escape responsibility when he noted that Whiting had not disciplined any of the officers who had actually operated the race. But Whiting was in command, and he took full responsibility. He knew *the full truth*, and he made sure it was known. Some of the other officers involved became admirals, but Whiting was passed over twice for promotion to rear admiral and mandatorily retired as a captain.[1]

Whiting's core beliefs included not kowtowing, which he probably learned as a young officer serving in the Far East and observing the Oriental practice of kowtowing. He also was deeply committed to never quitting and keeping up his efforts on anything on which he worked, unless and until relieved. He believed he was a naval officer first before he was a submariner or an aviator. He was not a religious man, but he was an American patriot and a political conservative.

Another personality trait that he exhibited throughout his life was a high level of personal modesty. Despite a significant list of professional achievements and contributions to his Navy, "never, even in his later years, would he talk about these and other personal accomplishments"[2]

He always blended in an element of fun into his work, which probably helped maintain the morale of his men and caused them to work harder and more effectively. His daughters said he had a kind of joking wildness about him. From the beginning of his life, he gave nicknames to most of the members of his family, his subordinates, and the pilots with whom he flew. He may have been part of starting the Naval Aviation tradition of assigning nicknames, or call signs, to all pilots. He sang humorous songs for fun, but had a "tin ear" and could not carry a tune. As the years passed, he asked that his cremated ashes be spread at the Long Island Sound buoy that marked the start of the nearly fifty years of sailboat races in which he participated so that after his death, he could "call out those who jumped the gun and crossed the starting line early!"

He was charming and totally unaware of it. From his youth, people wanted to follow him. He was always neat, always in shape, and always looked good in his clothes whether in a Navy uniform or in old sailing clothes. He was physically good-looking, with strong overall body coordination, and small hand-eye coordination, and a natural athlete. He played all sports well, but as a he grew older, he gravitated to sailing and became a champion handler and racer of sailboats. Despite his great natural coordination, his daughters said he was not a good automobile driver.

One of the constants in his career was the continuing care and concern he felt for the men under his command and their families, and as a consequence, he always enjoyed a high level of popularity with them. From the first days of the First Aeronautic Detachment in France when his men's complaints about French food caused Whiting to hire two French chefs to his command at NAS Pearl Harbor when he took care of the families in his command by building schools for their children, and finally to the ill-fated trip he made to Washington in April 1943 to advocate for sea duty for the junior ferry and test pilots he had commanded at NAS New York and as Third Naval District general inspector of naval aircraft, he used his command authority to support his subordinates and their families. The eulogy given in a hangar at NAS New York after Whiting's death testified to the continuing high level of concern and care he gave his men and their families.

With his strong sense of personal modesty, he found it difficult to advocate for himself; this was probably a factor in his being passed over for promotion to rear admiral. Yet he fought courageously and continuously for the Navy and for organizational goals, such as independence for Naval Aviation (Morrow Board, only aviators can command carriers and seaplane tenders) and the betterment of the Navy (honest investigations of airplane crashes, development of aircraft carriers). In his advocacy for the Navy, Whiting was agreeable and affable. He treated everyone respectfully and had a nice way about him. He could apparently advocate for new or divergent positions, argue and debate them without causing negative feelings.

As he pushed for radical new things, like aircraft carriers, he always worked within the organizational boundaries of the Navy. He never went outside those boundaries unless asked to do so (like testifying before Congress, the Morrow Board, or the Mitchell court-martial). In World War I, he did push the envelope of his authority in working with the French for the joint defense of their land, but he limited the scope of his decisions about French requests, did what he had to do to accomplish his mission, and submitted continuous written reports to the Department of the Navy.

He had a hardiness and toughness about him. He had a high level of stamina, could and would work long hours. One imagines the discomfort he experienced during his life from the loss of five teeth, probably from boxing or other sports. He had an extremely high level of courage. He was called a daredevil, particularly early in his career. If he needed to do something physically risky, he never shied away from it and would rarely be hurt. As he got older, he gained some control over taking physical risks and did it more and more for good purposes (to save someone's life or health or save a ship or piece of equipment). However, he never lost his desire for physical fun and excitement.

In his youth, he may have had a learning disability and had trouble applying himself to academic challenges; he sometimes failed written tests or underperformed academically. Yet he conquered this problem and became a thinker, a planner, a good problem-solver, and a good student. He commanded several experimental ships (or stations with an experimental mission) and became a good leader of experimental efforts. He had a great intellectual curiosity about the world and how it worked, people, animals, politics, and governments. He loved dogs and took care of animals that had been hurt.

Whiting loved his family, including his in-laws, but he loved the Navy first. He would have preferred to have sons, but he had two daughters. He raised them as tomboys and did not put them on a pedestal. With him and his wife, Edna, being gifted athletes, both their daughters participated strongly in sports. On long car trips, such as moving his family between assignments, although normally chums, his wife and he sometimes ended up not speaking, which amused his daughters greatly.

CHAPTER 17

THE CASE FOR RECOGNIZING KENNETH WHITING AS THE FATHER OF THE AMERICAN AIRCRAFT CARRIER

As a young naval officer, Kenneth Whiting began to make significant contributions to our American Navy. As a junior officer in submarines, he was the first man to escape from a submerged submarine. As a junior aviator, he was relieved from command of two organizations because they had grown too large for an officer of his rank. As he was promoted into more senior ranks, he was a major spokesman for Naval Aviation in its bureaucratic battle for the aircraft carrier with the battleship admirals and played seminal roles in the creation, planning, and operation of the first six carriers. These would prove to be the most important warship type ever created by our Navy, which ultimately eliminated the battleship from the fleet and turned many of them into floating museums.

Yet in 1938 and 1939, probably because of nonjudicial punishment recommended by two battleship admirals he had received in 1930 from the secretary of the Navy, two boards of nine different admirals twice failed to achieve a positive vote of six to select Kenneth Whiting for promotion to rear admiral. As required by law, he retired but was returned to active duty to serve, first, in an assignment far from the frontlines in a new global war, and finally, in an assignment that took much better advantage of his background. Then after his untimely death and perhaps realizing the price in his career, which Whiting had paid in Naval Aviation's battle with the battleship admirals, the Navy bestowed on Kenneth Whiting multiple honors, which seem a little overblown for an officer of his rank required to retire.

Eight decades hence, we are left with many references to Whiting in the biographies of his naval officer peers and in books about the history of Naval Aviation. But no biography of Whiting has ever been written, and no comprehensive listing of his contributions to the development of aircraft carriers has ever been compiled. No complete summary of his accomplishments over a four-decade Navy career has ever been prepared for naval leaders, scholars, and other readers to consider the totality of his career through a single lens, to draw conclusions about his contributions to our Navy and our country, and to make a final judgment about the informal salutation frequently given him—Father of the Aircraft Carrier.

The thesis of this book is that, either because of his sudden, untimely death in the middle of a massive world war or because his career ended without the high-profile title of admiral, his many contributions to the development of the American aircraft carrier, to Naval Aviation, and to submarines have been lost or forgotten. Except for his close friends like Ellyson and Chevalier who were killed in crashes, many of those who worked for him on his teams, ships, and stations throughout their careers, like Mitscher, Pennoyer, and Pride did achieve flag rank. This may have put Whiting's contributions in even more of a shadow, but instead of creating a shadow for him, perhaps the protégés whom Whiting nurtured and prepared for such high service should be counted on his list of accomplishments! Regardless of the timing of his death or his failure to achieve flag rank, a significant number of those who have reviewed his career and his accomplishments have given him the unofficial title of Father of the American Aircraft Carrier. Here, in rough chronological order, are documented accomplishments achieved or led by Kenneth

Whiting in the development of the aircraft carrier, which should be considered in the consensus and official award of that title:

1. In early 1916, Whiting began agitating for a new type of ship he called a plane carrier.[1]

2. Soon afterward, Whiting made his first formal carrier-related proposal, in which he recommended that the Navy should purchase the *Henry M. Flagler*, a large seagoing train ferry owned by the Florida East Coast Railway and convert it into an experimental plane carrier. Although this proposal was disapproved by the Navy Department on June 20, 1917, it was only implemented twenty-five years later in World War II.[2]

3. In 1916, to develop the first necessary evolution of operating airplanes from a ship, launching them into the air, Whiting and Holden C. Richardson invented and mounted an aircraft catapult on a coal barge at NAS Pensacola. They successfully launched an airplane from it and then, attempting to perfect it, launched several more.[3]

4. In 1917, Whiting installed the catapult on the armored cruiser USS *Seattle* and led a squadron of pilots in experimenting with it in launching seaplanes from it.[4]

5. On *Seattle*, Whiting supervised the first successful spotting of ship-mounted artillery from an airplane launched from the catapult.[5]

6. On *Seattle*, Whiting began perfecting retarding, or arresting gear, in pursuit of the second necessary evolution of airplane operations from a ship, being able to successfully land an aircraft on the ship's deck and control it without a crash.[6]

7. On August 27, 1917, Whiting submitted a major planning memo that included the concepts of ships carrying seaplanes on anti-submarine missions operating in the ocean and carrying seaplanes across the North Sea and close enough to German bases to be able to bomb them.[7]

8. In late summer 1917, in a plan that was to become the initial mission of NAS Killingholme, Whiting wrote a proposal to transport seaplanes on lighter plane carriers close enough to bomb German bases. He continued to lead the lighter experimental bombing effort in 1918 after taking command at Killingholme.[8]

9. After observing aircraft carriers built and used by the British in World War I, Whiting was the first in the American Navy to make the transition from aircraft tender ships with partial decks and cranes for transporting seaplanes for the limited purposes of reconnaissance and artillery spotting to expanding Naval Aviation's mission by building full, flat deck carriers and using them as offensive weapons for carrying, launching, and recovering fighters and land planes, to attack the enemy where he is to achieve air superiority and provide close air support on land and sea.[9]

10. In 1919, after his return from Europe, Whiting proposed that the Navy build an experimental airplane carrier to develop a doctrine of offensive carrier operations. He provided two options to do this—convert a large high-speed passenger ferry that the Navy acquired during the war and that had been used to transport passengers on the West Coast or convert the collier USS *Jupiter*.[10]

11. Whiting, Mustin, and Towers all testified before the General Board in support of the proposal, but only Whiting fully envisioned the concepts of the airplane carrier for offensive carrier operations.[11]

12. From the end of World War I, Whiting was one of the Navy's strongest advocates for creating aircraft carriers. Given the power of the battleship admirals and their ability to negatively influence an officer's career, Whiting had the courage, knowledge, drive, and personality to play a major role in working the Bureau of Aeronautics' *Langley* proposal through the Navy's bureaucracy. The General Board supported the proposal and selected the *Jupiter* option. Whiting was a strong spokesman for the proposal

and led in testifying before the House and Senate Naval Committees. Congress adopted and funded the proposal.[12]

13. Whiting led in the conversion of the *Jupiter* and in the design of the USS *Langley*, and he worked with the shipyard in getting the job done.[13]

14. Whiting supervised the team of Chevalier, Pride, and Pennoyer, who designed all the gear for the *Langley*, including the retarding or arresting gear, hydraulic gears, and catapults.[14]

15. Whiting was a strong spokesman in testifying before the House and Senate Naval Committees to get approval and funding for converting the USS *Lexington* and USS *Saratoga* from cruisers to aircraft carriers.[15]

16. As a junior member of the American delegation to the Washington Naval Conference of 1922, Whiting was the primary spokesman for successfully including aircraft carriers in the final Treaty.[16]

17. As the first executive officer of the *Langley* and senior officer present afloat for three months until Captain S. H. R. Doyle came aboard, Whiting commissioned the Navy's first aircraft carrier.[17]

18. As senior aviator aboard *Langley*, Whiting performed the first catapult launch, supervised perfecting the retarding or arresting gear, converted the pigeon coop used for communications into the executive officer's quarters, invented the landing-signal-officer function, invented using destroyers as plane guards, invented ready rooms for pilots, installed a darkroom and camera equipment to film all landings, perfected aviation gas and grain alcohol storage tanks, and created all the doctrine, orders, and procedures for the Naval Aviation operation of an aircraft carrier.[18]

19. Whiting planned and developed the USS *Lexington* and USS *Saratoga*.[19]

20. Whiting was instrumental in obtaining a recommendation from the Morrow Board that only aviators could command

aircraft carriers, seaplane tenders, and naval air stations and passing a law to implement that recommendation.[20]

21. Whiting made major contributions in constructing the USS *Wright*, the first seaplane tender, and developing her organization. While *Wright* was not an aircraft carrier until the development of the aircraft carrier, some in the Navy blended carriers and tenders together. Whiting's work with *Wright* served to clarify the large differences between aircraft carriers and seaplane tenders and made the point that they were two different kinds of ships.[21]

22. Whiting provided significant testimony before the Morrow Board, the Mitchell court-martial, and the House and Senate Naval Committees in the defeat of the concept and bill to merge naval and army aviation and to make an example of Mitchell for his attacks on Naval Aviation so no other service or agency would ever attempt to take Naval Aviation away from the Navy.[22]

23. Whiting supervised the construction and fitting out of the USS *Saratoga*.[23]

24. Beginning November 16, 1927, Whiting served as the executive officer of USS *Saratoga*.[24]

25. Beginning June 15, 1933, Whiting served as the commanding officer of the USS *Langley*.[25]

26. Whiting fitted out the USS *Ranger*, the first American aircraft carrier built from the keel up.[26]

27. Whiting supervised the construction of the USS *Yorktown* and USS *Enterprise*.[27]

28. From June 12, 1934, Whiting served as the commanding officer of the USS *Saratoga*.[28]

29. By twice taking over conning the USS *Saratoga* from Panama Canal pilots, Whiting saved the Saratoga from running aground and from damaging a propeller.[29]

30. The plaque on the parade ground monument in front of the headquarters of NAS Whiting Field contains the title "Father of the Aircraft Carrier" beneath Whiting's name.[30]

31. As part of the celebration of the fortieth anniversary of the
commissioning of NAS Whiting Field, a paper prepared by
the Station asserted the following:

> In addition to his remarkable understand-
> ing of their mechanical qualities, Ken Whiting
> also understood the tactical potential of aircraft
> carriers. He is considered by many scholars to
> have been the father of the fast carrier task group
> and Ken Whiting's thinking undoubtedly con-
> tributed in a very real way to the successes of
> Navy carriers during World War II.[31]

32. During the decade of the 1920s, in which the concept of
the aircraft carrier was created and the Navy's first carriers were developed, Kenneth Whiting carried out many
assignments in which he was the Navy's spokesman for this
revolutionary new type of warship.[32]

Kenneth Whiting played major roles in the development of
America's first six aircraft carriers—*Langley, Lexington, Saratoga,
Ranger, Yorktown,* and *Enterprise.* After playing an instrumental role
in all six from concept through fighting them through the political system for authorization and funding, construction, and fitting
out, his fingerprints were all over them. Then he served as executive officer and captain of *Langley* and *Saratoga.* The doctrine and
procedures he developed on the *Langley* for the operation of aircraft
carriers became standard operating procedures for every American
aircraft carrier from then on. On every aircraft carrier, whenever the
bugle call "Boots and Saddles" is played, the loud speakers announce
"Pilots, man your planes," or any other evolution is performed, they
are reading from the book Whiting wrote.

A paper prepared for the fortieth anniversary of the commissioning of NAS Whiting Field summarized his contributions and vision for the United States Navy:

> Whether on the sea, or beneath its surface, whether aloft or ashore, Ken Whiting made his mark; he knew where we were, and he never stopped working to move us to where we needed to be. He saw the future.[33]

Admiral Van Deurs summarized his impact on the creation of what became the Navy's primary capital ship.

> For 20 years, 1919–1938, ashore and afloat, Whiting labored to improve carriers and their operations. He never spoke of his accomplishments, nor of the ideas he contributed, and never hinted that he put carriers into the US Navy. But more than any other man, he did just that.[34]

CHAPTER 18

RENDERING HONORS

B ecause Kenneth Whiting did not achieve the high-level profile and broader responsibilities of flag rank achieved by Moffett, Reeves, and many of his peers and protégés, honoring him with his first biography requires some justification of why he deserves it. One rationale comes from the history of the US Navy and of the difficult growth of its aviation branch from birth and survival to a strong, independent strike arm.

The "black shoe" surface admirals who led the Navy at the birth of Naval Aviation, the Gun Club, were not at all sure they needed aviation. Many did not understand its purpose nor what it could do for the Navy. There were concerns that it wanted to grow to be *too big for its britches*. The commanding officer of the *Langley*, Captain S. H. R. Doyle believed that creating a ready room for a carrier's pilots would pamper them. Naval Aviation's early years included only a few senior officers, like Moffett and Reeves, who saw what it could be and worked to get it there. One of the strategies employed by this minority of seers was to identify articulate junior aviators who could explain aircraft carriers and what they could do for the Navy—there were to be no senior aviators for over a decade whom they could send into bureaucratic battles to fight for the vision of what aviation could be.

Aviator Henry Mustin was perhaps the first one identified for this battle, and his efforts to build Naval Aviation and those of non-aviator Mark Bristol to control him are documented in pages 53 to 60. It was fortunate for both Mustin and Naval Aviation that the punitive measures Bristol took to keep him and the new branch under control were soon reversed by CNO Benson.

A few years after Benson reversed Bristol's punitive measures and restored Naval Aviation on its path of growth, the first chief of the new Bureau of Aeronautics, Moffett, identified other young Naval Aviation warriors to carry Naval Aviation's banner into the bureaucratic fray, like Kenneth Whiting. Against the still strong headwinds from the battleship admirals, Whiting fought for Naval Aviation on many fronts, including air-crash investigations, the aircraft carrier, the Morrow Board's Billy Mitchell wars, and growing Naval Aviation and keeping it independent of the Army. He provides us another important window into the history of Naval Aviation and of its continuing efforts to achieve independence and equality with the surface force.

The Whiting window provides an opportunity for students of this bureaucratic struggle to analyze the strategies that a midlevel leader can use in a fight where he is *outgunned* and where his mentor, who also suffers from an unequal power relationship with the opponents, can only provide partial protection for his battle designee. Part of this analysis is to consider the impact when a more junior officer in the fray pursues a goal relentlessly but brings to the battles the softer skills that go with a charming, pleasing personality as another battle strategy.

A Whiting biography also enables a reader to compare what happens when a battle designee such as Mustin is finally protected from retribution for his acts to elevate Naval Aviation to equal and independent status with one like Whiting who is partially protected, but in the end may have paid a price for his pursuit of the aviation independence goal. With Burrage's untrained perspective on the 1930 NAS Norfolk air race and his unwillingness to accept the report of several experienced pilots about the altitude at which they flew the race, it certainly demonstrates the validity of the strong position Mustin took in his comprehensive 1916 paper to CNO Benson that non-aviators could not understand all the issues of aviation and that the opinion of an aviator about a Naval Aviation issue should be accepted as expert testimony. Over twenty-five years later and in the midst of World War II's carrier warfare, the Navy accepted the validity of Mustin's conclusions, but on the way to independent status for Naval Aviation, there were a few aviators who had paid the price. Whiting was probably one of them.

In a few cases, the American government or the military has recognized errors made which seriously affected the career of an officer. After Billy Mitchell passed away, during and after World War II, President Roosevelt and Congress recognized that Mitchell had been correct about much of what he had advocated in the 1920s [although communicating his issues outside the Army had been inappropriate and harmful], posthumously promoted him to the rank of major general, and awarded him the Congressional Medal of Honor. Based upon the facts about Whiting's career, the 1930 NAS Norfolk Admonition and the Billy Mitchell precedent, posthumous promotion of Whiting to the rank of rear admiral may be appropriate.

Other rationales for a Whiting biography are to provide documentation in one place of all his contributions to the Navy and of their level of importance. One paradigm to explain the role Kenneth Whiting played in the United States Navy and in birthing carriers comes from the field of *military innovation studies* or just innovation studies. This field has been well-focused by Paul Kennedy, internationally known for his writings and commentaries on global political, economic, and strategic issues. Whiting's career activities, lifetime achievements, and the role he played in the Navy's advancement fit this paradigm closely.

In his book *Engineers of Victory*, Kennedy began with several major strategic challenges faced by the Allies in World War II—moving war-critical cargoes in merchant ships across the oceans in the face of the Nazi U-boat threat, overcoming vast distances, and landing on enemy-held shores, defeating the Wehrmacht's blitzkrieg, gaining air superiority for both the protection of strategic bombers, and providing close air support to Allied soldiers fighting on the ground, and constructing runways and bases many lands and oceans away from the United States and Britain. In each case, he writes of the creation of a culture of innovation by senior Allied leaders like Roosevelt, Churchill, Marshall, Eisenhower, and Nimitz. Within this environment of innovation, new weapons like the atomic bomb, miniaturized cavity magnetron radar, Higgins boats, B-29 bombers, and P-51 fighters, perfected torpedoes, and many more had to be created. In the final step, new warfare techniques and organizations had to be developed to employ the new weapons.[1]

Another example of creating a culture of innovation were the first twelve years of the Navy's Bureau of Aeronautics, where Bureau Chief Moffett, who has been described as a bureaucratic savant and a savvy political player, presided over a climate of innovation where failure was allowed as long as some productive results, which could be analyzed to advance Naval Aviation, were achieved. Vital to maintaining such a climate by senior leaders like Moffett was providing some level of encouragement and protection to innovative, lower, midlevel managers and their teams of strategists, tweakers, and those who can carry a project or task through to success "by skillful or artful contrivance." Also required were many risk-taking thinkers and designers, organized into teams led by middle managers with the ability to take advantage of the climate of innovation and to lead and coordinate the work of their teams of engineers and designers. Serving as a leader of these teams also required some courage because the protective cover provided from above did not always provide complete protection from competitors in the organization who would attack the leader and his team for displaying too much creativity or independence or from political opponents opposed to the goals of the team.[2]

Kennedy applied his paradigm to the performance of the five principal World War II adversaries—the United States, Great Britain, the Soviet Union, Germany, and Japan. Because the US and Britain were democracies with relatively free and open societies, they performed at the highest level in developing many new weapons and strategies. The Soviet Union's Stalin, once he had purged the Red Army in the late 1930s and realized that he had finally assembled a group of generals he could trust, reduced his level of autocratic control, and provided some examples of strong weapons and strategy development. Autocratic Japan (after Admiral Yamamoto's death) and Germany operated farthest from the paradigm and thus faltered in their development or employment of new strategies and weapons as the war wore on.[3]

In explaining his paradigm, Kennedy pointed to such examples as Churchill's protection of Major General Percy Hobart's development of odd weapons like flail tanks and Churchill's return of Sir Wilfrid Freeman to the Air Ministry to administer aircraft design and production, which paved the way to the marriage of an underperforming earlier version of the P-51 Mustang with the Rolls-Royce Merlin V-12 engine and which turned the P-51 into the best Allied fighter of World War II. Roosevelt's creation of the Navy's construction battalions and his promotion of Ben Moreell to flag rank provide an excellent American example.[4]

This paradigm can be applied over and over to the life and pre-World War II career of Kenneth Whiting, with the role of senior leader provided by admirals like Moffett, who has been credited with creating a culture of innovation within Naval Aviation. From a leader of a gang of brothers and boys within the sheltered environment of 1890s Larchmont; command of the submarines *Porpoise* and *Shark* and their small crews under the more senior and democratic flotilla leadership of Guy Castle; taking the risks of command of the experimental submarine *Seal* operating under the umbrella of the Navy's acceptance of the unusual craft; command of the First Aeronautical Detachment in World War I under the senior leadership and protection of CNO Benson; leading *Langley* and his development team of Chevalier, Pennoyer, Griffin, and Pride under the leadership of Moffett into the unexplored, trackless void of developing the book on carrier operations; his *Saratoga* leadership in preparing other naval officers like Mitscher to become World War II legends; and to the risky world of Washington politics performing as a very public spokesman for the Navy for the First Aeronautic Detachment, the Langley proposal, the Washington Naval Conference, the Morrow Board, and the Billy Mitchell court-martial—Whiting was the Navy's go-to, midlevel officer in the high-stakes political world of advocating for Naval Aviation and in leading teams in the risky development of submarines and aircraft carriers. Within this paradigm, Whiting developed the ability to serve as a team leader in a culture of innovation. With some protection provided by a higher authority, with courage, with a willingness to take risks that seems to have been embedded in Whiting's DNA from early in life, with a pleasant personality capable of advocating for an idea within an organization in which others were not always supportive, and with the skills to lead his team and its work, Whiting's life and career can be seen as exemplifying the team leader role envisioned by Kennedy in his paradigm.

*****

Kenneth Whiting held the following individual awards—Navy Cross; French Croix de Guerre (Chevalier); World War I Victory Medal; Overseas Clasp; American Campaign Medal; American Defense Service Medal; and World War II Victory Medal.[5]

Edna had a bronze plaque hung in Larchmont's Saint John's Episcopal Church, the family's home church, telling about Whiting and his naval achievements and including submariner's dolphins and aviator's wings. Although he had qualified in submarines and then left them nearly thirty years before his death, including the dolphins was well-justified by Turnbull and Lord by their statement that Whiting's name was standstill a tradition in them.[6]

Edna spent a great deal of time and energy after Whiting's death trying to get the Navy to name one of the many aircraft carriers that were coming down the weighs in the last two years of the war for him. But she was told that all new carriers were now being named for battles, not people, and she was not successful. In the last two years of her life, she saw the Navy act contrary to that policy, though, when on February 1, 1945, it changed the name of the USS *Wright*, AV-1, the first seaplane tender, to USS *San Clemente*, AG-79, in order to name a new light aircraft carrier USS *Wright*, CVL-49, in honor of Orville. After her death and that of James Forrestal, World War I naval aviator and first secretary of Defense, the Navy named a carrier for him. Since the *Wright* and the *Forrestal*, the Navy has named multiple carriers after people.[7]

The Navy honored Whiting posthumously in a growing number of ways in the forty years after his death. A new seaplane tender had been launched in Seattle on December 15, 1943, by Seattle-Tacoma Shipbuilding Corporation, and the Navy convinced Edna to accept the ship as the USS *Kenneth Whiting* (AV-14). She was commissioned May 8, 1944, with Commander R. R. Lyons in command. Edna and Moira traveled to Seattle for the commissioning ceremony, where Edna, as the ship's sponsor, christened her.[8]

With Kenneth Whiting, the Navy started a new class of seaplane tenders. Her characteristics were as follows: displacement—8,510 tons (12,812 tons full load); length—492 feet; beam—69 feet, 6 inches; draft—23 feet; propulsion—1 shaft, 8,500 horsepower; speed—18.7 knots; complement—113 officers, 964 enlisted, 1,077 total, including pilots and crew for her seaplanes; armament—2 five-inch .38-caliber guns, 2 quad-40 MM gun mounts, 2 dual-40 MM gun mounts, 16 single-20 MM gun mounts. This defensive weaponry show that *Kenneth Whiting* was a warship, designed to operate squadrons of Catalina and Mariner seaplanes to perform her mission of long-distance aerial reconnaissance and patrol and protect herself from attack while anchored, sometimes alone, in sheltered waters like the Kossol Passage of the Palau Islands and the Kerama Retto archipelago southwest of Okinawa.[9]

After her shakedown cruise from Seattle to Pearl Harbor, bound for the South Pacific, *Kenneth Whiting* departed Pearl Harbor on August 1, 1944. Joining the ship on the day she weighed anchor at Pearl Harbor was the author's father, a lieutenant (junior grade) communications officer named Felix T. Haynes, who had already served as communications officer in USS *Thuban* (AKA-19) at the invasions of Kiska, Tarawa, and Kwajalein. Haynes was promoted to lieutenant on October 14, 1944, remained with the *Kenneth Whiting* for the rest of the war, and departed her on October 4, 1945. He remained in the Naval Reserve and retired as a lieutenant commander. A graduate of Catholic University's Columbus School of Law, after World War II, Haynes returned to his labor law specialist career and retired in 1986. The ship's bell from the *Kenneth Whiting* today hangs in front of the

Santa Rosa County Courthouse in Milton, Florida, a few miles from NAS Whiting Field.[10]

Edna and Moira traveled from Seattle to Coronado to visit Eddie and returned home to Larchmont where Edna got sick in October 1944. Moira entered the Women Accepted for Volunteer Emergency Service (WAVES) and then traveled alone to Pensacola, Florida, in January 1945, where the Navy was rendering still more honors to Kenneth Whiting. To fulfill the huge wartime need for new naval aviators, the Navy was building more airfields in West Florida and South Alabama and naming them for deceased aviators. The first such field was established in Milton, Florida, and named NAS Whiting Field. Moira attended Whiting Field's commissioning ceremony and made the dedication. Bestowing a new title on Kenneth Whiting for the first of many times, the monument dedicating the field to Whiting is inscribed "Father of the Aircraft Carrier."[11]

Soon, other nearby fields were named for other deceased close friends of Whiting—like Theodore G. "Spuds" Ellyson and Godfrey de Courcelles "Chevy" Chevalier. "Ken Whiting's Airfield... The Busiest Airport in the Navy," a paper prepared for the fortieth anniversary of the commissioning of NAS Whiting Field, described the magnitude to which the Whiting Field training complex grew. It included two entirely separate airfields and fourteen auxiliary fields spread through Florida and Alabama. The two separate airfields supported 320,000 takeoffs and landings in 1982, and the touch-and-go landings at the other fourteen outlying fields brought the total to just short of two million.[12]

Moira left the WAVES in April 1945, to take care of her mother, who had suffered a series of strokes. On December 4, 1946, Edna died and was cremated. Her ashes were spread at C-1 buoy in Long Island Sound, her husband's, Ken's, final resting place.[13]

Edna's older daughter, Eddie, and her husband, Andy Nisewaner, went on to have six children. Eddie died on April 22, 2000, and is buried in the United States Naval Academy Columbarium. After commanding USS *Albert W. Grant* (DD-649) in the Battle of Surigao Strait and earning the Navy Cross for his actions there, Andy retired as a captain, USN, and died in 1995. He is also buried in the USNA Columbarium.[14]

On June 15, 1946, Moira Whiting married Howard T. Walden Jr. at Saint John's Episcopal Church in Larchmont, the same church at which her parents and older sister, Eddie, were married. Walden received his commission as a US Navy officer in 1930 at Yale University, from the first Naval Reserve Officer Training Corps unit in the United States to have graduates. Lieutenant Walden commissioned LST 128 in Evansville, Indiana, on October 11, 1943, and commanded her until April 1945, participating in the occupation of Kwajalein and Majuro atolls and the capture and occupation of Saipan, Peleliu, and Tinian. After the war, Howard returned to the legal profession. Moira and Howard had six children, including Moira Matilda (Tilly) Walden, a major contributor to this book. Howard died on October 14, 1983, and is buried in Greenwood Union Cemetery in Rye, New York. Second daughter Moira Whiting Walden died in Galisteo, New Mexico, on January 11, 2011.[15]

In late fall 1959, Kenneth Whiting's nephew and then-US ambassador to Costa Rica Whiting Willauer read an article on page 45 in *Time* magazine's Latin American edition on the history of escape from submarines. Noting no mention of his uncle Kenneth's feat of April 15, 1909, and believing it to be the first time a man had ever escaped from a submarine, he wrote to the Naval History and Heritage Command and asked for documentation of his uncle's feat. Confirming the facts of Kenneth Whiting's achievement, the Command responded.[16]

While the Command is to be thanked for preserving this important event in naval history, *Time* magazine's failure to find information to document Whiting's first-ever submarine escape supports the title and thesis of this book. Kenneth Whiting's significant contributions to naval history, both in submarines and Naval Aviation, have indeed been forgotten. By drawing together Whiting's many achievements, his life, and all his accomplishments will be documented in one place.

Whiting's last honor took place at the National Aviation Hall of Honor, located at the Naval Aviation Museum at NAS Pensacola. As the first child born on a naval air station, a Navy junior, and the wife of an Annapolis graduate, first daughter Edna Whiting Nisewaner knew the vocabulary to use to compose and deliver the speech to nominate her father for membership in the Hall of Honor. She gave that nominating speech in May 1984 at the Pensacola Museum. Criteria for induction into the Hall are sustained superior performance in and for Naval Aviation, superior contributions in the technical and tactical development of Naval Aviation, and unique and superior flight achievement in combat or noncombat flight operations.[17]

She began by emphasizing that, while other nominators had never met their nominee, she had known her father well for nearly thirty years. Among other comments, she said the following:

> Kenneth Whiting was a modest man. He believed that an officer was a naval officer first and a submariner or aviator second. He had very strong principles, two of which were kowtow to no one; don't quit. He believed the United States Navy should straddle the world through the use of big, fast carriers that were capable of carrying planes of all types to defeat the enemy.[18]
>
> With these beliefs and principles, he testified at the court-martial of Brigadier General William Mitchell and before the Morrow Board very forcefully in a successful effort to keep Naval Aviation under control of the Navy. This was a major contribution.[19]

Summarizing his work on early carrier and tender design, she said between 1920 and 1934, Whiting worked on the design of his country's first six aircraft carriers—*Langley, Saratoga, Lexington, Ranger, Yorktown, Enterprise*, and its first seaplane tender, *Wright*.[20]

Tracing the history of the *Langley*, she recounted that in 1919, Whiting, with the approval of his superiors, went before the General Board to request a ship be converted to an airplane carrier. It took a year of testifying by Whiting at all levels before the request was approved from the General Board through congressional committee hearings to the enactment of appropriation legislation. Whiting stayed in Washington while *Jupiter* was under conversion in direct charge of the development of arresting gear, supported in Norfolk by a team he had handpicked—Chevalier, Griffin, Pennoyer, Pride, and others. Pride was the mechanical genius who made arresting gear work and developed the hydraulic gear. Then Whiting commissioned *Langley* on March 10, 1922, and was the senior officer present afloat until relieved by S. H. R. "Stiffy" Doyle in June, 1922.[21]

As executive officer of *Langley*, he invented the landing signal officer and was also responsible for the use of destroyers as plane guards.[22]

As early as 1919, Whiting recommended a chain of islands from Oahu to Midway, Kure, Wake, and Johnston Islands be surveyed. During his four years at Pearl Harbor, 1935–1939, he continued the surveys, including many other islands in the Pacific, making a special effort to prepare some for seaplane bases.[23]

Edna gave special credit to Lieutenant Commander Godfrey "Chevy" de Chevalier, Captain Virgil C. "Squash" Griffin, Vice Admiral F. W. "Horse" Pennoyer, Admiral Marc "Pete" Mitscher, Rear Admiral William A. Moffett, Admiral J. W. "Bull" Reeves, and Admiral A. M. "Mel" Pride.[24]

Kenneth Whiting was inducted into the Naval Aviation Hall of Honor on May 4, 1984, the twenty-second man so honored, and a bronze plaque with Whiting's likeness commemorating his induction was hung in the Hall of Honor on that day.[25]

Like the author, the reader may be struck by the unusual and significant number of posthumous honors that the Navy bestowed on Captain Kenneth Whiting. Whether these actions were intended to make up for its treatment of Whiting in the wake of the 1930 Norfolk NAS air-racing incident and in the last five years of his career, we may never know, but it does bear scrutiny.

Having read this book, the reader now has the benefit of seeing, in one document, a complete picture of Kenneth Whiting's career-long contributions to our American Navy. We can now compare this holistic perspective with the posthumous honors the Navy bestowed on him. For those who conclude that he is worthy of more accolades, here are some possibilities for consideration.

In a goal for which his wife, Edna, unsuccessfully campaigned between Whiting's death and hers, only to have the Navy deny her and repeatedly violate its own policy about not naming aircraft carriers for people. Should the US Navy have an aircraft carrier named for the man recognized as the Father of the Aircraft Carrier?

If Whiting's premature death prevented the Navy from applying the independence and control of its own destiny earned by Naval Aviation in World War II to the judgment of battleship admirals and the secretary of the Navy in Whiting's 1930 NAS Norfolk admonition, should the Navy consider following the corrective precedents provided by CNO Benson in Bristol's punishment of Mustin and by Roosevelt and Congress in the Billy Mitchell affair and posthumously promote Whiting to rear admiral?

Rationale for this posthumous promotion would be based not only on the precedents established in the Mustin and Mitchell cases. Navy Lieutenant Philip Mayer has written of the importance of reaching into Naval Aviation's past, capturing the climate of innovation created by aviation leaders like Moffett and Reeves, and recreating it in the future. Mayer reminds us that, just as the April 1918 merger of the Royal Naval Air Service and the Royal Flying Corps stifled innovation and caused the British loss of world leadership in Naval Aviation between World Wars I and II, the underdevelopment of critical technologies and tactics will be the result of an overly conservative approach. Navy leaders must be committed to countering bureaucratic inertia and to rewarding increases in efficiency, and they should expect that some of those efforts will fail. Accepting the risk of failure will be vital to maintaining US naval superiority, and to promote innovation this acceptance should include insulating tactical commanders from the penalties of failure.[26]

Publicly telling the story of Kenneth Whiting's career and accomplishments within an era of great change and efforts to maintain a climate of innovation and honoring him by his posthumous promotion to rear admiral will send the message to the entire Navy that risk-taking and innovation will be protected in the future to maintain our sea power leadership around the world.

*****

Every time you see the 1,100-foot-long USS *Chester W. Nimitz* or USS *George H. W. Bush* flying through the water at 30-plus knots, surrounded by cruisers and destroyers, catapulting jet fighters off her flight deck every 20 seconds, arresting aircraft at the same time, and projecting American power to an international hot spot, think about Kenneth Whiting. The man who wanted to study art in Paris was the first person to accurately envision that scene you are seeing before you and to paint it for his fellow naval officers, the nation's political leaders, and all of us to see.

If you think of Kenneth Whiting on the bridge of that carrier or in the cockpit of one of those jets, smiling and humming off-key a verse of the "Armored Cruiser Song" and "looking for someone to put on the bum" to fulfill the offensive mission of the aircraft carrier, this book will have achieved its intended purpose.

The Whiting boys, "Butts",
"Pete", and Kenneth

Kenneth Whiting, first son of
his mother, Daisy. Courtesy of a
copyright grant for Whiting Family
Journal materials to the author.

Kenneth, age 4.

Midshipman First Class
Whiting as Captain of the Naval
Academy Color Company

Early Porpoise-class submarines of the type
commanded by Kenneth Whiting.

Kenneth Whiting in the
cockpit of an early aircraft.

Edna "Eddie" and Moira, daughters
of Kenneth and Edna Whiting.

USS Langley CV-1, America's first aircraft carrier.

USS Saratoga CV-3

Kenneth Whiting, winner
of many sailing races on
Long Island Sound

Theodore G. "Spuds" Ellyson
and Kenneth Whiting.

Commander Kenneth Whiting,
executive officer of the aircraft
carrier USS Saratoga.

Speakers at the August 19, 1940 dedication
of the Wright Brothers Monument at
Dayton, Ohio—left to right: Edward P.
Warner, Captain Kenneth Whiting, Orville
Wright, US Army Air Corps Commanding
General Henry "Hap" Arnold.

Younger daughter Moira Whiting
with the Pensacola plaque dedicating
Whiting Field for Kenneth Whiting
as "Father of the Aircraft Carrier".

USS Kenneth Whiting
AV-14 seaplane tender.

Plaque in St. John's Episcopal Church
Larchment, NY. Placed by Edna Whiting
in honor of her husband Kenneth.

Kenneth Whiting's bride, Edna Andresen, and Kenneth with
his brother and best man, Butler "Butts", April 24, 1912.

Eliot Whiting, father of Kenneth.

Captain S.H.R. "Stiffy" Doyle and Commander
Kenneth Whiting escort President Warren
G. Harding on a visit to the Langley, 1922.

Brigadier General Barton Yount, commanding Army Air Corps in Hawaii; Amelia Earhart; Colonel R.C. Hammond, commanding Luke Field, Hawaii; and Captain Kenneth Whiting, commanding fleet air base at Pearl Harbor, Hawaii. Courtesy of Purdue University Libraries, Karnes Archives and Special Collections.

Fifteen-year-old Kenneth Whiting (with cigarette) leading his Larchmont Gang.

Bronze plaque of Kenneth Whiting, Naval Aviator #16, in the Naval Aviation Museum's Hall of Honor, Pensacola, Florida, May 4, 1984.

NOTES

Chapter 1: Where Are the Carriers?

[1] "Aircraft Carriers-CVN," Chief of Information, United States Navy, from Naval Sea Systems Command (September 17, 2020), accessed September 14, 2021, https://www.navy.mil/DesktopModules/ArticleCS/Print.aspx?.

[2] "Pearl Harbor Ships on the Morning of the Attack," Pearl Harbor Visitors Bureau, accessed October 22, 2019, www.visitpearlharbor.org/pearl-harbor-ships-on-december-7th/.

[3] Morison, *The Two-Ocean War*, p. 578.

[4] "World War II: Grumman F6F Hellcat," ThoughtCo., accessed October 22, 2019, www.thoughtco.com/grumman-f6f-hellcat-2361521; "Ship Characteristics," Battleship Missouri Memorial, Pearl Harbor, Hawaii, accessed October 22, 2019, www.ussmissouri.org/learn-the-history/the-ship/ship-characteristics; "F/A-18 Super Hornet Strike Fighter," US Navy Fact File, Department of the Navy, accessed October 22, 2019, www.navy.mil/navydata/factdisplay.asp?cid=1100&tid=1200&ct=1.

[5] Joseph Reilly, "Power of an Aircraft Carrier," *The Physics Handbook: An Encyclopedia of Scientific Essays*, accessed September 14, 2021, https:hypertextbook.com/facts/2000/JosephReilly.shtml; "The Carriers," Chief of Information, United States Navy, accessed October 22, 2019, www.navy.mil/navydata/ships/carriers/cv-why.asp.

[6] Steve Cohen, "Where are the Carriers?" *Forbes* (October 25, 2010), accessed September 14, 2021, forbes.com/Sites/stevecohen/2010/10/25/where-are-the-Carriers??sh=63823199fdOe.

[7] "William Moffett Facts," Your Dictionary: Biography, *Encyclopedia of World Biography* (Gale Group, 2010), www.biography.yourdictionary.com/willliam-moffett.

[8] Wildenberg, *Proceedings* (September 1998), pp. 70–73.

[9] "Kenneth Whiting, Pioneer Naval Aviator," *Out of the Box* (blog), August 14, 2014, www.libraries.wright.edu/community/out of the box/2014/o8/14/kenneth-whiting-pioneer-naval-aviator.

[10] Kenneth Whiting file, ZB personnel files.

[11] National Personnel Records Center, St. Louis, Missouri.

Chapter 2: The Family of Kenneth Whiting

1   Edna Whiting Nisewaner and Moira Whiting Walden, journal of family memories.
2   Ibid.
3   *The Lucky Bag* (1905), p. 92.
4   Van Deurs, *Wings for the Fleet*, p. 118; "The USS *Porpoise* and Ken Whiting," p. 86.
5   Van Deurs, *Wings for the Fleet*, p. 118; "The USS *Porpoise* and Ken Whiting," p.82.
6   *Annual Registry of the United States Naval Academy* (1905), p. 100.
7   National Personnel Records Center, St. Louis, Missouri.
8   Wortman, p. 121; Rossano, pp. 7–8.

Chapter 3: Making a Man and Transforming a Nation

1   "Alfred Thayer Mahan," *Encyclopedia Britannica*, accessed June 11, 2022,.
2   Bailey, pp. 606–649.
3   Ibid.
4   "Alfred Thayer Mahan," *Encyclopedia Britannica*, accessed June 11, 2022, https://www.britannica.com/biography/Alfred-Thayer-Mahan.
5   "Alfred Thayer Mahan," *Encyclopedia Britannica*, accessed June 11, 2022,; "Mahan's *The Influence of Sea Power upon History: Securing International Markets in the 1890s*," Office of the Historian, Foreign Service Institute, US Department of State.
6   Bailey, pp. 615–618.
7   Ibid., pp. 625–628.
8   Lemelin, "Theodore Roosevelt as Assistant Secretary of the Navy: Preparing America for the World Stage," pp. 21, 29–30.
9   Ibid., pp. 30–31.
10 "The Rough Riders Storm San Juan Hill, July 1, 1898," This Day in History, Eyewitness to History, (2004), accessed September 23, 2019, www.eyewitnesstohistory.com.
11 McCullough, *The Path Between the Seas*, pp. 202–203, 251, 609–611.
12 JO2 (Journalist Second Class) Mike McKinley, "Cruise of the Great White Fleet," Naval History and Heritage Command, accessed October 23, 2019, www.history.navy.mil/research/library/online-reading-room/title-list-alphabetically/cruise-great-white-fleet-mckinley.html.
13 "Recovery of the Remains of Patriot John Paul Jones," Order of the Founders and Patriots of America, accessed October 23, 2019, www.founderspatriots.org/articles/jones.php; "John Paul Jones," United States Naval Academy Public Affairs Office, accessed October 23, 2019, www.usna.edu/PAO/faq_pages/JPJones.php.

14 "Address of President Roosevelt at Annapolis Commemoration, April 24, 1906," SeacoastNH.com, accessed October 23, 2019, www.seacoastnh.com/Maritime-History/John-Paul-Jones/farewell-paul-jones/.

Chapter 4: Refining a Man
1 Kenneth Whiting Papers, MS 294, Nimitz Library; Bureau of Naval Personnel, "Re: Service of Captain Kenneth Whiting, United States Navy, Retired, Active, Deceased," May 12, 1943.
2 "The Armored Cruiser Squadron," *Navy Song Book*, #23; Nisewaner and Walden, Journal of Family Memories.
3 Van Deurs, *Wings for the Fleet*, p. 118; Bureau of Naval Personnel, "Re: Service of Captain Kenneth Whiting, United States Navy, Retired, Active, Deceased," May 12, 1943.
4 Nisewaner and Walden, Journal of Family Memories.
5 Brennan, p. 22; Tate, p. 2; Nisewaner and Walden, Journal of Family Memories.
6 Brennan, p. 22.
7 Nisewaner and Walden, Journal of Family Memories.
8 Brennan, p. 22.
9 Ibid., p. 27.
10 Van Deurs, "The USS *Porpoise* and Kenneth Whiting," p. 81–82.
11 Van Deurs, *Wings for the Fleet*, p. 118.
12 "A-6," *Dictionary of American Naval Fighting Ships*, Naval History and Heritage Command vol. IA, pp. 3–4, accessed October 23, 2019, www.hazegray.org/danfs/submar/ss7.htm; "The A-Boats," PigBoats.com, accessed October 23, 2019, www.pigboats.com/subs/a-boats.html.
13 Bureau of Naval Personnel, "Re: Service of Captain Kenneth Whiting, United States Navy, Retired, Active, Deceased," May 12, 1943; Nisewaner and Walden, Journal of Family Memories.
14 Nisewaner and Walden, Journal of Family Memories.
15 Van Deurs, "The USS *Porpoise* and Kenneth Whiting," p. 81–82; "A-6," *Dictionary of American Naval Fighting Ships*, Naval History and Heritage Command.
16 Ibid.
17 USS *Porpoise* A-6 (Submarine Torpedo Boat Number 7), Naval History and Heritage Command; Van Deurs, "The USS *Porpoise* and Kenneth Whiting," p. 82.
18 Van Deurs, "The USS *Porpoise* and Kenneth Whiting," p. 82.
19 Nisewaner and Walden, Journal of Family Memories.
20 Kenneth Whiting file, ZB personnel file, Naval History and Heritage Command.
21 Ibid.
22 "USS *Porpoise* A-6 (Submarine Torpedo Boat Number 7)," *Dictionary of American Naval Fighting Ships*, Naval History and Heritage Command vol. IA,

pp. 3–4, www.hazegray.org/danfs/submar/ss7.htm; Van Deurs, "The Old Navy: The USS *Porpoise* and Ken Whiting," *Proceedings* (United States Naval Institute, September 1972), pp. 82–83, www.usni.org/magazines/proceedings/1972/september.

23 Nisewaner and Walden, Journal of Family Memories.

24 "How It Feels Traveling under Sea: a Trip in a US Submarine," *Tacoma Times*, August 21, 1909.

25 Nisewaner and Walden, Journal of Family Memories

26 National Personnel Records Center, St. Louis, Missouri.

27 Kenneth Whiting file, ZB personnel file, Naval History and Heritage Command; Nisewaner and Walden, journal of family memories.

28 Kenneth Whiting Papers, MS 294, Nimitz Library.

29 Nisewaner and Walden, Journal of Family Memories.

30 Ibid.

31 Ibid.

32 Ibid.

33 Ibid.

34 Ibid.

35 Ibid.

36 Ibid.

37 Ibid.

38 Kenneth Whiting Papers, MS 294, Nimitz Library; Johnston, "The Wackiest Ship in the Navy," National Personnel Records Center, St. Louis, Missouri.

39 Johnston, "The Wackiest Ship in the Navy."

40 "NavSource Online: Submarine Photo Archive, Seal/G-1 (SS-19 1/2)," www.navsource.org/archives/08/08019a.htm; Rod Mather, University of Rhode Island Applied History Lab, www.oceanexplorer.noaa.gov/technology/development-partnerships/18Kraken/uss-g1.html.

41 Johnston, "The Wackiest Ship in the Navy."

42 Kenneth Whiting file, ZB personnel file, Naval History and Heritage Command.

43 Nisewaner and Walden, Journal of Family Memories.

44 Ibid.

45 Ibid.

46 "Guy Wilkinson Stuart Castle, Commander, United States Navy," Arlington National Cemetery website, accessed October 23, 2019, www.arlingtoncemetery.net/gwscastl.htm.

47 Richard J. Bauman, "The Strange Disappearance of Admiral Wilcox," *Naval History Magazine*, United States Naval Institute, February 2018.

48 Nisewaner and Walden, Journal of Family Memories.

49 Ibid.

50 Ibid.; National Personnel Records Center, St. Louis, Missouri.

51 Ibid.

52 Ibid.

53 Ibid.

54 Ibid.; Van Deurs, *Wings for the Fleet*, p. 119; Rod Mather, University of Rhode Island Applied History Lab, https://www.oceanexplorer.gov/technology/development-partnerships/18Kraken/uss-g1.html; "G-1," Naval History and Heritage Command, February 2, 2004, www.history.navy.mil/research/histories/ship-histories/danfs/g/g-1.html.

55 Ibid.; "The Clarkson Cowl Residence," Old Long Island, April 10, 2014, accessed October 24, 2019, www.oldlongisland.com/2014/04/the-clarkson-cowl-residence.html.

56 Ibid.

57 Ibid.

58 Ibid.; Van Deurs, *Wings for the Fleet*, p. 119; Rod Mather, University of Rhode Island Applied History Lab, https://www.oceanexplorer.gov/technology/development-partnerships/18Kraken/uss-g1.html.

59 "Patent No. 1,097,700," Official Gazette of the United States Patent Office vol. CCII, (Washington: Government Printing Office, 1914), pp. 990–991, www.books.google.com/books?id=Patent+1,097,700&source=bl&ots.

60 Kenneth Whiting Papers, MS 294, Nimitz Library.

61 Halsey, *Admiral Halsey's Story*, chapter 4 (Auckland, New Zealand: Pickle Partners Publishing, August 15, 2014).

62 Ibid.

63 Nisewaner and Walden, Journal of Family Memories.

64 Van Deurs, *Wings for the Fleet*, p. 119; "G-1," Naval History and Heritage Command," February 2, 2004, www.history.navy.mil/research/histories/ship-histories/danfs/g/g-1.html; National Personnel Records Center, St. Louis, Missouri; Bureau of Naval Personnel, "Re: Service of Captain Kenneth Whiting, United States Navy, Retired, Active, Deceased," May 12, 1943; Brennan, p. 23–24.

65 Van Deurs, *Wings for the Fleet*, p. 119.

66 Brennan, p. 24; "Papers of Commander Theodore G. Ellyson," 1918–1928, Archives Branch, Naval History and Heritage Command, Washington, DC, June 4, 2019. www.history.navy.mil/content/history/navalhistoryandheritagecommand/research/archives/research-guides-and-finding-aids/personal-papers/d-e/papers-of-theodore-g-ellyson.html.

Chapter 5: New Risk and a New Instrument to Project Sea Power

1 "Re: Service of Captain Kenneth Whiting, United States Navy, Retired, Active, Deceased," May 12, 1943, National Personnel Records Center, St. Louis, Missouri; Johnston, "The Wackiest Ship in the Navy."

2 "The Ultimate World War II Fleet Submarine Resource," accessed September 26, 2019, www.fleetsubmarine.com/S-class.html.

3 Turnbull and Lord, p. 238; Van Deurs, *Wings for the Fleet*, pp. 147, 161.

4   Kenneth Whiting files, NAS Whiting Field.

5   Eisenhower, *At Ease*, pp. 185–187; Cox, *Gray Eminence: Fox Conner and the Art of Mentorship*, pp. 16–17.

6   Nisewaner and Walden, Journal of Family Memories.

7   "Wright Timeline, 1910–1919," www.wrightbrothers.org; Towers, pp. 97–98, 110; Dennis Parks, "Flight Training the Wright Way," *General Aviation News*, March 8, 2015, generalaviationnews.com/2015/03/08/flight-training-the-wright-way/.

8   Nisewaner and Walden, Journal of Family Memories; Kenneth Whiting Papers, MS 294, Nimitz Library; Van Deurs, *Wings for the Fleet*, p. 119; Honios, chapter 9, *What Dreams We Have: The Wright Brothers and their Hometown of Dayton, Ohio*, online book; Van Deurs, appendix A: Early Naval Aviators, in *Wings for the Fleet*.

9   "1910–1914 Wright Model B," *Just the Facts*, Wright Brothers Aeroplane Co., accessed September 26, 2019, www.wrightbrothers.org/Information_Desk/Just_the_Facts/Airplanes/Model_B.htm.

10 Nisewaner and Walden, Journal of Family Memories.

11 "Kenneth Whiting, Pioneer Naval Aviator," Diary of Bishop Milton Wright, *Out of the Box*, Special Collections and Archives, Wright State University, accessed October 23, 2019, www.libraries.wright.edu/community/outofthebox/2014/08/14/kenneth-whiting-pioneer-naval-aviator/.

12 "Kenneth Whiting, Pioneer Naval Aviator," Diary of Bishop Milton Wright, *Out of the Box*, Special Collections and Archives, Wright State University, accessed October 23, 2019, www.libraries.wright.edu/community/outofthebox/2014/08/14/kenneth-whiting-pioneer-naval-aviator/; Nisewaner and Walden, Journal of Family Memories.

13 Nisewaner and Walden, Journal of Family Memories; Kenneth Whiting Papers, MS294, Nimitz Library.

14 "NAS Pensacola, FL History," accessed September 26, 2019, www.PensacolaNavalHousing.com; Goodspeed, "One Hundred Years at Pensacola," *Naval History Magazine*, United States Naval Institute Annapolis, Maryland, December 2014, usni.org/magazines/naval-history-magazine/2014/december/one-hundred-years-pensacola.

15 Van Deurs, *Wings for the Fleet*, p. 118.

16 Kenneth Whiting files, NAS Whiting Field; Nisewaner and Walden, Journal of Family Memories.

17 Van Deurs, *Wings for the Fleet*, p. 119.

18 Ibid.

19 Kenneth Whiting files, NAS Whiting Field.

20 Van Deurs, *Wings for the Fleet*, pp. 124–125.

21 Nisewaner and Walden, Journal of Family Memories.

22 Ibid.

23 Ibid.

24 Kenneth Whiting files, NAS Whiting Field.

25 Van Deurs, *Wings for the Fleet*, pp. 126–127; Kenneth Whiting Papers, MS294, Nimitz Library.

26 Nisewaner and Walden, Journal of Family Memories.

27 Van Deurs, *Wings for the Fleet*, pp. 148–153.

28 Ibid.; Kenneth Whiting Papers, MS294, Nimitz Library.

29 Dyer, p. 3.

30 Ibid., p. 4.

31 Ibid.

32 Ibid.

33 Turnbull and Lord, p. 132; Van Deurs, *Wings for the Fleet*, pp. 136–137.

34 Nisewaner and Walden, Journal of Family Memories.

35 Van Deurs, *Wings for the Fleet*, p. 157.

36 Ibid., p. 137.

37 Ibid.

38 Ibid., p. 138.

39 Ibid., p. 139.

40 Ibid., p. 152–153.

41 Brennan, p. 21.

42 Van Deurs, *Wings for the Fleet*, p. 151.

43 Brennan, p. 21.

44 Van Deurs, *Wings for the Fleet*, pp. 154–155.

45 Turnbull and Lord, pp. 131–132.

46 Mueller, pp. 204–206.

47 Ibid., pp. 206–210; Turnbull and Lord, p. 132.

48 Brennan, p. 21.

49 Bureau of Naval Personnel, "Re: Service of Captain Kenneth Whiting, United States Navy, Retired, Active, Deceased," May 12, 1943; Carroll Van West, "Albert Gleaves," *Tennessee Encyclopedia*, October 8, 2017, www.tennesseeencyclopedia.net/entries/albert-gleaves/; "USS *Seattle*," accessed September 27, 2019, www.history.navy.mil/research/histories/ship-histories/danfs/s/seattle-i.html.

50 "USS *Washington*/USS *Seattle* ACR-11," accessed September 27, 2019, www.freepages.rootsweb.com/~ncacunithistories/military/USS-Washington.html.

51 Nisewaner and Walden, Journal of Family Memories.

52 Turnbull and Lord, pp. 131–132.

53 Kenneth Whiting Papers, MS 294, Nimitz Library; Gleaves, p. 134.

54 Van Deurs, *Wings for the Fleet*, pp. 142–143.

55 Nisewaner and Walden, Journal of Family Memories.

56 Goodspeed, "Whiting Key in Several Military Milestones," *Pensacola News Journal*, Pensacola, Florida, June 17, 2017, www.pnj.com/story/news/military/2017/06/17/whiting-key-several-military-milestones/399443001/; Nisewaner and Walden, Journal of Family Memories.

Chapter 6: Whiting Leads the First Americans "Over There"

[1] Bailey, pp. 706, 722–727.

[2] Ibid., p. 724.

[3] Rossano, foreword; Turnbull and Lord, pp. 89–90.

[4] "US Navy Aeronautic Detachment No. 1: The First American Unit Overseas in World War I," Naval History and Heritage Command, September 16, 2019, accessed June 15, 2022; Rossano, pp. 2–4.

[5] Ibid.; Rossano, introduction, p. 11.

[6] Rossano, p. 7.

[7] Nisewaner and Walden, Journal of Family Memories.

[8] Rossano, pp. 6–7,12, 20–21,121; Wortman, p. 121.

[9] Vego, p. 2.

[10] Ibid., p. 1.

[11] Ibid., p. 2; Robert C. Rubel, "Deconstructing Nimitz's Principle of Calculated Risk," *Naval War College Review* vol. 68, no. 1, article 4, p. 1, www.digital-commons.usnwc.edu/cgi/viewcontent.cgi?referer=https://www.google.com/& httpsredir=1&article=1181&context=nwc-review; Potter, p. 87.

[12] Wortman, p. 121; Turnbull and Lord, p. 119; Rossano, pp. 7–8.

[13] Rossano, p. 9; Kenneth Whiting Papers, MS294, Nimitz Library.

[14] Wortman, p. 121.

[15] Turnbull and Lord, p. 119,

[16] Ibid.

[17] Wortman, p. 120; Goodspeed, "Whiting Key in Several Military Milestones," *PensacolaNewsJournal*,Pensacola,Florida,June17,2017,www.pnj.com/story/news/ military/2017/06/17/whiting-key-several-military-milestones/399443001/.

[18] Wortman, p. 120; "Remembering World War I: Gen. John J. Pershing Arrives in Europe," American Battle Monuments Commission, accessed October 23, 2019, www.abmc.gov/news-events/news/remembering-world-war-i-gen-john-j-pershing-arrives-europe; Evans and Grossnick, p. 31; Goodspeed, "Whiting Key in Several Military Milestones," *Pensacola News Journal*, Pensacola, Florida, June 17, 2017, www.pnj.com/story/news/military/2017/06/17/whiting-key-several-military-milestones/399443001/; "1917–1919: Test of Strength," Timeline, Naval History and Heritage Command, September 13, 2019, www. history.navy.mil/browse-by-topic/communities/naval-aviation/1917-1919. html.

[19] Turnbull and Lord, pp. 131–132; Mueller, pp. 207–210.

[20] Nisewaner and Walden, Journal of Family Memories.

[21] Ibid.

[22] Kenneth Whiting file, ZB Personnel file, Naval History and Heritage Command.

[23] Whiting to SecNav, "Report of Operations to Date," July 20, 1917, Box 910, ZGU, Records Group 45, National Archives and Records Administration, Washington, DC.

24 Ibid.

25 Rossano, introduction, pp. 17, 24–26.

26 Wortman, pp. 121–125.

27 "US Navy Aeronautic Detachment No. 1: The First American Unit Overseas in World War I," Naval History and Heritage Command, accessed June 15, 2022; Rossano, p. 13.

28 Rossano, p. 14.

29 "US Navy Aeronautic Detachment No. 1: The First American Unit Overseas in World War I," Naval History and Heritage Command, September 16, 2019, accessed June 15, 2022; Evans and Grossnick, *United States Naval Aviation 1910–1920*, p. 27, accessed June 15, 2022; Rossano, pp. 13–15.

30 Evans and Grossnick, *United States Naval Aviation 1910–1920*, p. 27, accessed June 15, 2022; Rossano, pp. 15–16.

31 Rossano, pp. 15–16.

32 Evans and Grossnick, *United States Naval Aviation 1910–1920*, p. 28, accessed June 15, 2022; Turnbull and Lord, p. 143; Rossano, p. 16.

33 Turnbull and Lord, pp. 119–120.

34 Ibid.

35 Rossano, pp. 17–20; Whiting, "Report of Operations to Date," July 20, 1917.

36 Ibid.; Whiting, "Report of Operations to Date," July 20, 1917.

37 National Personnel Records Center, St. Louis, Missouri.

38 Rossano, pp. 20–23; Evans and Grossnick, p. 32; Whiting, "Report of Operations to Date," July 20, 1917.

39 Ibid., pp. 24–25.

40 Turnbull and Lord, pp. 120–121; Evans and Grossnick, p. 34.

41 Whiting to Admiral Sims, "Information and Suggestions for the Use of Seaplanes," August 26, 1917, Box 910, ZGU, Records Group 45, National Archives and Records Administration, Washington, DC.

42 Ibid.

43 Ibid.

44 Turnbull and Lord, p. 121.

45 Evans and Grossnick, p. 34.

46 Rossano, p. 30; Evans and Grossnick, p. 36.

47 Ibid., p. 42.

48 Ibid.

49 Turnbull and Lord, p. 139; Rossano, p. 44; Rossano and Wildenberg, p. 39; "CDR Grattan Colley 'Dyke' Dichman," Find a Grave, accessed October 23, 2019, www.findagrave.com/34270567/grattan-colley-dichman; Captain Virgil Childers Griffin Jr., Find a Grave, accessed October 23, 2019, www.findagrave.com/memorial/34328248/virgil-childers-griffin; Mead, p. 207; "Lieutenant Sinton Returns," *Times Dispatch*, Richmond, Virginia, April 20, 1919, accessed October 23, 2019, www.newspapers.com/image/?clipping_id=9394094&fcfToken.

50 Tate, pp. 63–64; Memorandum to the Commanding Officer, from A.
    M. Pride, officer in charge, Experimental Division, US Naval Air Station
    Norfolk, November 11, 1930, National Personnel Records Center;
    Michael D. Withers, "Pride, Alfred Melville, ADM, Deceased," accessed
    October 2, 2019, www.navy.togetherweserved.com/servlet/twswebapp.
    WebApp?cmd=ShadowBoxProfile&type=Person&ID=454721; Mark L. Evans
    and Roy A. Grossnick, "The Great Depression 1930–1939," *United States Naval
    Aviation 1910–2010*, Naval History and Heritage Command, accessed October
    13, 2019, www.history.navy.mil/research/publications/publications-by-subject/
    naval-aviation-1910-2010.html.

Chapter 7: Whiting Takes Command at NAS Killingholme
1   Rossano, p. 42.
2   Turnbull and Lord, p. 120.
3   Rossano, p. 168.
4   Ibid., pp. 168–169; Lt. Col. T. H. Bane, US Army Signal Corps, "Report on
    RNAS Station, Felixstowe, England and General Intelligence," February 6,
    1918, p. 5.
5   Turnbull and Lord, p. 132; Kenneth Whiting Papers, MS 294, Nimitz Library.
6   Rossano, p. 170.
7   Ibid., p. 169.
8   Turnbull and Lord, p. 136; Rossano, p. 169.
9   Rossano, p. 169; Kenneth Whiting Papers, MS 294, Nimitz Library.
10 Ibid., p. 17.
11 Ibid., pp. 170–171.
12 Ibid., p. 173.
13 Ibid., p. 174; Evans and Grossnick, p. 47; Turnbull and Lord, p. 139.
14 Nisewaner and Walden, Journal of Family Memories.
15 Kenneth Whiting Papers, MS 294, Nimitz Library; National Personnel Records
    Center, St. Louis, Missouri.
16 Rossano, p. 182.
17 Ibid., p. 184.
18 Wortman, pp. 202–203.
19 Ibid., pp. 208–209.
20 Ibid., pp. 211–212.
21 National Personnel Records Center, St. Louis, Missouri.
22 Evans and Grossnick, p. 47; Kenneth Whiting file, MS294, Nimitz Library;
    "Kenneth Whiting," *Dictionary of American Fighting Ships*, accessed
    September 28, 2019, www.history.navy.mil/danfs/k2/kenneth_whiting.htm;
    "US Naval Air Station: England: Killingholme," *Naval History and Heritage
    Command*, accessed September 27, 2019, www.history.navy.mil/content/
    history/wwi-aviation/u-s-naval-air-stations/us-naval-air-stations-england/

england-Killingholme.html; www.larchmonthistory.org/memorials/individual/Times/19430429WhitingAnnouncement.html.

[23] Van Deurs, *Wings for the Fleet*, p. 119.

[24] Ibid., pp. 119–120; Kent Weekly, "Whiting, Kenneth, CAPT, Deceased," Togetherweserved.com, accessed October 23, 2019, www.navy.togetherweserved.com/usn/servlet/tws.webapp. WebApp?cmd=ShadowBoxProfile&type=Person&ID=458615.

Chapter 8: Continuing the Battle for a Plane Carrier

[1] Tate, p. 63; McDonald, p. 16; Muir, "Birth of the Aircraft Carrier," *Quarterly Journal of Military History* vol. 30, no. 2 (Winter, 2018), www.historynet.com/birth-aircraft-carrier.htm; Nisewaner and Walden, Journal of Family Memories.

[2] Muir, "Birth of the Aircraft Carrier," *Quarterly Journal of Military History* vol. 30, no. 2 (Winter, 2018) www.historynet.com/birth-aircraft-carrier.htm.

[3] Ibid.; "*HMS Ark Royal*: United Kingdom (1914) Seaplane Carrier," Naval Encyclopedia.com/ww1/UK/hms-ark-royal-1914.

[4] Tillman, p. 46.

[5] Muir, "Birth of the Aircraft Carrier," *Quarterly Journal of Military History* vol. 30, no. 2 (Winter, 2018), www.historynet.com/birth-aircraft-carrier.htm.

[6] Van Deurs, *Wings for the Fleet*, p. 30.

[7] R. L. Layman, "Furious and the Tondern Raid," *Warship International* vol. 10, no. 4, p. 381; Tillman, p. 49.

[8] Nisewaner and Walden, Journal of Family Memories.

[9] Ibid.

[10] Ibid.

[11] Ibid.

[12] Van Deurs, *Wings for the Fleet*, pp. 157–158.

[13] "Admiral William Shepherd Benson, 1st Chief of Naval Operations," September 10, 2019, www.Geni.com/people/Admiral-William-Benson-1st-Chief-of-Naval-Operations/6000000023433345777

[14] Jeffery S. Underwood, *The Wings of Democracy: the Influence of Airpower on the Roosevelt Administration, 1933–1941* (College Station: Texas A&M University Press, 1991), p. 11; Price, Scott T., "A Study of the General Board of the US Navy, 1929–1933," Naval History and Heritage Command, May 6, 2017, pp. 11–12, www.history.navy.mil/research/library/online-reading-room/title-list-alphabetically/s/study-general-board-usnavy-1929-1933.html.

[15] Van Deurs, *Wings for the Fleet*, pp. 142–143.

[16] Van Deurs, "The Aircraft Collier Langley," p. 25; Tate, p. 62.

[17] Ibid.; McDonald, p. 17; "Table 21-Ships on Navy List June 30, 1919," Congressional Serial Set, US Government Printing Office: 766, 1921; *Dictionary of American Fighting Ships* vol. IV, pp. 45–47, DANFS Online, www.hazegray.org/danfs/auxil/ac-3.htm.

18. Van Deurs, "The Aircraft Collier Langley," p. 26; Reynolds, p. 171; Tillman, p. 46.

19. Pennoyer, "Notes," p. 1; Kenneth Whiting files, NAS Whiting Field; Van Deurs, "The Aircraft Collier Langley," p. 25.

20. Ibid., pp. 1–2; Van Deurs, "The Aircraft Collier Langley," p. 26; Kenneth Whiting files, NAS Whiting Field.

21. Van Deurs, "The Aircraft Collier Langley," p. 26; Wadle, p. 13; Van Deurs, "The Aircraft Collier Langley," p. 27.

22. Wadle, p. 13.

23. Kenneth Whiting Papers, MS 294, Nimitz Library; Kenneth Whiting files, NAS Whiting Field.

24. Ibid.; Kenneth Whiting files, NAS Whiting Field.

25. Ibid.; Kenneth Whiting files, NAS Whiting Field.

26. Wadle, p. 13; McDonald, pp. 16–17.

27. Kenneth Whiting Papers, MS 294, Nimitz Library; McDonald, pp. 16–17.

28. *Dictionary of American Fighting Ships* vol. IV, pp. 45–47, DANFS Online, www.hazegray.org/danfs/auxil/ac-3.htm.

29. Tom D. Crouch, "Samuel Pierpont Langley," August 18, 2019, www.brittanica.com/biography/samuel-pierpont-langley.

30. Pennoyer, "Notes," pp. 2–3.

31. Van Deurs, *Wings for the Fleet*, p. 30.

32. Pennoyer, "Notes," p. 2; Kenneth Whiting file, NAS Whiting Field; National Personnel Records Center, St. Louis, Missouri.

33. Tate, p. 63.

34. Ibid., pp. 63–67; Pennoyer, "Notes," p. 9; Kenneth Whiting file, NAS Whiting Field.

35. Pennoyer, "Notes," pp. 9–10; Kenneth Whiting file, NAS Whiting Field.

36. Ibid., p. 10; Kenneth Whiting file, NAS Whiting Field.

37. Ibid., p. 10; Kenneth Whiting file, NAS Whiting Field.

38. Ibid., p. 5; Kenneth Whiting file, NAS Whiting Field.

39. Ibid., p. 6; Kenneth Whiting file, NAS Whiting Field.

40. Van Deurs, *Wings for the Fleet*, pp. 30–31.

41. Pennoyer, "Notes," p. 6; Van Deurs, *Wings for the Fleet*, p. 31.

42. Ibid., pp. 8–9; Kenneth Whiting file, NAS Whiting Field.

43. Tate, pp. 63–65, Pennoyer, "Notes," pp. 10–11; Kenneth Whiting file, NAS Whiting Field.

44. Pennoyer, "Notes," pp. 10–11; Kenneth Whiting file, NAS Whiting Field.

45. Ibid., p. 11; Kenneth Whiting file, NAS Whiting Field.

46. Ibid., p. 11; Kenneth Whiting file, NAS Whiting Field.

47. "William Moffett Facts," *Your Dictionary: Biography*, October 2, 2019, www.biography.yourdictionary.com/william-moffett; "William A. Moffett," Barron Hilton: Pioneers of Flight Gallery, Smithsonian Air and Space Museum, October 2, 2019, www.pioneers of flight.si.edu/content/william-moffett; Clark G.

Reynolds, "William A. Moffett" (Oxford University Press, September 16, 2019), www.encyclopedia.com/history/encyclopedias-almanacs-transcripts-and-maps/moffett-william.

48 "Re: Service of Captain Kenneth Whiting, United States Navy, Retired, Active, Deceased," May 12, 1943, National Personnel Records Center, St. Louis, Missouri; "Early Aircraft Carriers: Introduction of Aircraft Carriers following WWI," *Literary Digest*, February 18, 1922, www.1920-1930.com/military/aircraft-carriers.html.

49 McDonald, p. 21.

50 "HMS *Hermes* (D 95): Aircraft Carriers of the Hermes Class," *Fighting the U-Boats: Allied Warships*, October 3, 2019, www.uboat.net/allies/warships/ship/3256.html; "Aircraft Carrier: Ship," *Encyclopedia Britannica*, May 27, 1999, www.britannica.com/technology/aircraft-carrier.

51 "Washington Naval Conference," Encyclopedia.com, September 19, 2019, www.encyclopedia.com/history/dictionaries-thesauruses-pictures-and-press-releases/washington-naval-conference.

52 Tate, p. 63.

53 "Early Aircraft Carriers: Introduction of Aircraft Carriers following WWI," *Literary Digest*, February 18, 1922, www.1920-1930.com/military/aircraft-carriers.html; Wadle, p. 16.

54 Kennedy Hickman, "World War II: USS *Saratoga* (CV-3), Thought Co., accessed 10/3/2019, www.thoughtco.com/uss-saratoga-cv-3-2361553; "Interesting Facts about the Panama Canal," Panama Canal Museum, University of Florida, Gainesville, Florida, accessed October 3, 2019, www.cms.uflib.ufl.edu/pcm/facts/aspx.

55 Kenneth Whiting file, ZB Personnel files; Nisewaner and Walden, Journal of Family Memories.

56 Van Deurs, "The Aircraft Collier Langley," p. 27; Tate, p. 65; Lee, Bill, "Wings over Water," p. 13, www.nnapprentice.com/alumni/letter/Wings_Over_Water.pdf, C:/Users/Felix/Documents/Wings_Over_Water.pdf; Pennoyer, "Notes," p. 13; Kenneth Whiting file, NAS Whiting Field; Bureau of Naval Personnel, "Re: Service of: Captain Kenneth Whiting, United States Navy, Retired, Active, Deceased," May 12, 1943; Kermit Bonner, *Final Voyages* (Nashville: Turner Publishing Company, 1956), p. 178.

57 Nisewaner and Walden, Journal of Family Memories.

58 Ibid.

59 Ibid.

60 Ibid.; "The Clarkson Cowl Residence," (Old Long Island, April 10, 2014), accessed October 24, 2019, www.oldlongisland.com/2014/04/the-clarkson-cowl-residence.html.

61 Tate, pp. 63–65.

62 McDonald, p. 17.

63 Lee, "Wings over Water," pp. 2, 6.

64 Tate, pp. 62, 65.

65 Ibid., p. 65.

66 Ibid., p. 65.

67 McDonald, p. 19; Lee, "Wings over Water," pp. 15–16; Pennoyer, "Notes," pp. 15–16; Kenneth Whiting file, NAS Whiting Field.

68 Ibid., pp. 18–19.

69 ADM Scott H. Swift, "To Train the Fleet for War: The US Navy Fleet Problems, 1923–1940," US Naval War College Historical Monograph Series (Newport, R. I.: Naval War College Press, 2010); Corbin Williamson, review of *To Train the Fleet for War: The US Navy Fleet Problems, 1923–1940*, Albert A. Nofi, book review: *To Train the Fleet for War: The US Navy Fleet Problems, 1923–1940*, Naval Historical Foundation, September 29, 2011, www.navyhistory.org/2011//09/book-review-to-train-the-fleet-for-war-the u-s-navy-fleet-problems-1923-1940/.

70 Pennoyer, "Notes," p. 18; Kenneth Whiting file, NAS Whiting Field.

71 Ibid., p. 19; Kenneth Whiting file, NAS Whiting Field.

72 Ibid.; Kenneth Whiting file, NAS Whiting Field.

73 Tate, p. 67; Pennoyer, p. 16; Lee, "Wings over Water," p. 8.

74 Pennoyer, "Notes," p. 16; Kenneth Whiting file, NAS Whiting Field.

75 Ibid., pp. 11–12; "America's First Aircraft Carrier—USS *Langley* (CV-1)," *Naval History* (blog), Warfighting First, Platforms, People (Annapolis, MD: United States Naval Institute, March 20, 2014), www.navalhistory.org/2014/03/20/ americas-aircraft-carrier-uss-langley-cv-1-warfighting-first-platforms-people; VADM A. M. Pride, USN, "Comment and Discussion," *Proceedings* (Annapolis, Maryland: US Naval Institute, January 1979), p. 89; Kenneth Whiting file, NAS Whiting Field.

76 Tate, p. 64; Lee, "Wings Over Water," p. 6.

77 Reynolds, p. 198.

78 Pennoyer, "Notes," p. 12; Kenneth Whiting file, NAS Whiting Field.

79 Ibid., pp. 12–13; Kenneth Whiting file, NAS Whiting Field.

80 Ibid., p. 16; Kenneth Whiting file, NAS Whiting Field.

81 Tate, p. 68.

82 Ibid., p. 62–69; Pennoyer, "Notes," p. 6; Nisewaner and Walden, Journal of Family Memories.

83 Pennoyer, "Notes," p. 6; Kenneth Whiting file, NAS Whiting Field.

84 Ibid., pp. 6–7; Kenneth Whiting file, NAS Whiting Field.

85 Tate, pp. 64, 68.

86 Nisewaner and Walden, Journal of Family Memories.

87 Ibid.

88 "About John Hays Hammond Jr.," Hammond Castle Museum, accessed October 7, 2019, www.hammondcastle.org/about/john-hays-hammond-jr/; "John Hays Hammond Jr., American Inventor," *Encyclopedia Britannica*, July 20, 1998,

www.britannica.com/biography/John-Hays-Hammond-Jr;   Nisewaner   and Walden, Journal of Family Memories.

89 Nisewaner and Walden, Journal of Family Memories.

90 Tate, pp. 68–69; Pennoyer, "Notes," p. 13; Kenneth Whiting file, NAS Whiting Field; Sears, pp. 113–114; Bonner, p. 178.

91 National Personnel Records Center, St. Louis, Missouri.

92 Nisewaner and Walden, Journal of Family Memories.

93 Tate, pp. 68–69.

Chapter 9: Building More Carriers and Fighting the Billy Mitchell Wars

1   "Re: Service of Captain Kenneth Whiting, United States Navy, Retired, Active, Deceased," May 12, 1943, National Personnel Records Center, St. Louis, Missouri; Nisewaner and Walden, Journal of Family Memories, reprinted in *Naval Aviation News* (Ohio State University Library, June 25, 1979), p. 5, accessed March 11, 2020, books.google.com/books?id=z10zEtNQj80C&pg=RA9-PA8&1pg=RA9-.

2   "USS *Wright* AZ-1," *Dictionary of American Fighting Ships* vol. VIII, pp. 480–483, accessed October 9, 2019, www.hazegray.org/danfs/auxil/az-1.htm.

3   Ibid.

4   "Photo Archive: USS *San Clemente*, ex USS *Wright* (AV-1), USS *Wright* (AZ-1), *Nav Source Online: Service Ship*, www.navsource.org/archives/09/41/4101. htm; "Wright," *Dictionary of American Fighting Ships* vol. VIII, pp. 480–483, accessed October 9, 2019, www.hazegray.org/danfs/auxil/az-1.htm; Robert Jon Cox, "The Battle Off Samar: Taffy 3 at Leyte Gulf," BOSAMAR website, accessed October 20, 2019, www.bosamar.com.

5   "Wright," *Dictionary of American Fighting Ships*, Naval History and Heritage Command vol. VIII, p. 482, accessed October 21, 2019, www.hazegray.org/ dafs/auxil/azi.htm.

6   Kenneth Whiting Papers, MS 294, Nimitz Library.

7   Davis, *The Billy Mitchell Affair*, p. 25.

8   Ibid., pp. 26–27; Minnie L. Jones (IMCOM), "William 'Billy' Mitchell—the Father of the United States Air Force," (United States Army, January 28, 2010), accessed June 7, 2020, www.army.mil/article/33580/william_billy_mitchell_ the_father_of_the_united_states_air_force; C. V. Glines, "William 'Billy' Mitchell: Air Power Visionary," accessed June 7, 2020, www.historynet.com, william-billy-mitchell-an-air-power-visionary.

9   Ibid., pp. 28–38.

10 Ibid., pp. 38–42; C. V. Glines, "William 'Billy' Mitchell: Air Power Visionary," accessed June 7, 2020, www.historynet.com, william-billy-mitchell-an-air-power-visionary; Minnie L. Jones (IMCOM), "William 'Billy' Mitchell—the Father of the United States Air Force," (United States Army, January 28, 2010), accessed June 7, 2020, www.army.mil/article/33580/ william_billy_mitchell_the_father_of_the_united_states_air_force.

11 Ibid., p. 42, 44; Minnie L. Jones (IMCOM), "William 'Billy' Mitchell—the Father of the United States Air Force," (United States Army, January 28, 2010), accessed June 7, 2020, www.army.mil/article/33580/william_billy_mitchell_the_father_of_the_united_states_air_force.

12 Ibid., p. 47; Minnie L. Jones (IMCOM), "William 'Billy' Mitchell—the Father of the United States Air Force" (United States Army, January 28, 2010), accessed June 7, 2020, www.army.mil/article/33580/william_billy_mitchell_the_father_of_the_united_states_air_force

13 Ibid., p. 49.

14 Ibid., p. 49, 52; C. V. Glines, "William 'Billy' Mitchell: Air Power Visionary," accessed June 7, 2020, www.historynet.com, william-billy-mitchell-an-air-power-visionary.

15 Ibid., p. 53, 58; C. V. Glines, "William 'Billy' Mitchell: Air Power Visionary," accessed June 7, 2020, www.historynet.com, william-billy-mitchell-an-air-power-visionary; Minnie L. Jones (IMCOM), "William 'Billy' Mitchell—the Father of the United States Air Force," June 7, 2020, United States Army, January 28, 2010, www.army.mil/article/33580/william_billy_mitchell_the_father_of_the_united_states_air_force.

16 Ibid., pp. 88–89.

17 Ibid., p. 225, 239.

18 Nisewaner and Walden, Journal of Family Memories; Charles F. Downs II, "Calvin Coolidge, Dwight Morrow, and the Air Commerce Act of 1926," *Essays, Papers, and Addresses* (Calvin Coolidge Presidential Foundation), accessed October 9, 2019, www.coolidgefoundation.org/resources/essays-papers-addresses-13/.

19 *Report of President's Aircraft Board: November 30, 1925*, title page; Charles F. Downs II, "Calvin Coolidge, Dwight Morrow, and the Air Commerce Act of 1926," *Essays, Papers, and Addresses* (Calvin Coolidge Presidential Foundation, June 20, 2001), www.coolidgefoundation.org/resources/essays-papers-addresses-13/; Turnbull and Lord, p. 252; Davis, pp. 228–232.

20 Ibid.; Charles F. Downs II, "Calvin Coolidge, Dwight Morrow, and the Air Commerce Act of 1926," *Essays, Papers, and Addresses* (Calvin Coolidge Presidential Foundation, June 20, 2001), www.coolidgefoundation.org/resources/essays-papers-addresses-13/; Turnbull and Lord, p. 252.

21 Statement of Commander Kenneth Whiting, United States Navy, *Hearings before the President's Aircraft Board: November 30, 1925* vol. 2, pp. 819–865.

22 Davis, pp. 12, 13, 26.

23 Statement of Commander Kenneth Whiting, United States Navy, *Hearings before the President's Aircraft Board: November 30, 1925* vol. 2, pp. 820, 849.

24 Ibid., pp. 820–823.

25 Ibid., pp. 820–821, 846.

26 Ibid., p. 820.

27 Ibid., p. 822–832.

28 Ibid., pp. 824–832, 848–850,

29 Ibid., p. 823.

30 Ibid., pp. 835–836, 840, 847.

31 Ibid., pp. 858–861.

32 Ibid., pp. 863–864.

33 *Report of President's Aircraft Board: November 30, 1925*, pp. 13, 22.

34 Ibid., p. 23, 25.

35 Ibid.

36 Ibid., p. 24.

37 Ibid., p. 25.

38 Ibid.

39 Downs, "Calvin Coolidge, Dwight Morrow, and the Air Commerce Act of 1926," *Wortman*, pp. 270–271; Van Tol, p. 82; Turnbull and Lord, p. 256.

40 Rossano, pp. 369–370; Kenneth Whiting file, NAS Whiting Field; Tillman, p. 48.

41 Turnbull and Lord, p. 195; C. V. Glines, "William 'Billy' Mitchell: Air Power Visionary," accessed June 7, 2020, www.historynet.com/william-billy-mitchell-an-air-power-visionary.htm; Minnie L. Jones (IMCOM), "William 'Billy' Mitchell—the Father of the United States Air Force," accessed June 7, 2020, www.army.mil/article/33680/william_billy_mitchell_the-father-of_the_united_states_air_force.

42 Nisewaner and Walden, Journal of Family Memories.

43 R. D. Layman, *Naval Aviation in the First World War* (Annapolis, Maryland: Naval Institute Press, 1996), p. 195; Manley R. Irwin, "A Note on Public Sector Integration: the Decline of British Naval Aviation, 1914–1945," *Review of Industrial Organization*, February 1999, pp. 85–86; Lieutenant Philip D. Mayer, US Navy, "Incubate Innovation: Aviation Lessons from the Interwar Period," *Proceedings* (Annapolis, Maryland: United States Naval Institute, December 2019), p. 41; Nisewaner and Walden, Journal of Family Memories.

44 Rossano, pp. 369–370; Sears, pp. 41–42; Kenneth Whiting Papers, MS 294, Nimitz Library; Nisewaner and Walden, Journal of Family Memories.

45 Kennedy Hickman, "Military Aviation: Brigadier General Billy Mitchell," ThoughtCo., accessed October 9, 2019, www.thoughtco.com/military-aviation-brigadier-general-billy-mitchell-2360544; Minnie L. Jones (IMCOM), "William 'Billy' Mitchell—the Father of the United States Air Force," accessed June 7, 2020, United States Army, January 28, 2010, www.army.mil/article/33580/william_billy_mitchell_the_father_of_the_united_states_air_force; "Brigadier General William 'Billy' Mitchell," National Museum of the United States Air Force, April 9, 2015, www.nationalmuseum.af.mil/Visit/Museum-Exhibits/Fact-Sheets/Display/Articles/196418/brig-gen-william-billy-mitchell/; Rebecca Maksel, "The Billy Mitchell Court-Martial," Air and Space Museum, accessed October 26, 2019, www.airspacemag.com/history-of-the-billy-mitchell-court-martial-136828592/; Davis, p. 344; "Letter from the Secretary of the Navy to Commander Kenneth Whiting, USN, Bureau of Aeronautics, Navy Department," November 11, 1925, National Personnel Records Center, St. Louis, Missouri; C. V. Glines, "William 'Billy' Mitchell: Air Power Visionary," accessed June 7, 2020, www.historynet.com, william-billy-mitchell-an-air-power-visionary.

46 Davis, pp. 306–308; C. V. Glines, "William 'Billy' Mitchell: Air Power Visionary," accessed June 7, 2020, www.historynet.com, william-billy-mitchell-an-air-power-visionary.

47 Kennedy Hickman, "Military Aviation: Brigadier General Billy Mitchell," ThoughtCo., accessed October 9, 2019, www.thoughtco.com/military-aviation-brigadier-general-billy-mitchell-2360544; Minnie L. Jones (IMCOM), "William 'Billy' Mitchell—the Father of the United States Air Force," accessed June 7, 2020, United States Army, January 28, 2010, www.army.mil/article/33580/william_billy_mitchell_the_father_of_the_united_states_air_force; "Brigadier General William 'Billy' Mitchell," National Museum of the United States Air Force, April 9, 2015, www.nationalmuseum.af.mil/Visit/Museum-Exhibits/Fact-Sheets/Display/Articles/196418/brig-gen-william-billy-mitchell/; Rebecca Maksel, "The Billy Mitchell Court-Martial," Air and Space Museum, accessed October 26, 2019, www.airspacemag.com/history-of-the-billy-mitchell-court-martial-136828592/, Copyright YYYY Smithsonian Institution, Reprinted with permission from Smithsonian Enterprises, All rights reserved, Reproduction in any medium is strictly limited without permission from Smithsonian magazine; Davis, p. 344; "Letter from the Secretary of the Navy to Commander Kenneth Whiting, USN, Bureau of Aeronautics, Navy Department," November 11, 1925, National Personnel Records Center, St. Louis, Missouri; Davis, pp. 339, 341; C. V. Glines, "William 'Billy' Mitchell: Air Power Visionary," accessed June 7, 2020, www.historynet.com, william-billy-mitchell-an-air-power-visionary.

48 Eisenhower, p. 173; Hickman, "Military Aviation: Brigadier General Billy Mitchell"; Turnbull and Lord, p. 195; Rossano, pp. 369–370; Van Deurs, pp. 157–158.

49 "Re: Service of Captain Kenneth Whiting, United States Navy, Retired, Active, Deceased," May 12, 1943, National Personnel Records Center, St. Louis, Missouri; "USS Saratoga," Dictionary of American Fighting Ships vol. VI (1979), pp. 339–342, accessed October 10, 2019, www.hazegray.org/danfs/carriers/cv-3.htm; Hickman, "World War II: USS Saratoga (cv-3)," ThoughtCo., July 3, 2019, www.thoughtco.com/uss-saratoga-cv-3-2361553; Nisewaner and Walden, Journal of Family Memories.

50 Nisewaner and Walden, Journal of Family Memories; Reynolds, p. 215.

51 Ibid.; Nisewaner and Walden, Journal of Family Memories.

52 Ibid.; Nisewaner and Walden, Journal of Family Memories.

53 National Personnel Records Center, St. Louis, Missouri; Nisewaner and Walden, Journal of Family Memories.

54 Nisewaner and Walden, Journal of Family Memories.

55 "Early Birds of Aviation Inc. Collection," Smithsonian Online Virtual Archives, Smithsonian Institution, accessed October 10, 2019, www.sova.si.edu/details/NASM.XXXX.0566#ref364, Kenneth Whiting documentation available in Contained Box 36, folder 41.

56 Nisewaner and Walden, Journal of Family Memories.

57 Van Deurs, *Wings for the Fleet*, p. 157; "Saratoga V (CV-3)," *Dictionary of American Fighting Ships*, Naval History and Heritage Command, September 2, 2015, www.history.navy.mil/research/histories/ship-histories/danfs/s/saratoga-v. html; "Interesting Facts about the Panama Canal," Panama Canal Museum, University of Florida, Gainesville, Florida. accessed October 3, 2019, www. cms.uflib.ufl.edu/pcm/facts/aspx.; Nisewaner and Walden, Journal of Family Memories

58 Van Deurs, *Wings for the Fleet*, p. 157; Curtis Utz, "Fleet Problem IX: January 1929," Naval History and Heritage Command, September 5, 2019, www.history. navy.mil/browse-by-topic/heritage/usn-lessons-learned/fleet-problem-ix.html.

59 Nisewaner and Walden, Journal of Family Memories.

60 Ibid.

61 Kenneth Whiting file, ZB Personnel files; "Re: Service of Captain Kenneth Whiting, United States Navy, Retired, Active, Deceased," May 12, 1943, National Personnel Records Center, St. Louis, Missouri.

62 Nisewaner and Walden, Journal of Family Memories.

63 National Personnel Records Center, St. Louis, Missouri.

64 Ibid.

65 Ibid.; "Re: Service of Captain Kenneth Whiting, United States Navy, Retired, Active, Deceased," May 12, 1943, National Personnel Records Center, St. Louis, Missouri; Keith Allen, "Notes on US Fleet Organisation [sic] and Disposition," September 30, 2001, www.gwpda.org/naval/fdus0001.htm.

66 Nisewaner and Walden, Journal of Family Memories.

67 Ibid. Nisewaner and Walden, Journal of Family Memories.

68 Ibid. Nisewaner and Walden, Journal of Family Memories.

69 Ibid. Nisewaner and Walden, Journal of Family Memories.

70 Ibid. Nisewaner and Walden, Journal of Family Memories.

71 Ibid. Nisewaner and Walden, Journal of Family Memories.

72 National Personnel Records Center, St. Louis, Missouri.

Chapter 10: Command at Hampton Roads and Norfolk Casts a Shadow over Whiting's Career

1 National Personnel Records Center, St. Louis, Missouri

2 "The Origins of Navy Day," Military.com, accessed October 10, 2019, www. military.com/military-appreciation-month/origins-of-navy-day.html; National Personnel Records Center, St. Louis, Missouri.

3 National Personnel Records Center, St. Louis, Missouri.

4 Ibid.

5 Ibid.

6 Ibid.

7 Ibid.

8 Ibid.

9 Ibid.

10 Steven Loomis (Saigon Shipyard), "Burrage, Guy, VADM, Deceased," Togetherweserved.com, accessed October 11, 2019, www.navy.togetherweserved.com/usn/servlet/tws.webapp. WebApp?cmd=ShadowBoxProfile&type=Person&ID=693906; Kent Weekly; "Upham, Frank Brooks, ADM, Deceased," Togetherweserved.com, accessed October 11, 2019, www.navy.togetherweserved.com/usn/servlet/tws.webapp. WebApp?cmd=ShadowBoxProfile&type=Person&ID=508011; "ADM Frank Brooks Upham, ID:669," Military Hall of Honor, accessed October 11, 2019, www.militaryhallofhonor.com/honoree-record.php?id=669; Reynolds, p. 223, 225.

11 National Personnel Records Center, St. Louis, Missouri.

12 Title 32, Code of Federal Regulations, National Personnel Records Center, St. Louis, Missouri, p. 332.

13 Michael D. Withers, OSCS, "Pride, Alfred Melville, ADM, deceased," Togetherweserved.com, accessed October 11, 2019, www.navy.togetherweserved.com/usn/servlet/tws.webapp. WebApp?cmd=ShadowBoxProfile&type=Person&ID=454721; Steven Loomis (SaigonShipyard), IC3, "Ingersoll, Stuart, VADM, Deceased," Togetherweserved. com, accessed October 11, 2019, www.navy.togetherweserved.com/usn/servlet/ tws.webapp.WebApp?cmd-ShadowBoxProfile&type=Person&ID=674039; Nisewaner and Walden, Journal of Family Memories.

14 "VADM Guy Hamilton Burrage," Find a Grave, May 25, 2009, accessed May 13, 2022, www.findagrave.com/memorial/37484552/guy-hamilton-burrage.

15 Nisewaner and Walden, Journal of Family Memories; Kenneth Whiting Papers, MS 294, Nimitz Library.

16 Ibid.

17 Ibid.

18 Ibid.; "Norman Schwartzkopf, United States General," *Encyclopedia Britannica*, accessed October 24, 2019, www.britannica.com/biography/ Norman-Schwartzkopf.

19 Ibid.; "VADM Guy Hamilton Burrage," Find a Grave, May 25, 2009, www. findagrave.com/memorial/37484552/guy-hamilton-burrage.

20 Ibid.

21 Ibid.; "Suspect in Lindbergh Kidnapping Case Held in New York," *The Evening Citizen* (Ottawa, Canada, September 21, 1934), p. 4, accessed October 25, 2019, www.news.google.com/newspapers?nid=2194&dat=19340921&id.

22 "Lindbergh Kidnapping," FBI: History: Famous Cases and Criminals, accessed October 11, 2019, fbi.gov/history/famous-cases/lindbergh-kidnapping.

23 "Re: Service of Captain Kenneth Whiting, United States Navy, Retired, Active, Deceased," May 12, 1943, National Personnel Records Center, St. Louis, Missouri.

24 Nisewaner and Walden, Journal of Family Memories.

Chapter 11: Moffett Fights to Remove the Shadow
1 "Re: Service of Captain Kenneth Whiting, United States Navy, Retired, Active, Deceased," May 12, 1943, National Personnel Records Center, St. Louis, Missouri; Reynolds, p. 255; Kent Weekly, "Kenneth Whiting, CAPT, Deceased," accessed October 12, 2019, www.navy.togetherweserved.com/usn/servlet/tws.webapp.WebApp?cmd=ShadowBoxProfile&type=Person&ID=4586.15; Nisewaner and Walden, Journal of Family Memories.

2 Reynolds, p. 255.

3 Nisewaner and Walden, Journal of Family Memories.

4 Ibid.; Robert J. Cressman, "Akron (ZRS-4), 1931–1933," *Dictionary of American Fighting Ships* (Naval History and Heritage Command, May 4, 2017), www.history.navy.mil/research/histories/ship-histories/danfs/a/akron.html; "May 6, 1937, Hindenberg Disaster," This Day in History, History.com, A & E Television Networks, www.history.com/this-day-in-history/the-hindenberg-disaster; "Fleet Admiral Ernest J. King, US Navy," National Sojourners, accessed October 12, 2019, www.nationalsojourners.org.wp-content/uploads/2017,08/King.

5 Kenneth Whiting Papers, MS 294, Nimitz Library; Nisewaner and Walden, Journal of Family Memories.

6 Nisewaner and Walden, Journal of Family Memories.

7 "Re: Service of Captain Kenneth Whiting, United States Navy, Retired, Active, Deceased," May 12, 1943, National Personnel Records Center, St. Louis, Missouri; "Ranger IX (CV-4), 1936–1946," *Dictionary of American Fighting Ships* (Naval History and Heritage Command, September 16, 2005), www.history.navy.mil/research/histories/ship-histories/danfs/r/ranger-ix.html; "USS *Ranger* (CV-4): Conventionally-Powered Aircraft Carrier," Military Factory, accessed October 12, 2019, www.militaryfactory.com/ships/detail.asp?ship_id=USS-Ranger-CV-4; "World War II: USS *Yorktown* (CV-5), ThoughtCo., accessed October 12, 2019, www.thoughtco.com/uss-yorktown-com-cv-5-2361555; *Wadle*, pp. 21, 104–105; Kenneth Whiting Papers, MS 294, Nimitz Library.

8 Wadle, p. 106.

9 National Personnel Records Center, St. Louis, Missouri.

10 Ibid.

11 Ibid.

12 "Re: Service of Captain Kenneth Whiting, United States Navy, Retired, Active, Deceased," May 12, 1943, National Personnel Records Center, St. Louis, Missouri; "ADM Frank Brooks Upham, ID:669," Military Hall of Honor, accessed October 11, 2019, www.militaryhallofhonor.com/honoree-record.php?id=669; Nisewaner and Walden, Journal of Family Memories; Kenneth Whiting Papers, MS 294, Nimitz Library; Herbert Hoover, p. 179, *Public Papers of Presidents of the United States*, 1930; National Personnel Records Center, St. Louis, Missouri.

13 Nisewaner and Walden, Journal of Family Memories; Kenneth Whiting Papers, MS 294, Nimitz Library; Kenneth Whiting file, NAS Whiting Field.

14 Scot McDonald, "Last of the Fleet Problems," September 1962, p. 37, C:/users/Felix/Downloads/car-6.pdf; "Casualties: US Navy and Marine Corps Personnel Killed and Injured in Selected Accidents and Other Incidents Not Directly the Result of Enemy Action," Naval Historical Center, Department of the Navy, accessed October 24, 2019, www.ibiblio/hyperwar/NHC/accidents; Nisewaner and Walden, Journal of Family Memories.

15 Nisewaner and Walden, Journal of Family Memories; "Re: Service of Captain Kenneth Whiting, United States Navy, Retired, Active, Deceased," May 12, 1943, National Personnel Records Center, St. Louis, Missouri.

16 "Villa Riviera: A General History," Villa Riviera, accessed October 13, 2019, www.villariviera.net/page/18138-307064/General-History.

17 Nisewaner and Walden, Journal of Family Memories.

18 Ibid.

19 Ibid.

20 Ibid.

21 Ibid.; "USS *Saratoga*," *Dictionary of American Fighting Ships* vol. VI (1979), pp. 339–342, accessed October 10, 2019, www.hazegray.org/danfs/carriers/cv-3.htm.

22 Ibid.; Reynolds, p. 223.

23 Ibid.

24 National Personnel Records Center, St. Louis, Missouri.

25 Nisewaner and Walden, Journal of Family Memories.

Chapter 12: Command Ashore in Beautiful Hawaii

1 "Re: Service of Captain Kenneth Whiting, United States Navy, Retired, Active, Deceased," May 12, 1943, National Personnel Records Center, St. Louis, Missouri; Kenneth Whiting Papers, MS 294, Nimitz Library.

2 Nisewaner and Walden, Journal of Family Memories.

3 Ibid.

4 Ibid.

5 Ibid.

6 Kenneth Whiting file, NAS Whiting Field.

7 Nisewaner and Walden, Journal of Family Memories.

8 Ibid.

9 Kenneth Whiting file, MS 294, Nimitz Library.

10 National Personnel Records Center, St. Louis, Missouri; William C. Shiel Jr., MD, FACP, FACR, "Medical Definition of Albuminuria," Medicine Net, accessed October 25, 2019, www.medicinenet.com/script/main/art.asp?articlekey=6851.

11 Ernest J. King and Walter Muir Whitehill, *Fleet Admiral King: A Naval Record* (New York City: W. W. Norton & Company, 1952), p. 266; "Kenneth Whiting

Papers 1901–1943: Finding Aid," February 2009, Kenneth Whiting Papers, MS 294, Special Collections & Archives Department, Nimitz Library, United States Naval Academy, www.edu/Library/sca/man-findingaids/view.php?f=MS_294; Nisewaner and Walden, Journal of Family Memories.

12 "PBY Catalina," Catalina Preservation Society, accessed October 13, 2019, www.pbycatalina.com/society-profile/.

13 Nisewaner and Walden, Journal of Family Memories

14 Ibid.

15 Thomas B. Buell, *Master of Sea Power: A Biography of Fleet Admiral Ernest J. King* (Annapolis, Maryland: Naval Institute Press, 2012), p. 223; Nisewaner and Walden, Journal of Family Memories

16 Nisewaner and Walden, Journal of Family Memories.

17 Ibid.

18 Ibid.

19 "S-Class (Herreshoff)," Sailboat Data.Com, accessed June 27, 2022, www.sailboatdata.com/sailboat/s-class-herreshoff, https://classicsailboats.org/n-g-herreshoff-c-class, www.s-class.org/new-page.

20 Doris L. Rich, *Amelia Earhart: A Biography* (Washington, DC: Smithsonian Institution Press, 1989), p. 245; "Amelia Earhart: First Lady of the Sky," Life Hero of the Week Profile, May 19, 1997, reprinted in Internet Archive: Wayback Machine, accessed October 13, 2019, www.webarchive.org/web/20021005082222/http://www.life.com/Life/heroes/newsleters/nlearhart.html; Kenneth Whiting file, NAS Whiting Field.

21 Kenneth Whiting file, NAS Whiting Field.

22 Ibid.; Sarina Houston, "Learn about Amelia Earhart's Lockheed Model 10 Electra: the Aircraft She Flew on Her Attempted Flight Around the World," Balance Careers, accessed October 13, 2019, www.thebalancecareers.com/earhart-lockheed-model-10-electra-282579.

23 Nisewaner and Walden, Journal of Family Memories.

24 "Amelia Earhart with Three Military Men," March 18, 1937, e-archive, Purdue University Libraries, www.lib.purdue.edu/aearhart; Brennan, p. 23.

25 "Amelia Earhart Biography," Biography.com website, A & E Television Networks, April 2, 2014, www.biography.com/explorer/amelia-earhart; Nisewaner and Walden, Journal of Family Memories.

26 National Personnel Records Center, St. Louis, Missouri

27 Ibid.

28 Ibid.

29 Ibid.

30 Ibid.

31 Nisewaner and Walden, Journal of Family Memories.

32 Ibid.; Reynolds, p. 278.

33 Ibid.

Chapter 13: As the Navy Prepares for War, Whiting Fights His Own Battles
1   Evans and Grossnick, United States Naval Aviation, 1910–2010, p. 127.
2   H. R. 9997, June 23, 1938; Chisholm, p. 733; Reynolds, p. 284.
3   Reynolds, p. 262.
4   Chisholm, p. 757; Reynolds, pp. 284, 594.
5   Ibid.
6   Nisewaner and Walden, Journal of Family Memories.
7   Herbert Hoover, *Public Papers of Presidents of the United States*, p. 179; National Personnel Records Center, St. Louis, Missouri.
8   Nisewaner and Walden, Journal of Family Memories; Kenneth Whiting Papers, MS 294, Nimitz Library.
9   National Personnel Records Center, St. Louis, Missouri.
10 Kenneth Whiting Papers, MS 294, Nimitz Library; National Personnel Records Center, St. Louis, Missouri.
11 Reynolds, pp. 265–270.
12 Ibid.
13 Ibid.
14 "William Moffett Facts," *Your Dictionary: Biography*, October 2, 2019, www. biography.yourdictionary.com/william-moffett; "Re: Service of Captain Kenneth Whiting, United States Navy, Retired, Active, Deceased," May 12, 1943, National Personnel Records Center, St. Louis, Missouri, Kenneth Whiting Papers, MS 194, Nimitz Library.
15 Kenneth Whiting Papers, MS 294, Nimitz Library.
16 Ibid.
17 Ibid.
18 Nisewaner and Walden, Journal of Family Memories.
19 Ibid.
20 Ibid.
21 Ibid.

Chapter 14: A New World War without a Front-Line Role for Whiting
1   Kenneth Whiting Papers, MS 294, Nimitz Library; Nisewaner and Walden, Journal of Family Memories.
2   Nisewaner and Walden, Journal of Family Memories.
3   Ibid.; Kenneth Whiting Papers, MS 294, Nimitz Library; Herman, *Freedom's Forge*, preface.
4   Bailey, *American Pageant*, pp. 828, 876.
5   National Personnel Records Center, St. Louis, Missouri; *McGraw-Hill Dictionary of Scientific and Technical Terms 6E*, (McGraw-Hill Companies, 2003), www.encyclopedia2.thefreedictionary.com/periodontium.
6   Ibid.
7   Ibid.
8   Ibid.

9   Kenneth Whiting Papers, MS 294, Nimitz Library.

10 Ibid.

11 Ibid.

12 Ibid.

13 Ibid.

14 Ibid.

15 Ibid.

16 Ibid.

17 Ibid.

18 Ibid.

19 Ibid.

20 Ibid.

21 Ibid.

22 Ibid.

23 Ibid.

24 "Navy Promotions Announced by President Roosevelt," *Coronado Eagle and Journal*, December 14, 1939, California Digital Newspaper Collection, Center for Bibliographical Studies and Research, accessed October 24, 2019, www. cdnc.ucr.edu/?a=d&d/=CJ19391214.2.20&e.

25 Reynolds, pp. 286–287; Raymond Wong, "John Henry Towers, ADM-Military Timeline," Togetherweserved.com, accessed October 21, 2019, www.navy.togetherweserved.com/usn/servlet/tws.webapp. WebApp?cmd=SBVTimeLine&type=Person&ID=437046.

26 William F. Trimble, *Admiral John S. McCain and the Triumph of Naval Air Power* (Annapolis, Maryland: Naval Institute Press, 2019), pp. 42–43.

27 National Personnel Records Center, St. Louis, Missouri.

28 Ibid.

29 Ibid.

30 Ibid.

31 Ibid.; Kenneth Whiting Papers, MS 294, Nimitz Library.

32 Ibid.

33 Ibid.

34 Bailey, p. 878.

35 Sears, p. 113.

36 Ibid., pp. 113–114.

37 Ibid., p. 114; E. B. Potter, *Nimitz* (Annapolis, Maryland: US Naval Institute Press, 1976), p. 85.

38 Robert C. Rubel, "Deconstructing Nimitz's Principle of Calculated Risk," *Naval War College Review* vol. 68, no. 1, Article 4, p. 1, www.digital-commons.usnwc. edu/cgi/viewcontent.cgi?referer=https://www.google.com/&httpsredir=1&article =1181&context=nwc-review; Potter, p. 87; Sears, pp. 136–137; Morison, p. 161; Jonathan Parshall and Anthony Tully, *Shattered Sword: The Untold Story of the Battle of Midway* (Dulles, Virginia: Potomac Books, 2005), pp. 378, 380, 383.

[39] *All Hands: The Bureau of Naval Personnel Information Bulletin*, June, 1947, p. 35, www.navy.mil/ah_online/archpdf/ah194706.pdf.

[40] Nisewaner and Walden, Journal of Family Memories.

[41] Ibid.

[42] Ibid.

[43] Ibid.

[44] Ibid.

[45] Ibid.

[46] Ibid.

[47] Ibid.

[48] Ibid.; William Henry Drummond, "The Wreck of the 'Julie Plante' (A Legend of Lac St. Pierre)," Bartleby.com, Great Books Online, accessed October 25, 2019, www.bartleby.com/335/78.html.

[49] Ibid.; Frank Crumit, "Abdul Abulbul Amir," accessed October 25, 2019, www.genius.com/Frank-crumit-abdul-abulbul-admir-lyrics; Leonard Barry, editor, "The Armored Cruiser Squadron," arranged from the version in the Book of Navy Songs, edited by the Trident Society, U. S. Naval Academy, Garden City, New York: Doubleday, Doran and Co., Inc. 1937, accessed October 25, 2019, www.books.google.com/books?id=InlPOIrsvwC&pg=PA2&lpg=PA2&d-q=The=Armored+Cruiser+Squadron+Navy+Song+Book&source=bl&ots.

[50] Ibid.

Chapter 15: A Notable Life and Career of Achievement Suddenly Interrupted

[1] Nisewaner and Walden, Journal of Family Memories; Kenneth Whiting file, ZB Personnel file.

[2] Ibid.

[3] National Personnel Records Center, St. Louis, Missouri.

[4] Ibid.

[5] Ibid.

[6] Ibid.

[7] Nisewaner and Walden, Journal of Family Memories.

[8] National Personnel Records Center, St. Louis, Missouri.

[9] Ibid.

[10] Ibid.

[11] "Waterhouse-Friderichsen Syndrome," Genetic and Rare Diseases Information Center, National Institutes of Health, accessed October 15, 2019, www.rarediseases.info.nih.gov/diseases/9449/waterhouse-friderichsen-syndrome.

[12] National Personnel Records Center, St. Louis, Missouri; "Waterhouse-Friderichsen Syndrome," Genetic and Rare Diseases Information Center, National Institutes of Health, accessed October 15, 2019, www.rarediseases.info.nih.gov/diseases/9449/waterhouse-friderichsen-syndrome.

[13] Nisewaner and Walden, Journal of Family Memories.

[14] Ibid.

15 Ibid.

16 Ibid.; National Personnel Records Center, St. Louis, Missouri.

17 "Capt. Whiting Dies Suddenly in Bethesda, MD," *Larchmont Times*, April 29, 1943, www.larchmonthistory.org/memorials/individual/Times/19430429WhitingAnnouncement.html

18 "Capt. Whiting Dies Suddenly in Bethesda, MD," *Larchmont Times*, April 29, 1943; Nisewaner and Walden, Journal of Family Memories.

19 Nisewaner and Walden, Journal of Family Memories.

20 Ibid.

21 Ibid.

22 Kenneth Whiting Papers, MS 294, Nimitz Library; Kenneth Whiting file, NAS Whiting Field; Mark L. Evans, "Forrestal (CVA-59), 1955–1993," Naval History and Heritage Command, August 2, 2007, www.history.navy.mil/research/histories/ship-histories/danfs/f/forrestal-cva-59.html.

23 Ibid.; Kenneth Whiting file, NAS Whiting Field; "Artemus Gates, aviator, businessman," *Prabook*, World Biographical Encyclopedia Inc., accessed October 15, 2019, www.prabook.com/web/artenus.gates/2599443.

24 Ibid.; Kenneth Whiting file, NAS Whiting Field; "Re: Service of Captain Kenneth Whiting, United States Navy, Retired, Active, Deceased," May 12, 1943, National Personnel Records Center, St. Louis, Missouri; "Thomas Tingey Craven," Find a Grave, accessed October 15, 2019, www.findagrave.com/memorial/3870.

25 "NH 82802 Vice Admiral John H. Newton, USN," Naval History and Heritage Command, accessed October 16, 2019, www.history.navy.mil/our-collections/photography/numerical-list-of-images/nhhc-series/nh-series/NH-82000/NH-82802.html; Smith, *One Hundred Years of US Navy Air Power*; Michael Robert Patterson, webmaster, "John Sidney McCain, admiral, United States Navy," Arlington National Cemetery website, accessed October 22, 2019, www.arlingtoncemetery.net/jsmccain.htm; Mike Weeks, "Adm. George Dominic Murray," Find a Grave, 35611018, accessed October 22, 2019, www.findagrave.com; Kenneth Whiting Papers, MS; Nimitz Library; Kenneth Whiting file, NAS Whiting Field; Smith, *Carrier Battles: Command Decision in Harm's Way*, p. 9.

26 "Edward O. McDonnell: Vice Admiral, USNR (Retired), 1891–1960," Naval History and Heritage Command, accessed October 15, 2019, www.history.navy.mil/our-collections/photography/us-people/m/mcdonnell-edward-o.html; Wortman, p. 90; Kenneth Whiting Papers, MS 294, Nimitz Library; Kenneth Whiting file, NAS Whiting Field.

27 Kenneth Whiting Papers, MS 294, Nimitz Library; Kenneth Whiting file, NAS Whiting Field; "Falaise," Sands Point Preserve Conservancy, accessed October 24, 2019, www.sandspointpreserveconservancy.org/about/welcome/; "Guggenheim, Harry Frank, Naval Aviator," National Aviation Hall of Fame, accessed October 24, 2019, www.nationalaviation.org/our-enshrinees/guggenheim-harry-frank/.

28 Nisewaner and Walden, Journal of Family Memories.
29 Ibid.
30 National Personnel Records Center, St. Louis, Missouri.
31 Ibid.
32 Ibid.
33 Ibid.
34 Kenneth Whiting Papers, MS 294, Nimitz Library.
35 Ibid.; National Personnel Records Center, St. Louis, Missouri.
36 "Capt. Whiting Dies Suddenly in Bethesda, MD," *Larchmont Times*, April 29, 1943.
37 Nisewaner and Walden, Journal of Family Memories.
38 "Meningococcal Meningitis," Rare Disease Database, National Organization of Rare Disorders, accessed October 24, 2019, www.rarediseases.org/rare-diseases/meningococcal-meningitis/.
39 Moira Matilda Walden, granddaughter of Kenneth Whiting, interview, August 2018.
40 Nisewaner and Walden, Journal of Family Memories.

Chapter 16: The Kenneth Whiting Persona

1 "Honor Concept," United States Naval Academy, accessed October 16, 2019, www.usna.edu/About/honorconcept.php.
2 Van Deurs, *Wings for the Fleet*, p. 118; Van Deurs, "The Aircraft Collier Langley," p. 27.

Chapter 17: The Case for Recognizing Kenneth Whiting as the Father of the American Aircraft Carrier

1 Van Deurs, p. 157.
2 Ibid., pp. 136–137; Turnbull and Lord, p. 131; Mueller, pp. 207–210.
3 Ibid., p. 139.
4 Kenneth Whiting Papers, MS 294, Nimitz Library.
5 Van Deurs, pp. 142–143.
6 Nisewaner and Walden, Journal of Family Memories.
7 Rossano, pp. 24–25.
8 Ibid., pp. 168–169, 182.
9 Tate, p. 63; Van Tol, p. 100–101; Reynolds, p. 171; Tillman, p. 46; Nisewaner and Walden, Journal of Family Memories.
10 Ibid., p. 62; Pennoyer, p. 2.
11 Reynolds, p. 171.
12 Wadle, p. 13; McDonald, "Langley, Lex, and Sara," p. 16; Pennoyer, pp. 1–2; Van Deurs, *Wings for the Fleet*, pp. 118–119; C:/Users/Felix/Documents/Wings_Over_Water.pdf, p. 3.
13 Tate, p. 63.
14 Ibid., pp. 63–64, 65, 67.

[15] "Early Aircraft Carriers: Introduction of Aircraft Carriers following WWI," *Literary Digest*, February 18, 1922, www.1920-1930.com/military/aircraft-carriers.html.

[16] Tate, p. 63.

[17] Ibid., p. 65; Lee, "Wings over Water," p. 3; "Langley (CV-1)," *Dictionary of American Naval Fighting Ships*, Naval History and Heritage Command, August 21, 2019; "Re: Service of Captain Kenneth Whiting, United States Navy, Retired, Active, Deceased," May 12, 1943, National Personnel Records Center, St. Louis, Missouri.

[18] McDonald, pp. 18–19; Lee, "Wings over Water," pp. 3, 8; Pennoyer, p. 16; Reynolds, p. 198; Tate, p. 64, 67; Van Deurs, p. 30; Nisewaner and Walden, Journal of Family Memories.

[19] Kenneth Whiting Papers, MS 294, Nimitz Library; Nisewaner and Walden, Journal of Family Memories; "Re: Service of Captain Kenneth Whiting, United States Navy, Retired, Active, Deceased," May 12, 1943, National Personnel Records Center, St. Louis, Missouri; Van Deurs, p. 157–158.

[20] Van Tol, p. 88; Tate, p. 68; Turnbull and Lord, p. 256.

[21] Kenneth Whiting Papers, MS 294, Nimitz Library.

[22] Kennedy Hickman, "Military Aviation: Brigadier General Billy Mitchell," ThoughtCo., accessed October 9, 2019, www.thoughtco.com/military-aviation-brigadier-general-billy-mitchell-2360544; Minnie L. Jones (IMCOM), "William 'Billy' Mitchell—The Father of the United States Air Force," United States Army, January 28, 2010, www.army.mil/article/33580/william_billy_mitchell_the_father_of_the_united_states_air_force; Rossano, pp. 369–370; Kenneth Whiting Papers, MS 294, Nimitz Library; Kenneth Whiting file, NAS Whiting Field; Turnbull and Lord, p. 195; Van Deurs, p. 157–158; Nisewaner and Walden, Journal of Family Memories.

[23] Van Deurs, pp. 157–158; Nisewaner and Walden, Journal of Family Memories; "Re: Service of Captain Kenneth Whiting, United States Navy, Retired, Active, Deceased," May 12, 1943, National Personnel Records Center, St. Louis, Missouri.

[24] Nisewaner and Walden, Journal of Family Memories; "Re: Service of Captain Kenneth Whiting, United States Navy, Retired, Active, Deceased," May 12, 1943, National Personnel Records Center, St. Louis, Missouri.

[25] Ibid.; "Re: Service of Captain Kenneth Whiting, United States Navy, Retired, Active, Deceased," May 12, 1943, National Personnel Records Center, St. Louis, Missouri.

[26] "Re: Service of Captain Kenneth Whiting, United States Navy, Retired, Active, Deceased," May 12, 1943, National Personnel Records Center, St. Louis, Missouri; "Ranger IX (CV-4), 1934–1946," *Dictionary of American Naval Fighting Ships*, Naval History and Heritage Command, September 16, 2005, www.history.navy.mil/research/histories/ship-histories/danfs/r/ranger-ix.html.

27 Wadle, pp. 21, 104–105; "Re: Service of Captain Kenneth Whiting, United States Navy, Retired, Active, Deceased," May 12, 1943," National Personnel Records Center, St. Louis, Missouri.

28 Nisewaner and Walden, Journal of Family Memories; "Re: Service of Captain Kenneth Whiting, United States Navy, Retired, Active, Deceased," May 12, 1943, National Personnel Records Center, St. Louis, Missouri.

29 Ibid.; Kenneth Whiting Papers, MS 294, Nimitz Library.

30 Kenneth Whiting file, NAS Whiting Field; Nisewaner and Walden, Journal of Family Memories.

31 Ibid.

32 National Personnel Records Center, St. Louis, Missouri.

33 Kenneth Whiting file, NAS Whiting Field.

34 Van Deurs, "The Aircraft Collier Langley," p. 27.

Chapter 18: Rendering Honors

1 Kennedy, xvi.

2 Ibid., xvi; Lisle A. Rose, *Power at Sea* (Columbia, Missouri: University of Missouri Press, 2007), p. 178; Robert G. Albion, *Makers of Naval Policy 1798–1947* (Annapolis, Maryland: Naval Institute Press, 1980), pp. 374–375.

3 Ibid., p. 367.

4 Ibid., pp. 328, 371.

5 Weekly, "Kenneth Whiting, Capt., Deceased," Togetherweserved.com, accessed October 19, 2019; "Re: Service of Captain Kenneth Whiting, United States Navy, Retired, Active, Deceased," May 12, 1943, National Personnel Records Center, St. Louis, Missouri.

6 Nisewaner and Walden, Journal of Family Memories; Turnbull and Lord, p. 238.

7 Ibid.; "USS *Wright* AV-1," *Dictionary of American Naval Fighting Ships* vol. VIII, Naval History and Heritage Command, pp. 480–483, accessed October 18, 2019, www.hazegray.org/danfs/auxil/az1.htm; "CVA-59," *Dictionary of American Naval Fighting Ships* vol. III, Naval History and Heritage Command (1963), p. 432, accessed October 18, 2019, www.hazegray.org/danfs/carriers/cva59.htm; "DANFS Online: Aircraft Carriers," Naval History and Heritage Command, accessed October 18, 2019, www.hazegray.org/danfs/carriers/.

8 "Kenneth Whiting," *Dictionary of American Naval Fighting Ships*, Naval History and Heritage Command, accessed October 19, 2019, www.history.navy.mil/research/history/ship-histories/danfs/k/kenneth-whiting.html; Nisewaner and Walden, Journal of Family Memories.

9 Ibid.

10 Ibid.; "USS *Thuban* (LKA-19 ex USS *Thuban* (AKA-19) (1943–1969)," NavSource Online: Amphibious Photo Archives, accessed October 19, 2019, www.navsource.org/archives/10/02/02019.htm; Felix Haynes file, Dover, Florida.

[11] Nisewaner and Walden, Journal of Family Memories.

[12] Ibid.; Kenneth Whiting file, NAS Whiting Field.

[13] Ibid.

[14] Ibid.; "Terrell Andrew Nisewaner," Hall of Valor Project, accessed October 22, 2019, www.valor.militarytimes.com/hero/21424; Edna Whiting Nisewaner," Find a Grave, accessed October 22, 2019, www.findagrave.com/memorial/75860889/edna-nisewaner#source.

[15] Ibid.; "LST 128," *Dictionary of American Naval Fighting Ships*, Naval History and Heritage Command, accessed October 22, 2019, www.history.navy.mil/research/histories/ship-histories/danfs/l/lst-128. Htm.

[16] Kenneth Whiting file, ZB Personnel files.

[17] "Naval Aviation Museum Hall of Honor," OPNAVINST 5750.10J, July 29, 1994, accessed October 19, 2019, www.web.archive.org/web/20110716084907/http://doni.daps.dla.mil/Directions.pdf; Nisewaner and Walden, Journal of Family Memories.

[18] Nisewaner and Walden, Journal of Family Memories; Kenneth Whiting Papers, MS 294, Nimitz Library

[19] Ibid.; Kenneth Whiting Papers, MS 294, Nimitz Library.

[20] Ibid.; Kenneth Whiting Papers, MS 294, Nimitz Library.

[21] Ibid.; Kenneth Whiting Papers, MS 294, Nimitz Library.

[22] Ibid.; Kenneth Whiting Papers, MS 294, Nimitz Library.

[23] Ibid.; Kenneth Whiting Papers, MS 294, Nimitz Library.

[24] Ibid.; Kenneth Whiting Papers, MS 294, Nimitz Library.

[25] Roy Grossnick, *United States Naval Aviation, 1910–1995*, Appendix 19 (Washington, DC: Naval Historical Center, Department of the Navy, 1997).

[26] Lieutenant Philip D. Mayer, US Navy, "Incubate Innovation: Aviation Lessons from the Interwar Period," *Proceedings* (Annapolis, Maryland: United States Naval Institute, December 2019), p. 41.

BIBLIOGRAPHY

INTERNET SOURCES

"1917–1919: Test of Strength." Timeline, Naval History and Heritage Command, September 13, 2019. www.history.navy.mil/browse-by-topic/communities/mava;-aviation0/1917-1919.html.

"A-6." *Dictionary of American Naval Fighting Ships* vol. IA. Naval History and Heritage Command, pp. 3–4. Accessed October 23, 2019. www.hazegray.org/danfs/submar/ss7.htm.

"Address of President Roosevelt at Annapolis Commemoration, April 24, 1906." SeacoastNH.com. Accessed October 23, 2019. www.seacoastnh.com/Maritime-History/John-Paul-Jones/farewell-paul-jones/.

"About John Hays Hammond Jr." Hammond Castle Museum. Accessed October 7, 2019. www.hammondcastle.org/about/john/hays/hammond-jr/.

"Aeronautics and Astronautics Chronology, 1925–1929." National Aeronautics and Space Administration. Accessed October 4, 2022. https://www.hq.nasa.gov/office/pao/History/Timeline/1925-1929.html.

"Amelia Earhart Biography." Biography.com. A & E Television Networks, April 2, 2014. www.biography.com/explorer/amelia-earhart.

"Amelia Earhart: First Lady of the Sky." Life Hero of the Week Profile, May 19, 1997. Reprinted in Internet Archive: Wayback Machine. Accessed October 13, 2019. www.webarchive.org/

web/20021005082222/http://www.life.com/Life/heroes/news-leters/nlearhart.html.

"Amelia Earhart with Three Military Men." March 18, 1937. e-archive of newspaper photograph. Courtesy of Purdue University Libraries, Karnes Archives and Special Collections. www.lib.purdue.edu/aearhart.

Annual Registry of the United States Naval Academy, Annapolis, Md., 1905. Washington: Government Printing Office at https://babel.hathitrust.org/cgi/pt?id=ucl.b3041888;view=1up;seq=436.

"ADM Frank Brooks Upham, ID:669." Military Hall of Honor. Accessed October 11, 2019. www.militaryhallofhonor.com/honoree-record.php?id=669.

"Admiral William Shepherd Benson, 1st Chief of Naval Operations." September 10, 2019. www.Geni.com/people/Admiral-William-Benson-1st-Chief-of-Naval-Operations/6000000023433345777.

"Aircraft Carriers-CVN." Chief of Information, United States Navy, from Naval Sea Systems Command, September 17, 2020. Accessed September 14, 2021. https://www.navy.mil/DesktopModules/ArticleCS/Print.aspx?.

"Albert Gleaves." Naval History and Heritage Command. Accessed October 4, 2022. https://www.history.navy.mil/research/histories/biographies-list/bios-g/gleaves-albert.html.

"Alfred Thayer Mahan." *Encyclopedia Britannica.* Accessed June 11, 2022. https://www.britannica.com/biography/Alfred-Thayer-Mahan.

Allen, Keith. "Notes on US Fleet Organisation [sic] and Disposition." September 30, 2001. www.gwpda.org/naval/fdus0001.htm.

"Artemus Gates, Aviator, Businessman." *Prabook.* World Biographical Encyclopedia, Inc. Accessed October 15, 2019. www.prabook.com/web/artenus.gates/2599443.

Barry, Leonard, editor. "The Armored Cruiser Squadron." Arranged from the version in the *Book of Navy Songs*, edited by the Trident Society, US Naval Academy. Garden City, New York: Doubleday, Doran and Co., Inc., 1937. Accessed October 25, 2019. www.

books.google.com/books?id=InlPOIrsvwC&pg=PA2&lp-g=PA2&dq=The=Armored+Cruiser+Squadron+Navy+Song+-Book&source=bl&ots.

Bauman, Richard J., "The Strange Disappearance of Admiral Wilcox," *Naval History Magazine*. United States Naval Institute, February 2018. www.usni.org/magazines/naval-history-magazine/2018/february/strange-disappearance-admiral-wilcox.

"Brigadier General William 'Billy' Mitchell." National Museum of the United States Air Force. April 9, 2015. www.national-museum.af.mil/Visit/Museum-Exhibits/Fact-Sheets/Display/Articles/196418/brig-gen-william-billy-mitchell/

"Capt. Whiting Dies Suddenly in Bethesda, MD." *Larchmont Times*. April 29, 1943. www.larchmonthistory.org/memorials/individual/Times/19430429WhitingAnnouncement.html.

"Casualties: US Navy and Marine Corps Personnel Killed and Injured in Selected Accidents and Other Incidents Not Directly the Result of Enemy Action." Naval Historical Center, Department of the Navy. Accessed October 24, 2019. www.ibiblio/hyperwar/NHC/accidents.

"CDR Grattan Colley 'Dyke' Dichman." Find a Grave. Accessed October 23, 2019. www.findagrave.com/34270567/grattan-colley-dichman.

Cohen, Steve. "Where are the Carriers?" *Forbes*. October 25, 2010. Accessed September 14, 2021. forbes.com/Sites/stevecohen/2010/10/25/where-are-the-Carriers??sh=63823199fdOe.

Cohen, Steve. "Where Are the Carriers?" *Forbes*. Accessed October 4, 2022. https://www.forbes.com/sites/stevecohen/2010/10/25/where-are-the-carriers/2/#104fb56f7cf6.

Cox, Edward. *Gray Eminence: Fox Conner and the Art of Mentorship*. Institute of Land Warfare, Association of the United States Army, No. 78W, September 2010, ausa.org/sites/default/files/LWP-78-Gray-Eminence-Fox-Conner-and-the-Art-of-Mentorship.pdf.

Cox, Robert Jon, Webmaster. "The Battle Off Samar: Taffy 3 at Leyte Gulf." BOSAMAR website. Accessed October 20, 2019. www.bosamar.com.

Crouch, Tom D. "Samuel Pierpont Langley." August 6, 2019. www.brittanica.com/biography/samuel-pierpont-langley.

Crumit, Frank. "Abdul Abulbul Amir." Accessed October 25, 2019. www.genius.com/Frank-crumit-abdul-abulbul-admir-lyrics.

"C-V List." United States Navy. Accessed October 5, 2022. https://www.navy.mil/navydata/ships/carriers/c-v-list.

"CVA-59." *Dictionary of American Naval Fighting Ships* vol. III. Naval History and Heritage Command (1963), p. 432. Accessed October 18, 2019. www.hazegray.org/danfs/carriers/cva59.htm.

"DANFS Online: Aircraft Carriers." Naval History and Heritage Command. Accessed October 18, 2019. www.hazegray.org/danfs/carriers/.

Downs II, Charles F. "Calvin Coolidge, Dwight Morrow, and the Air Commerce Act of 1926." *Essays, Papers, and Addresses.* Calvin Coolidge Presidential Foundation, June 20, 2001. www.coolidgefoundation.org/resources/essays-papers-addresses-13/.

Drummond, William Henry. "The Wreck of the 'Julie Plante' (A Legend of Lac St. Pierre)." Bartleby.com. Accessed October 25, 2019. www.bartleby.com/335/78.html.

Dyer, George C. "Chapter 4: In and Out of Big Time Naval Aviation." *The Amphibians Came to Conquer: The Story of Admiral Richmond Kelly Turner.* Accessed October 4, 2022. https://www.ibiblio.org/hyperwar/USN/ACTC/actc-4/html.

"Early Aircraft Carriers: Introduction of Aircraft Carriers following WWI." *Literary Digest.* February 18, 1922. www.1920-1930.com/military/aircraft-carriers.html.

"Early Birds of Aviation Inc. Collection." Smithsonian Online Virtual Archives. Smithsonian Institution. Accessed October 10, 2019. www.sova.si.edu/details/NASM.XXXX.0566#ref364.

"Edward O. McDonnell: Vice Admiral, USNR, (Retired), 1891–1960." Naval History and Heritage Command. Accessed October 15, 2019. www.history.navy.mil/our-collections/photography/us-people/m/mcdonnell-edward-o.html.

Evans, Mark L. "Forrestal (CVA-59), 1955–1993." Naval History and Heritage Command. August 2, 2007. www.history.navy.

mil/research/histories/ship-histories/danfs/f/forrestal-cva-59. html.

Evans, Mark L. and Grossnick, Roy A. "The Great Depression 1930–1939," *United States Naval Aviation, 1910–2010*. Naval History and Heritage Command. Accessed October 13, 2019. www. history.navy.mil/research/publications/publications-by-subject/ naval-aviation-1910-2010. Html.

Evans, Mark L. and Grossnick, Roy A. *United States Naval Aviation, 1910–2010*. Naval History and Heritage Command. file:///C:/Users/ Felix/Documents/United%20States%20Aviation%201910-2010. html.

"F/A-18 Super Hornet Strike Fighter." US Navy Fact File, Department of the Navy. Accessed October 22, 2019. www.navy.mil/navy-data/factdisplay.asp?cid=1100&tid=12008ct=1.

"FA-18 Hornet." FAS Military Analysis Network. Accessed October 4, 2022. https://www.fas.org/man/dod-101/sys/ac/f-18.htm.

"Falaise." Sands Point Preserve Conservancy. Accessed October 24, 2019. www.sandspointpreserveconservancy.org/about/welcome/.

Glines, C. V. "William 'Billy' Mitchell: Air Power Visionary." Accessed June 7, 2020. www.historynet.com/ william-billy-mitchell-an-air-power-visionary.

Goodspeed, Hill. "One Hundred Years at Pensacola." *Naval History Magazine*, December 2014. United States Naval Institute, Annapolis, Maryland. www.usni.org/magazines/naval-history-magazine/2014/ december/one-hundred-years-pensacola.

Goodspeed, Hill. "Whiting Key in Several Military Milestones." *Pensacola News Journal*. June 17, 2017. http://www.pnj.com/story/news/military/2017/06/17/ whiting-key-several-military-milestones/399443001.

Griffin, Virgil Childers, Jr. Find a Grave. Accessed October 23, 2019. www.findagrave.com/memorial/34328248/ virgil-childers-griffin.

"Guggenheim, Harry Frank, Naval Aviator." National Aviation Hall of Fame. Accessed October 24, 2019. www.nationalaviation. org/our-enshrinees/guggenheim-harry-frank/.

"Guy Wilkinson Stuart Castle, Commander, United States Navy." Arlington National Cemetery website. Accessed October 23, 2019. www.arlingtoncemetery.net/gwscastl.htm.ZZZZZZz

"Hammond Castle Museum." Accessed October 4, 2022. https://www.hammondcastle.org.

Hickman, Kennedy. "Military Aviation: Brigadier General Billy Mitchell." ThoughtCo., Accessed October 9, 2019. www.thoughtco.com/military-aviation-brigadier-general-billy-mitchell-2360544.

Hickman, Kennedy. "World War II: USS *Saratoga* (CV-3)." ThoughtCo. July 3, 2019. www.thoughtco.com/uss-saratoga-cv-3-2361553.

"HMS *Ark Royal*: United Kingdom (1914) Seaplane Carrier." *Naval Encyclopedia*. Accessed September 28, 2019. www.naval-encyclopedia.com/ww1/UK/hms-ark-royal-1914.

"Honor Concept." United States Naval Academy. Accessed October 16, 2019. www.usna.edu/About/honorconcept.php.

Houston, Sarina. "Learn About Amelia Earhart's Lockheed Model 10 Electra: The Aircraft She Flew on Her Attempted Flight Around the World." Balance Careers. Accessed October 13, 2019. www.thebalancecareers.com/earhart-lockheed-model-10-electra-282579.

"How It Feels Traveling under Sea: A Trip on US Submarine," *Tacoma Times*, August 21, 1909. www.navsource.org/archives/08/pdf/0800717.pdf.

"Interesting Facts about the Panama Canal." Panama Canal Museum. University of Florida, Gainesville, Florida. Accessed October 3, 2019. www.cms.uflib.ufl.edu/pcm/facts/aspx.

"John Hays Hammond Jr., American Inventor." *Encyclopedia Britannica*. July 20, 1998. www.britannica.com/biography/John-Hays-Hammond-Jr.

"John J. Pershing." *Encyclopedia Britannica*, in Biography. Accessed October 4, 2022. https://www.britannica.com/biography/John-J-Pershing.

"John Paul Jones." United States Naval Academy Public Affairs Office. Accessed October 23, 2019. www.usna.edu/PAO/faq_pages/JPJones.php.

Johnston, David L., "The Wackiest Sub in the Navy or a Short History of the USS G-1 SS-19 1/2," 2007. http://www.pigboats.com/dave2.html, February 23, 2018.

Jones, Minnie L. (IMCOM). "William 'Billy' Mitchell—"The Father of the United States Air Force." United States Army. January 28, 2010. www.army.mil/article/33680/ william_billy_mitchell_the-father_of_the_united_ states_air_force.

"Kenneth Whiting." *Dictionary of American Naval Fighting Ships*. Naval History and Heritage Command. Accessed October 19, 2019. www.history.navy.mil/research/history/ship-histories/ danfs/k/kenneth-whiting.html.

"Kenneth Whiting Papers, 1901–1943: Finding Aid." February 2009. Kenneth Whiting Papers, MS 294, Special Collections & Archives Department: Nimitz Library, United States Naval Academy. www.edu/Library/sca/man-findingaids/view. php?f=MS_294.

"Kenneth Whiting, Pioneer Naval Aviator." *Out of the Box* (blog). August 14, 2014. www.libraries. wright.edu/community/outofthetbox/2014/08/14/ kenneth-whiting-pioneer-naval-aviator.

"Kenneth Whiting, Pioneer Naval Aviator." Out of the Box. Wright State University Libraries *Special Collections and Archives.* Accessed October 4, 2022. https://www.libraries.wright.edu/community/outofthetox/2014/08/14/ kenneth-whiting-pioneer-naval-aviator/.

Lee, Bill. "Wings over Water." July 2, 2016. Accessed October 17, 2019. www.nnapprentice.com/alumni/letter/Wings_Over_ Water.pdf. C:/Users/Felix/Documents/Wings_Over_Water. pdf. July 2, 2016.

Lemelin, David. "Theodore Roosevelt as Assistant Secretary of the Navy: Preparing America for the WorldStage." www.historymatters.appstate.edu/sites/historymatters.appstate.edu/files/ David%20Lemelin%20Final_0.pdf.

Loomis, Steven (Saigon Shipyard), IC3. "Burrage, Guy, VADM, Deceased." Togetherweserved.com. Accessed October 11, 2019.

www.navy.togetherweserved.com/usn/servlet/tws.webapp.
WebApp?cmd=ShadowBoxProfile&type=Person&ID=693906.

"Lieutenant Sinton Returns." *Times Dispatch* (Richmond, Virginia),
April 20, 1919. Accessed October 23, 2019. www.newspapers.
com/image/?clipping_id=9394094&fcfToken.

Loomis, Steven (Saigon Shipyard), IC3. "Ingersoll, Stuart, VADM
Deceased." Togetherweserved.com Accessed October 11, 2019.
www.navy.togetherweserved.com/usn/seervlet/tws.webapp.
WebApp?cmd=ShadowBoxProfile&type=Person&ID=674039.

"LST 128." *Dictionary of American Naval Fighting Ships*. Naval
History and Heritage Command. Accessed October 22, 2019.
www.history.navy.mil/research/histories/ship-histories/danfs/l/
lst-128. Htm.

Maksel, Rebecca. "The Billy Mitchell Court-Martial." Air and Space
Museum. Accessed October 26, 2019. www.airspacemag.co
m/history-of-the-billy-mitchell-court-martial-136828592/.
Copyright YYYY Smithsonian Institution. Reprinted with
permission from Smithsonian Enterprises. All rights reserved.
Reproduction in any medium is strictly limited without permission from Smithsonian magazine.

Mather, Rod. "NOAA Ocean Exploration." National Oceanic and
Atmospheric Administration, U. S. Department of Commerce.
Accessed October 5, 2022. https://www.oceanexplorer.gov/
technology/development-partnerships/18Kraken/uss-g-1.html.

Mather, Rod. University of Rhode Island Applied History Lab.
Accessed October 5, 2019. https://www.oceanexplorer.gov/
technology/development-partnerships/18Kraken/uss-g1.html.

McDonald, Scot, "Langley, Lex, and Sara," *Naval Aviation News*,
May 1962. Ohio State University Library, June 25, 1979,
pp. 16–21. Accessed March 11, 2020, books.google.com/
books?id=z10zEtNQj80C&pg=RA9-PA8&1pg=RA9-
PA8&dq=kenneth+whiting+larchmont+times+obituary&source.

McDonald, Scot. "Last of the Fleet Problems." September 1962, p.
37, C:/Users/Felix/Downloads/car-6.pdf.

McKinley, JO2 (Journalist Second Class) Mike. "Cruise of the Great
White Fleet." Naval History and Heritage Command. Accessed

October 23, 2019. www.history.navy.mil/research/library/online-reading-room/title-list-alphabetically/cruise-great-white-fleet-mckinley.html.

"Meningitis Rash: Pictures and Symptoms." *Healthline.* Accessed October 4, 2022. https://www.healthline.com/health/meningitis-pictures-rask-symptons.

"Meningococcal Meningitis." Rare Disease Database. National Organization of Rare Disorders. Accessed October 24, 2019. www.rarediseases.org/rare-diseases/meningococcal-meningitis/.

"NAS Pensacola, FL History." Accessed September 26, 2019, www.PensacolaNavalHousing.com.

"Naval Aviation Museum Hall of Honor." OPNAVINST 5750.10J. July 29, 1994. Accessed October 19, 2019. www.web.archive.org/web/20110716084907/http://doni.daps.dla.mil/Directions.pdf.

"Navy Promotions Announced by President Roosevelt." *Coronado Eagle and Journal,* December 14, 1939. California Digital Newspaper Collection, Center for Bibliographical Studies and Research. Accessed October 24, 2019. www.cdnc.ucr.edu/?a=d&d/=CJ19391214.2.20&e.

"Nisewaner, Edna Whiting." Find a Grave. Accessed October 22, 2019. www.findagrave.com/memorial/75860889/edna-nisewaner#source.

"Nisewaner, Terrell Andrew." Hall of Valor Project. Accessed October 22, 2019. www.valor.militarytimes.com/hero/21424.

"Norman Schwartzkopf." *Biography.com.* Accessed October 4, 2022. https://www.biography.com/people/norman-schwartzkopf-9476401.

"Norman Schwartzkopf, United States General." *Encyclopedia Britannica.* Accessed October 24, 2019. www.britannica.com/biography/Norman-Schwartzkopf.

"Orville Wright." *Biography.* Accessed October 4, 2022. https://www.biography.com/people/orville-wright-20672999.

"Papers of Commander Theodore G. Ellyson, 1918–1928," Archives Branch, Naval History and Heritage Command, Washington, DC, June 4, 2019, www.history.navy.mil/content/history/

navalhistoryandheritagecommand/research/archives/research-guides-and-finding-aids/personal-papers/d-e/papers-of-theodore-g-ellyson.html.

"Patent No. 1,097,700." *Official Gazette of the United States Patent Office* vol. CCII, pp. 990–991. Washington: Government Printing Office, 1914. www.books.google.com/books?id=Patent+1,097,700&source=bl&ots.

Patterson, Michael Robert, Webmaster. "John Sidney McCain, Admiral, United States Navy." Arlington National Cemetery Website. Accessed October 22, 2019. www.arlingtoncemetery.net/jsmccain.htm.

"PBY Catalina." Catalina Preservation Society. Accessed October 13, 2019. www.pbycatalina.com/society-profile/.

"Pearl Harbor Ships on the Morning of the Attack." Pearl Harbor Visitors Bureau. Accessed October 22, 2019. www.visitpearl-harbor.org/pearl-harbor-ships-on-december-7th/pwencycl.kgbudge.com/N/e/Newton_John_H.htm.

"Periodontoclasia." *The Free Dictionary by Farley*. Accessed October 4, 2022. https://medicaldictionary.thefreedictionary.com/periodontoclasia.

"Photo Archive: USS *San Clemente*, ex USS *Wright* (AV-1), USS *Wright* (AZ-1). Nav Source Online: Service Ship. Accessed October 9, 2019. www.navsource.org/archives/09/41/4101.htm.

Price, Scott T. "A Study of the General Board of the US Navy, 1929–1933." Naval History and Heritage Command, May 6, 2017, pp. 11–12. www.history.navy.mil/research/library/oline-reading-room/title-list-alphabetically/s/study-general-board-us-navy-1929-1933.html.

"*Ranger* IX (CV-4), 1936–1946." *Dictionary of American Fighting Ships*. Naval History and Heritage Command. September 16, 2005. www.history.navy.mil/research/histories/ship-histories/danfs/r/ranger-ix.html.

"Recovery of the Remains of Patriot John Paul Jones." Order of the Founders and Patriots of America. Accessed October 23, 2019. www.founderspatriots.org/articles/jones.php.

Reilly, Joseph. "Power of an Aircraft Carrier." *The Physics Handbook: An Encyclopedia of Scientific Essays*. Accessed September 14, 2021. https:hypertextbook.com/facts/2000/JosephReilly.shtml.

"Remembering World War I: Gen. John J. Pershing Arrives in Europe." American Battle Monuments Commission. Accessed October 23, 2019. www.abmc.gov/news-events/news/remembering-world-war-i-gen-john-j-pershing-arrives-europe.

Reynolds, Clark G. "William A. Moffett." Encyclopedia.com. Oxford University Press, September 16, 2019. www.encyclopedia.com/history/encyclopedias-almanacs-transcripts-and-maps/moffett-william.

Rofe, J. S. "Under the Influence of Mahan: Theodore and Franklin Roosevelt and their Understanding of American National Interest, Diplomacy & Statecraft." 19:4, pp. 732–745. DOI:10:1080/09592290802564536.

Rubel, Robert C. "Deconstructing Nimitz's Principle of Calculated Risk." *Naval War College Review* vol. 68, no. 1, article 4, p. 1. www.digital-commons.usnwc.edu/nwc-review/vol68/iss1/4.

"S-Class (Herreshoff)." Sailboat Data.Com. Accessed June 27, 2022. www.sailboatdata.com/sailboat/s-class-herreshoff; www.classic-sailboats.org/n-g-herreshoff-s-class; www.s-classorg/new-page.

"Seal/G-1 (SS-19-1/2)." NavSource Online: *Submarine Photo Archive*. Accessed October 5, 2022. https://www.navsource.org/archives/08/08019a.htm.

Shiel, William C. Jr., "Medical Definition of Albuminaria." Medicine Net. Accessed October 25, 2019. www.medicinenet.com/script/main/art.asp?articlekey=6851.

"Ships and District Craft Present at Pearl Harbor 0800 7 December 1941. Naval History and Heritage Command. Accessed October 4, 2022. https://www.history.navy.navy.mil/research/library/online-reading-room/title-list-alphabetically/s/ships-present-at-pearl-harbor.html.

"Ship Characteristics." Battleship Missouri Memorial, Pearl Harbor, Hawaii. Accessed October 22, 2019. www.ussmissouri.org/learn-the-history/the-ship/ship-characteristics.

"Suspect in Lindbergh Kidnapping Case Held in New York." *Evening Citizen.* Ottawa, Canada, September 21, 1934, p. 4. Accessed October 25, 2019. www.news.google.com/ newspapers?nid=2194&dat=19340921&id.

Tate, Rear Admiral Jackson R. "We Rode the Covered Wagon." *Proceedings* vol. 104/10/908. US_Naval Institute, October 1978.

"Terrell Andrew Nisewaner." *The Hall of Valor Project.* Accessed October 4, 2022. https://valor.militarytimes.com/hero/21424.

"The A-Boats." PigBoats.com. Accessed October 23, 2019. www. pigboats.com/subs/a-boats.html.

"The Carriers." Chief of Information, United States Navy. Accessed October 22, 2019. www.navy.mil/navydata/ships/carriers/ cv-why.asp.

"The Clarkson Cowl Residence." Old Long Island. April 10, 2014. Accessed October 24, 2019. www.oldlongisland.com/2014/04/ the-clarkson-cowl-residence.html.

The Lucky Bag. 1905. Annapolis, MD: First Class, United States Naval Academy. Last modified January 18, 2013. https:// archive.org/details/luckybag1905unse/page92.

"The Origins of Navy Day." Military.com. Accessed October 10, 2019. www.military.com/military-appreciation-month/origins- of-navy-day.html.

"The Rough Riders Storm San Juan Hill, July 1, 1898." This Day in History, Eyewitness to History. Accessed September 23, 2019. www.eyewitnesstohistory.com (2004).

"The Ultimate World War II Fleet Submarine Resource." Accessed September 26, 2019, www.fleetsubmarine.com/S-class.html.

"Thomas Tingey Craven." Find a Grave. Accessed October 15, 2019. www.findagrave.com/memorial/3870.

Tillman, Barrett. "William Bull Halsey: Legendary World War II Admiral." Accessed June 4, 2002. https://www.historynet.com/ william-bull-halsey-legendary-world-war-ii-admiral.htm.

"Tropical Cyclone History for Southeast South Carolina and Northern Portions of Southeast Georgia." National Weather Service. Accessed October 5, 2022. https://www.weather.gov. chs/TChistory.

Turnbull, Archibald D. and Lord, Clifford L. *History of United States Naval Aviation*. New Haven: Yale University Press, 1949. Internet reprint. penelope.uchicago.edu/Thayer/E/Gazetteer/places/America/United_States/Navy/_Texts/TLHUNA/18*.html.

"US Naval Air Station: England: Killingholme." Naval History and Heritage Command. Accessed September 27, 2019. www.history.navy.mil/content/history/wwi-aviation/u-s-naval-air-stations/us-naval-air-stations-england/england-Killingholme.html.

"US Navy Aeronautic Detachment No. 1: The First American Unit Overseas in World War I. Naval History and Heritage Command. Accessed June 15, 2022.

"USS *A-6*, ex USS *Porpoise* (SS-7), 1903–1922." Naval History and Heritage Command. Accessed October 4, 2022. https://www.history.navy.mil/research/histories/ship.histories/danfs/a/a-6.html.

"USS *Langley* (CV-1)." *Dictionary of American Fighting Ships* vol. IV. DANFS Online, pp. 45–47. www.hazegray.org/danfs/auxil/ac-3.

"USS *LST-128*." NavSource Online: *Amphibious Photo Archives*. Accessed October 5, 2022. https://www.navsource.org/archives/10/16/160128.htm.

"USS *Ranger* (CV-4): Conventionally-Powered Aircraft Carrier." Military Factory. Accessed October 12, 2019. www.militaryfactory.com/ships/detail.asp?ship_id=USS-Ranger-CV-4.

"USS *Saratoga*." *Dictionary of American Fighting Ships* vol. VI. 1979, pp. 339–342. Accessed October 10, 2019. www.hazegray.org/danfs/carriers/cv-3.htm.

"USS *Seattle*." Naval History and Heritage Command. www.history.navy.mil/research/histories/ship-histories/danfs/s/seattle-i.html.

"USS *Thuban* (LKA-19) ex-USS *Thuban* (AKA-19) (1943–1969)." NavSource Online: Amphibious Photo Archives. Accessed October 19, 2019. www.navsource.org/archives/10/02/02019.htm.

"USS *Washington*/USS *Seattle* ACR-11." Accessed September 27, 2019. www.freepages.rootsweb.com/~cacunithistories/military/USS-Washington.html.

"USS *Wright.*" *Dictionary of American Fighting Ships* vol. VIII, pp. 480–483. Accessed October 9, 2019. www.hazegray.org/danfs/auxil/az-1.htm.

Utz, Curtis. "Fleet Problem IX." January 1929. Naval History and Heritage Command. September 5, 2019. www.history.havy.mil/browse-by-topic/heritage/usn-lessons-learned/fleet-problem-ix.html.

"VADM Guy Hamilton Burrage." Find a Grave. May 25, 2009. Accessed May 13, 2022. www.findagrave.com/memorial/37484552/guy-hamilton-burrage.

Van Deurs, Rear Admiral George. "The USS Porpoise and Ken Whiting." *Proceedings.* US Naval Institute, September 1972, pp. 82–83. www.usni.org/magazines/proceedings/1972/september.

Van Deurs, Rear Admiral George. "The Aircraft Collier Langley." *Proceedings.* US Naval Institute, April 1986, Supplement, pp. 24–27. www.usni.org/magazines/proceedings/1986/April.

Van Tol, Jan M. "Military Innovation and Carrier Aviation—The Relevant History." https://fas.org/man/dod-101/sys/ship/docs/1516pgs.pdf.

Van West, Carroll. "Albert Gleaves." *Tennessee Encyclopedia.* October 8, 2017. www.tennesseeencyclopedia.net/entries/albert-gleaves/.

"Villa Riviera: A General History." The Villa Riviera. Accessed October 13, 2019. www.villariviera.net/page/18138-307064/General-History.

"Washington Naval Conference." Encyclopedia.com. September 19, 2019. www.encyclopedia.com/history/dictionaries-thesauruses-pictures-and-press-releases/washington/naval/conference.

"Waterhouse-Friderichsen Syndrome." Genetic and Rare Diseases Information Center, National Institutes of Health. Accessed October 15, 2019. www.rarediseases.info.nih.gov/diseases/9449/waterhouse-friderichsen-syndrome.

Weekly, Kent. "Upham, Frank Brooks, ADM, Deceased." Togetherweserved.com. Accessed October 11, 2019. www.

navy.togetherweserved.com/usn/servlet/tws.webapp.
WebApp?cmd=ShadowBoxProfile&type=Person&ID=508011.

Weekly, Kent. "Whiting, Kenneth, CAPT, Deceased." Togetherweserved.com. Accessed October 23, 2019. www. navy.togetherweserved.com/usn/servlet/tws.webapp. WebApp?cmd=ShadowBoxProfile&type=Person&ID=458615.

Weeks, Mike. "Adm. George Dominic Murray." Find a Grave, 35611018. Accessed October 22, 2019. www.findagrave.com.

"William A. Moffett." *Barron Hilton: Pioneers of Flight Gallery*. Smithsonian Air and Space Museum, October 2, 2019. www. pioneers of flight.si.edu/content/william-moffett.

"William Adger Moffett." National Aviation Hall of Fame. Accessed October 4, 2022. https://www.nationalaviation.org/enshrinees/ william-adger-moffett.

"William Moffett Facts." Your Dictionary: Biography. *Encyclopedia of World Biography*. Gale Group. 2010. www.biography.yourdic-tionary.com/willliam-moffett.

Williamson, Corbin. *To Train the Fleet for War: The US Navy Fleet Problems, 1923–1940* by Albert A. Nofi. Book review. Naval Historical Foundation, September 29, 2011. www.navyhistory. org/2011//09/book-review-to-train-the-fleet-for-war-the-u-s-navy-fleet-problems-1923-1940/.

Withers, Michael D. "Pride, Alfred Melville, ADM, Deceased." Accessed October 2, 2019. www.navy.togetherweserved.com/ servlet/two.webapp.WebApp?cmd=
ShadowBoxProfile&type=Person&ID=454721.

Wong, Raymond. "John Henry Towers, ADM-Military Timeline." Togetherweserved.com. Accessed October 21, 2019. www. navy.togetherweserved.com/usn/servlet/tws.webapp. WebApp?cmd=SBVTimeLine&type=Person&ID=437046.

"World War II: Grumman F6F Hellcat." ThoughtCo. Accessed October 22, 2019. www.thoughtco.com/grumman-f6f-hellcat-2361521.

"World War II: USS *Yorktown* (CV-5). ThoughtCo. Accessed October 12, 2019. www.thoughtco.com/uss-yorktown-com-cv-5-2361555.

"Wright Timeline 1910 to 1919." History Wing. *The Wright Story*. Accessed October 5, 2022. https://wright-brothers.org/

History_Wing/Wright_Story_Timeline/Wright-Timeline 1910_1919.

Illustrations

All illustrations are courtesy of a copyright grant for the use of all materials in the Whiting Family Journal, except the following:

The picture of four men, including Kenneth Whiting and Orville Wright, in front of the Wright Brothers Monument at Dayton, Ohio, which is used courtesy of permission from the copyright holder, Special Collections and Archives, Wright State University.

The picture of Amelia Earhart and three men, including Kenneth Whiting, which is used courtesy of Purdue University Libraries, Karnes Archives and Special Collections.

Other Sources

Albion, Robert G. *Makers of Naval Policy 1798–1947*. Annapolis, Maryland: Naval Institute Press, 1980.

"America's First Aircraft Carrier—USS *Langley* (CV-1). Warfighting First, Platforms, People. *Naval History* (blog). Annapolis, MD: US Naval Institute, March 20, 2014.

An Act to Regulate Distribution, Promotion, and Retirement of Officers of the Line of the Navy, and for other purposes, H. R. 9997, June 30, 1938. Code of Federal Regulations, Title 32, National Defense Federal Register, National Archives and Records Service, General Services Administration, January 1, 1970.

"Arthur Clayton Sinton." Sinton Family Trees. Accessed October 5, 2022. www.sinton-family-trees.uk/ft_main.php?rin=1574.

Bonner, Kermit. *Final Voyages*. Nashville: Turner Publishing Company, 1956.

Bailey, Thomas A. *The American Pageant: A History of the Republic*. Boston: D. C. Heath and Company, 1966.

Brennan, Captain Lawrence B., "No Guts, No Air Medals!" Universal Ship Cancellation Society Log, July 2011.

Buell, Thomas B. *Master of Sea Power: A Biography of Fleet Admiral Ernest J. King*. Annapolis, Maryland: Naval Institute Press, 2012.

Chisholm, Donald. *Waiting for Dead Men's Shoes: Origin and Development of the US Navy's Officer Personnel System 1793–1941*. Stanford, California: Stanford University Press, 1941.

Dane, T. H., Lt. Col., Signal Corps, US Army. "Report on R.N.A.S. Station, Felixstowe, England and General Intelligence, February 6, 1918." Washington, DC: Smithsonian Air and Space Museum.

Davis, Burke. *The Billy Mitchell Affair*. New York, New York: Random House, 1967.

Dyer, Vice Admiral George C., "Learn to Say 'No' to the Admiral," *Proceedings*. United States Naval Institute, July 1963.

Eisenhower, Dwight D. *At Ease: Stories I Tell to Friends*. New York City: Eastern Acorn Press, 1993.

"Frank Brooks Upham." Military Hall of Honor. Accessed October 5, 2022. www.militaryhallofhonor.com/honoree-record.php?id=669.

Gleaves, Albert. *The Admiral: The Memoirs of Albert Gleaves, Admiral, USN*. Pasadena, California: Hope Publishing House, 1985.

Grossnick, Roy. *United States Naval Aviation, 1910–1995*. Appendix 19, Hall of Valor Inductees. Washington, DC: Naval Historical Center, Department of the Navy, 1997.

Halsey, Fleet Admiral William F., USN. *Admiral Halsey's Story*. Auckland, New Zealand: Pickle Partners Publishing, August 15, 2014.

Haynes, Felix file, Dover, Florida.

Herman, Arthur. *Freedom's Forge: How America's Business Produced Victory in World War II*. New York: Random House, 2012.

Honious, Ann. *What Dreams We Have: The Wright Brothers and Their Hometown of Dayton, Ohio*. Ft. Washington, Pennsylvania: Eastern National, 2003.

Hoover, Herbert *Public Papers of Presidents of the United States*, 1930.

Irwin, Manley R. "A Note on Public Sector Integration: The Decline of British Naval Aviation, 1914–1945." *Review of Industrial Organization*. February 1999.

"January 6, 1919: Theodore Roosevelt Dies." *History*. Accessed October 5, 2022. www.history.com/this-day-in-history/theodore-roosevelt-dies.

Kennedy, Paul. *Engineers of Victory: The Problem Solvers Who Turned the Tide in the Second World War*. New York: Random House Trade Paperbacks, 2013.

Kenneth Whiting file, NAS Whiting Field, Milton, Florida.

Kenneth Whiting, ZB file, Navy Department, Rare Book Room, Washington Navy Yard.

Kenneth Whiting Papers, MS 294. Special Collections & Archives Department: Nimitz Library, United States Naval Academy.

King, Ernest J. and Walter Muir Whitehill. *Fleet Admiral King: A Naval Record*. New York City: W. W. Norton & Company, 1952.

Layman, R. D. *Naval Aviation in the First World War*. Annapolis, Maryland: Naval Institute Press, 1996.

Layman, R. L. "Furious and the Tondern Raid." *Warship International* vol. 10, no. 4, 1973.

Leonard, Barry, editor. *Navy Song Book*. Annapolis, Md.: United States Naval Institute, Diane Publishing Company, 1928.

"Mahan's *The Influence of Sea Power upon History* in the 1890's." Office of the Historian, Foreign Service Institute, US Department of State.

Mayer, Philip D., Lieutenant, U. S. Navy. "Incubate Innovation: Aviation Lessons from the Interwar Period." *Proceedings*, Annapolis, Maryland: United States Naval Institute, December, 2019.

McCullough, David. *The Path Between the Seas*. New York: Simon and Schuster, 1977.

McDonald, Scot. *USN Carrier Evolution VI: The Last of the Fleet Problems*. Reprinted in Ships, by Geoffrey Cole, The Naval Officers Club of Australia. Accessed October 5, 2022. www.navalofficer.com.au/carriers6/.

Mead, Frederick S., editor. *Harvard's Military Record in the World War*. Boston: Harvard Alumni Association, 1921.

Mitchell, William and Robert S. Ehlers Jr. *Winged Defense: The Development and Possibilities of Modern Air Power—Economics and Military.* Tuscaloosa, Alabama: University of Alabama Press, 2009.

Morison, Samuel Eliot. *The Two-Ocean War: A Short History of the United States Navy in the Second World War.* Boston: Little, Brown, and Company, 1963.

Mueller, Edward A. *Steamships of the Two Henrys: Being an Account of the Maritime Activities of Henry Morrison Flagler and Henry Bradley Plant.* DeLeon Springs, FL: E. O. Painter Printing Co., 1996.

National Personnel Records Center, Military Personnel Records, St. Louis, Missouri.

Nisewaner, Edna Whiting and Moira Whiting Walden. Journal of Family Memories. Boothbay, Maine.

Patterson, Michael Robert. "Guy Wilkinson Stuart Castle, Commander, United States Navy." Arlington National Cemetery. Accessed October 5, 2022. www.arlingtoncemetery. net./guywscastl.htm.

Parshall, Jonathan and Anthony Tully. *Shattered Sword: The Untold Story of the Battle of Midway.* Dulles, Virginia: Potomac Books, 2005.

Pennoyer, Jr., Vice Admiral F. W., "Notes on USS *Langley* (CV-1)." National Personnel Records Center, St. Louis, Missouri.

Potter, E. B. *Nimitz.* Annapolis, Maryland: US Naval Institute Press, 1976.

Pride, A. M., VADM, US Navy. "Comment and Discussion." *Proceedings.* Annapolis, MD: US Naval Institute, January 1979. p. 89.

"Re: Service of Captain Kenneth Whiting, United States Navy, Retired, Active, Deceased." May 12, 1943. National Personnel Records Center, St. Louis, Missouri.

Report of President's Aircraft Board: November 30, 1925. Washington: Government Printing Office, 1925, provided by Documents Division, University of California Library, October 20, 1944, through the National Archives and Records

Administration, Records Group 80, Entry 131F, College Park, MD, in Google Books.

Reynolds, Clark G. *Admiral John H. Towers: The Struggle for Naval Air Supremacy.* Annapolis, Maryland: Naval Institute Press, 1991.

Rich, Doris L. *Amelia Earhart: A Biography.* Washington, DC: Smithsonian Institution Press, 1989.

Rose, Lisle A. *Power at Sea.* Columbia, Missouri: University of Missouri Press, 2007.

Rossano, Geoffrey L. *Stalking the U-Boat: US Naval Aviation in Europe during World War I.* Gainesville: University of Florida Press, 2010.

Rossano, Geoffrey L. and Thomas Wildenberg. *Striking the Hornet's Nest: Naval Aviation and the Origin of Strategic Bombing in World War I.* Annapolis, Maryland: Naval Institute Press, 2015.

Sears, David. *Pacific Air: How Fearless Flyboys, Peerless Aircraft, and Fast Flattops Conquered the Skies in the War with Japan.* Cambridge, Ma: Da Capo Press. Pertaining to chapter 13, the quotes in notes 35, 36, and 37: From Pacific Air by David Sears, copyright 2011, reprinted by permission of Hachette Books, an imprint of Hachette Book Group Inc.

Smith, Douglas V. *Carrier Battles: Command Decision in Harm's Way.* Annapolis, Maryland: Naval Institute Press, 2006.

Smith, Douglas. *One Hundred Years of US Navy Air Power.* Annapolis, MD: US Naval Institute Press, 2010.

Statement of Commander Kenneth Whiting, United States Navy. *Hearings before the President's Aircraft Board* vol. 2, pp. 819–865. Washington: Government Printing Office, 1925, provided by Transportation Library, University of Michigan through the National Archives and Records Administration, Records Group 80, Entry 131F, College Park, MD, in Google Books.

Swift, ADM Scott H. "To Train the Fleet for War: The US Navy Fleet Problems, 1923–1940." US Naval War College Historical Monograph Series. Newport, RI: Naval War College Press, 2010.

"Table 21-Ships on Navy List June 30, 1919." *Congressional Serial Set*. US Government Printing Office: 766, 1921.

Tillman, Barrett, "The Tondern Raid: Strike Fighter Centennial," *Proceedings*, US Naval Institute, September 2018, pp. 46–50.

Tillman, Barrett. "William Bull Halsey: Legendary World War II Admiral." *History.net*. Accessed October 5, 2022. www.historynet.com/william-bull-halsey-legendary-world-war-ii-admiral.htm.

Trimble, William F. *Admiral John S. McCain and the Triumph of Naval Air Power*. Annapolis, Maryland: Naval Institute Press, 2019.

Underwood, Jeffery S. *The Wings of Democracy: the Influence of Airpower on the Roosevelt Administration, 1933–1941*. College Station: Texas A & M University Press, 1991, p. 11.

"USS *Houston* (CL) CA 30." NavSource Online: *Cruiser Photo Archive*. Accessed October 5, 2022. www.navsource.org/archives/04/030/04030.htm.

"USS *Missouri* (BB-63)." Military Factory. Accessed October 5, 2022. www.militaryfactory.com/ships.detail.asp?ship_id=USS-Missouri-BB63.

Van Deurs, Rear Admiral George. *Wings for the Fleet: A Narrative of Naval Aviation's Early Development, 1910–1916*. US Naval Institute, 1966. Paperback edition published 1916.

Vego, Milan. "Mission Command and Zero Error Tolerance Cannot Coexist." *Proceedings*. US Naval Institute, July 2018.

Wadle, Ryan David. "United States Navy Fleet Problems and the Development of Carrier Aviation, 1929–1933." Master's thesis, Texas A&M University, August, 2005.

"War and Military Affairs." Theodore Roosevelt Center at Dickinson State University. Accessed October 5, 2022. www.theodorerooseveltcenter.org/Learn-About-TR/TR-Encyclopedia/War-and-Military-Affairs/Great-White-Fleet.aspx.

Whiting, Lieutenant Commander Kenneth. "Information and Suggestions for the Use of Seaplanes." Box 910, ZGU, Records Group 45, National Archives and Records Administration, Washington, DC. August 26, 1917.

Whiting, Lieutenant Commander Kenneth. "Report of Operations to Date." Box 910, ZGU, Records Group 45, National Archives and Records Administration, Washington, DC. July 20, 1917.

Wildenberg, Thomas. "Admiral with Wings." *Proceedings*. US Naval Institute Press, September 1998, pp. 70–73.

Wortman, Marc. *The Millionaires' Unit: The Aristocratic Flyboys Who Fought the Great War and Invented American Air Power*. Public Affairs, 250 West 57th Street, Suite 1321, New York, NY.

ACKNOWLEDGMENTS

Writing a biography about a subject who has been deceased for nearly eighty years, who no one living now ever knew, presents special challenges. Many of those challenges were overcome by the support given the author by two direct descendants of Kenneth Whiting—Tilly Walden, granddaughter of Kenneth; and Karna Nisewaner, great-great-granddaughter of Whiting's daughter Edna, or Eddie. They opened the Whiting Family files and journals to the author, which allowed the book to be enriched with much family history and personal stories. They provided the background that enabled the book to be a social history as much as a military one.

Many others provided valuable assistance, frequently going above and beyond the call of duty as the COVID-19 pandemic affected the completion of the work. These included the following:

Ed Verner—a good friend of the author and a licensed pilot, licensed boat captain, and owner of a midsized sailboat. He provided valuable assistance in reading and commenting on drafts of the book.

Lt. Col. Bob Hervatine—lifelong friend and career US Air Force pilot. He passed away during the writing of this book.

National Personnel Records Center, St. Louis, Missouri—Christopher Dyroff.

National Archives and Records Administration, Washington, DC—Alicia Henneberry, Chris Killilay, Nathaniel Patch.

United States Naval Institute, Annapolis, Maryland—Paul Merzlak, Richard Russell.

Smithsonian Institute, Air and Space Museum, Washington, DC—Phil Edwards, Antoine Watson, Elizabeth C. Borja.

Saint John's Episcopal Church, Larchmont, New York—Rev. Alissa Anderson, assistant rector.

NAS Whiting Field, Pensacola, Florida—Julie Ziegenhorn, Jamie Link, Francie North.

Nimitz Library, US Naval Academy, Annapolis, Maryland—Jennifer Bryan, David D'Onofrio, Adam Minakowski.

US Navy Office of Information East, New York, New York—Lauren Cole, Eric Durie.

Naval War College, Newport, Rhode Island—Stacie Parillo.

Naval History and Heritage Command, Washington, DC—Sandra Fox.

National Naval Aviation Museum, Pensacola, Florida—Buddy Makin.

Plant City Photo Archives and History Center, Plant City, Florida—Samantha Poirier, Gil Gott.

Wright State University Library, Dayton, Ohio—Toni Vanden Bos.

Purdue University Libraries—Neal Harmeyer.

Cox Media Group Worldwide—Yuming Zhang.

Kenneth Whiting: Remembering a Forgotten Hero of Naval Aviation and Submarines could not have been written without the help of everyone on this list. I owe you much.

ABOUT THE AUTHOR

Felix Haynes began his career as an Army ROTC graduate and with service in Vietnam. Leaving the Army, he earned three University of Florida degrees and spent a career serving in community college administration. He served as president of three community colleges or campuses in Florida, Illinois, and Maryland, and attended the Military History Fellowship program at West Point. Turning to a lifelong interest in writing, Haynes published three historical fiction novels about important places in his life—Panama, Scotland, and Vietnam—before deciding to make the transition to nonfiction. After listening to the stories told by his father about a World War II ship he had served on called the USS Kenneth Whiting, the author researched Whiting's significant accomplishments in submarines and naval aviation and chose to write the first-ever biography of Kenneth Whiting. Along with his continuing interest in writing, Haynes and two friends established a community newspaper a decade ago. He has been a member of Rotary since 1985. He also serves on an Episcopal church vestry and on several nonprofit and community boards. He and his wife, Susan, have been married for fifty-three years and have four adult children, all adopted.

Printed in the USA
CPSIA information can be obtained
at www.ICGtesting.com
LVHW041244191223
766591LV00063B/1532